# The Sinfulness
# of Sin

# The Sinfulness of Sin

## RALPH VENNING

THE BANNER OF TRUTH TRUST

**THE BANNER OF TRUTH TRUST**
*3 Murrayfield Road, Edinburgh EH12 6EL*
*P.O. Box 621, Carlisle, Pennsylvania 17013, USA*

\*

*© The Banner of Truth Trust 1965*
*First published 1669*
*First Banner of Truth Trust edition under the title*
The Plague of Plagues *1965*
*Reprinted as* The Sinfulness of Sin *1993*
*Reprinted 1997*
*Reprinted 2001*
*ISBN 0 85151 647 5*

\*

*Printed in Finland by*
*WS Bookwell*

# CONTENTS

## SECTION THREE

### The Witnesses Against Sin

1. God himself bears witness against sin

[7]

# PUBLISHERS' INTRODUCTION

In the year 1633 a minor Great Ejection took place, several Puritan ministers being forced to quit their charges because of their nonconformity to the ceremonies prescribed by the Prayer Book and enforced by Archbishop Laud. Among these was George Hughes, a young Fellow of Pembroke College, Cambridge, who had been born in Southwark in 1603, when the first Stuart, James I, came to the throne of England. When his brilliant academic and ministerial career was thus so abruptly curtailed, Hughes resolved to emigrate to New England, and was only dissuaded from this course by the Puritan patriarch, John Dod. Shortly afterwards he moved to Devon as Rector of Tavistock. One feature of his ministry there, commented upon in Edmund Calamy's *Account* of the ejected ministers was that at least three who were subsequently useful ministers were first awakened spiritually under Hughes' preaching. One of these, interestingly enough, was to become a popular and fruitful preacher in Hughes' own native Southwark. His name was Ralph Venning.

Venning was born in Devonshire possibly at King's Teignton in about 1621. He entered Emmanuel College, Cambridge, in 1643, and obtained his Bachelor's and Master's degrees in 1646 and 1650 respectively. After leaving Cambridge, he became lecturer at St. Olave's Church in Southwark where he remained until forced to leave in 1662 by the Act of Uniformity. When the severity of the Great Persecution abated, Venning was able to continue his public ministry as co-pastor with Robert Bragge of an Independent congregation at Pewterer's Hall, Lime Street. He died, still in his early fifties, in 1674 and was buried at Bunhill Fields in the presence of many nonconformists.

As the occupant of a city pulpit in the Commonwealth period, Venning, it almost goes without saying, was a popular preacher. A less obvious feature of his ministry which has come down to us is that he was a great pleader for the poor. He lived and preached, it must be remembered, in days when the poor were poorer, and when they were much more dependent on private charity than is the case now. It was estimated that Venning collected hundreds of pounds annually for distribution among the needy, and it is recorded that, like George Whitefield a hundred years later, he was so persuasive that he often prevailed with those who had gone to church resolved to give nothing.

An interesting literary association between Venning and the noted John Goodwin is the 'Epistle Dedicatory' or Preface written by Venning to Goodwin's treatise, *A Being Filled with the Spirit*. Goodwin – not to be confused, of course, with the renowned Dr. Thomas Goodwin – was a Puritan in church order and politics, but not in theology. He was, indeed, described by a contemporary, Thomas Edwards, as 'a monstrous sectary, a compound of Socinianism, Arminianism, Libertinism, Antinomianism, Independency, Popery, yea and of Scepticism'. In the light of this, it may seem strange that Venning, an orthodox divine, should be commending one of Goodwin's works. Closer examination, however, suggests that the latter was, in fact, a fairly thoroughgoing Arminian, of a type similar to John Wesley, and that Edwards was a bigot. Venning, in fact, candidly expresses his reserve with regard to Goodwin's Arminianism, but recognizes that his writings may still be of spiritual profit: 'Though I confess myself not to be of the same mind and opinion with the learned author in some other controverted points, yet I cannot but give my testimony concerning this piece, that I find an excellent spirit moving on the face, and acting in the heart of it, to promote

[14]

the glory of God, the power of godliness, and consequently the good of men, especially of Christian men.'

Whatever one's view of John Goodwin, Venning's own writings can be read without reserve or qualification. In the present volume, for example, he shuns philosophizing, and consistently reasons from and applies Scripture. His familiarity with the Word of God is matched by his ability rightly to divide it. This is undoubtedly the chief reason for the power of his writing. In his 'Epistle to the Reader' Venning disclaims any pretensions to style and deplores the kind of eloquence which draws attention to itself, believing that 'words are for the matter's sake'. His own preference is clearly for the plain, homely and direct style of writing which most of the Puritans used. At the same time, *The Plague of Plagues*, for all the solemnity of its theme, has a charm and character of its own, which sustains the reader's interest. Moreover, the author shows no little skill in his use of plays on words and epigrams.

*The Plague of Plagues*, though first published in 1669, four years after the Great Plague of London, was, in the author's own words, 'begun, and almost finished before the late sore and great plague began. And therefore, though for a memorial of it I have taken occasion to give it a name or title from thence, yet it is not calculated particularly thereunto, but with a more general aspect upon the universal mischief that sin has done mankind. . . .' There is, in fact, scarcely one allusion to the Great Plague in the book, which is an experimental treatise on sin. Venning concedes in his prefatory Epistle that 'As to the sinfulness of sin, I have indeed handled it most fully, as it is against man's good and happiness'. He justifies such an emphasis from the fact that God 'is so condescending that he is pleased to treat man as a self-lover, and so to gain him, and win him by his own advantages'. Accordingly, in this book we are confronted with a massive and unanswerable indictment of sin as a foolish and evil thing.

To many in our day, Venning's treatment of his subject would appear horrifying or simply laughable – such is the wisdom of men! It is the foolishness of the thing preached, however which God blesses, and the author could testify 'I know that it was not then delivered (when first preached) without good effects on many, and, I hope, on more than I know of'. It is not difficult to believe this, after reading *The Plague of Plagues*, and it is the prayer of the Publishers that this new edition may be attended with like blessing, in a generation which knows little of the truth about sin, though much of the thing itself.

August, 1965

# INTRODUCTION

***

*'Was then that which is good made death to me? God forbid. But sin, that it might appear sin, working death in me by that which is good; that sin by the commandment might become exceeding sinful.'* (Romans 7. 13)

Being about to treat of the exceeding sinfulness of sin, it is not only expedient, but necessary that I preface and premise certain things: (1) *That God made all things very good* (Genesis 1. 31). They were all endowed with the perfections which were suitable to their several beings, so that none of them could find fault with or complain of God, as if he had owed them anything or had made them defective. (2) *Yet of these the two most eminent and principal degrees of creatures quickly degenerated.* Some of the angels sinned, and kept not their first estate, but left their own habitation (Jude 6). And by giving way to their subtle insinuations, the man Adam, who was a common person, sinned also (Genesis 3). And thus 'by one man sin entered into the world, and death by sin; and so death passed upon all men, for that all have sinned' (Romans 5. 12). (3) *As to the angels that fell, God left them irrecoverable.* For God spared not the angels that sinned, but cast them down to hell (2 Peter 2. 4), and has reserved them in everlasting chains under darkness, unto the judgment of the great day (Jude 6). Christ Jesus, the Mediator and Redeemer, took not on him angels, or, as it is in the margin, takes not hold of angels (Hebrews 2. 16). But it pleased God to pity man; his saving grace

[17]

and loving-kindness have appeared to man, and that, in Christ Jesus (Titus 2. 11; 3. 4). His delight was with the sons of men, the habitable parts of the earth (Proverbs 8. 31), and therefore he took on him the seed of Abraham (Hebrews 2. 16). (4) *This doctrine of God our Saviour, the Gospel-doctrine, supposes that man is a sinner.* It is a faithful saying, and worthy of the best and all acceptance and reception, that Christ Jesus came into the world (on this very errand and for this purpose) to save sinners (1 Timothy 1. 15). The doctrine of repentance supposes also that man has done amiss (Matthew 9. 13). The doctrine of faith in another for righteousness and hope concludes man to be without righteousness and hope in himself (Ephesians 2. 12, 13). The end of Christ's sending the Holy Spirit was that he might, in the first place, convince of sin (John 16. 8).

These things being so, beside others which might be considered, it cannot but be extremely useful to let men see what sin is: how prodigiously vile, how deadly mischievous, and therefore how monstrously ugly and odious a thing sin is. Thus a way may be made (1) For admiring the free and rich grace of God. (2) For believing in our Lord Jesus Christ. (3) For vindicating the holy, just and good law of God, and his condemnation of sinners for breaking it. (4) For hating sin, and repenting for and from it, thereby taking a holy, just and good revenge on it and ourselves. (5) That we may love and serve God at a better rate than we ever did in the little and short time of innocence itself. (6) And, lastly, that this black spot may serve to set off the admirable, incomparable and transcendent beauty of holiness.

And now to the text itself, which may have this for its title: The just vindication of the Law of God, and no less just accusation and condemnation of the sin of man. Its connexion with what precedes is as follows: the Apostle had said that the commandment which was ordained to life, he found to be unto death. Hence an objection is raised, in verse 13: Seeing the commandment is good, how then can it be unto death? 'Was that which was good made death to me?' To this he answers: (1) By way of negation and abhorrence, 'God forbid!' Far be it from me or anyone else to think so! No! By no means! To find fault with the law would be to find fault with God. The law is not to be blamed. What is, then? for something is to be blamed. (2) To this he answers, by way of affirmation and accusation, that sin is the true cause of death. The commandment condemns, or is death to man, not of itself, but because of sin. Hereby sin appears – not only like itself, but itself – sin, yea sinful, yea exceeding sinful sin; not in a disguise, as it is when committed, but in its own lively colours, or as we should rather and more appropriately say, its dead and deadly colours.

It is, he says, '*Hamartia*', sin in the abstract, and that is reiterated and repeated for certainty and assurance, as Pharaoh's dream was. It is sin, it is sin, and this sin is '*Hamartolos*', sinful or a sinner; it is nothing else but sinning and sinful sin. It is masculinely and vigorously sinful – for though Erasmus concludes that this conjunction of masculine and feminine in the Greek is the Attic dialect, others think that the Apostle brings in sin as if it were a person. In verses 17 and 20 he says: 'It is not I, but sin', as if it were a person. Unless we may read it as Faius does: that the '*Hamartolos*', the sinner, might become sin; this is the same sense as the objection made in verse 7, Is the law sin?; that is, Is it criminal and guilty? But, however we read it, we are sure of this, that it denotes the malignant, pestilent and pernicious nature and operation of sin, its own name being the worst that can be given to it. Yet, as if this were not meaningful enough, it is so *Kath huperbolon*, exceeding, above measure, excessively, or in the highest degree sinful. For a hyperbole is an extraordinary and the highest degree of speaking. The Arabic version has it *superans excessum*; it is extremely, indeed beyond all expression, sinful.

I may illustrate the scope and meaning of all this by a common occurrence: It is as if a criminal said to the judge, Oh, my Lord, how cruel and unmerciful you are to condemn me to die! No, says the judge, it is not I, it is the law. I am only the mouth of the law. No, says the law, it is not I, it is sin. If you had not sinned, I would not have condemned, for 'the law is not against the righteous' (1 Timothy 1. 9). No, against such there is no law

(Galatians 5. 23), no condemnation from it. You may then in me, as in a glass, see what a deadly, destructive and killing thing your sin is. Every mouth must be stopped, there is no room for complaint against God or his law, for, like all others, by becoming guilty you have fallen short of the glory, and are subject to the judgment of God (Romans 3. 19–23). So, by the commandment, sin appears to be a desperate, malignant thing, the proper, true and only cause of man's condemnation and death.

From this brief yet clear account of the text and context, the following truths are deducible:

1. *The law of God as a whole and in every part is good.* It is not only not sin, i.e. not culpable or criminal (verse 7), or only just (verse 12), or spiritual (verse 14), but good (verses 12, 13). It is good, not only in itself, but relatively in its institution with respect to man, for it was ordained to life (verse 10).

2. *This good law, when transgressed, makes man over to death.* Patience, that temperate and harmless thing, if abused, turns to rage and fury. So the law, good though it be, when abused condemns and kills.

3. *Though the law condemns man's fault, and man for his fault, yet still the law is good and not to be blamed.* The law is as good as ever it was; it is to be justified by man, even when it condemns man. Man had no reason to break the law, and he has none to find fault with the law, though it binds men over to death for breaking it.

4. *It is not the law, but sin, that works man's death and ruin.* Sin aims at no less, and if grace does not prevent, it will end in no less, for the end and wages of sin is death (Romans 6. 21, 23).

5. *Sin works man's death and destruction by that which is good, namely, the law.* When sin has used man to break the law, it uses the law to break man, to undo him by condemnation and death.

6. *Sin is therefore exceedingly sinful and wicked.* It is most immeasurably spiteful, poisonous and pernicious, because it kills men. And not only so, but it kills them by that which is good, and was appointed to man for life; it turns food into

[20]

poison. *Ut agnoscatur quam sceleratus peccator sit hoc peccatum, et quam pestifera res, dum per mandatum rem salutiferam, exserit virus suum* (In order that it may be recognised how vicious is the sinner, and how pernicious the matter, this sin, while through the commandment yielding a healthy result, produces its own poison), Clarius. This is like the horrid and cursed wickedness our stories tell us of, whereby a King was wickedly poisoned by the Cup of Blessing.

7. *Lastly, sin by the commandment appears to be excessively sinful.* If we look on this through the microscope-glass of the law, it will appear a most hideous, devilish and hellish thing, the most wicked, mischievous, virulent, villainous and deadly thing that ever was. Sinful sin! Worse than the Devil! More will be said of this later.

I will not pursue any of these divisions separately, for I shall have occasion enough to speak of each and every one of them in handling the sinfulness of sin, in relation to which I intend to observe the following order, showing: (1) What sin is, the thing so much and so deservedly evil spoken of. None can speak well of it, but they who speak ill of it, for they speak best who speak the worst of sin.

(2) In what the sinfulness of sin especially consists: So we may lay open not only its effects but also its nature.

(3) What witness and evidence there is to make good this indictment and charge against sin, that it is so vile and abominable, so sinful, as the Apostle calls it.

(4) And what use and improvement is to be made of the doctrine of sin's excessive sinfulness.

# SECTION ONE

# WHAT SIN IS

Sin is the transgression of a law, yea of a good law, yea of God's law. Sin presupposes that there is a law in being, for where is no law there is no transgression (Romans 4. 15). But where there is sin, there is a law, and a transgression of the law. Whosoever committeth sin transgresseth also the law, for sin is a transgression of the law (1 John 3. 4). That this is the sin intended in our text is apparent from Romans 7. 7.

Now the law not only forbids the doing of evil, whether by thought, word or deed, but also commands the doing of good. So to omit the good commanded is sin, as well (or ill) as is the doing of the evil that is forbidden. Against the fruit of the Spirit there is no law, but against the works of the flesh (for the antithesis holds) there is law, for they are all against the law, as the Apostle tells us (Galatians 5. 19–24). Whatever, then, transgresses the law of God – in whole or in part (James 2. 10) – is therefore and therein a sin, whether it break an affirmative or a negative precept i.e. whether it is the omission of good or the commission of evil.

# SECTION TWO

# THE SINFULNESS OF SIN

We now proceed to lay open in what especially the sinfulness of sin consists, which is easily and readily known from the description or definition just now set before us. Sin is a transgression of God's law, which is not only holy and just, as made and given by a holy and just God, but also good, as it respects man, for whom God made it, according to our text and its context, and as it is in Deuteronomy 5. 29 and 6. 24, and many other places. I say, sin being a transgression of God's law, which was made for man's good, the sinfulness of sin must needs lie in this, that it is contrary (1) to God, (2) to man. These then are the two heads I shall dwell upon, to declare the malignity and wicked nature of sinful sin. These are both evident from the law, for by it, as our text says, sin appears sin, and by the commandment sin, clearly and undeniably, becomes most exceeding, hyperbolically, or above measure sinful, i.e. extremely guilty of displeasing and dishonouring God, and of debasing and destroying man. On both accounts, it is justly obnoxious to, and deservedly worthy of the hatred of God and man. And I heartily wish that the outcome will be that man may hate it as God does, who hates it, and nothing else but it; or (to be sure) he hates none but for it.

## 1. SIN'S CONTRARIETY TO GOD

The sinfulness of sin not only appears from, but consists in this, that it is contrary to God. Indeed, it is contrariety and enmity itself. Carnal men, or sinners are called by the name of enemies to God (Romans 5. 8 with 10; Colossians 1. 21); but the carnal mind or sin is called enmity itself (Romans 8. 7). Accordingly, it and its acts are expressed by names of enmity and acts of hostility, such as, walking contrary to God (Leviticus 26. 21), rebelling against God (Isaiah 1. 2), rising up against him as an enemy (Micah 2. 8), striving and contending with God (Isaiah 45. 9), and despising God (Numbers 11. 20). It makes men haters of God (Romans 1. 30), resisters of God (Acts 7. 51), fighters against God (Acts 5. 39 and 23. 9), even blasphemers of God, and in short very atheists, who say there is no God (Psalm 14. 1). It goes about to ungod God, and is by some of the ancients called *Deicidium*, God-murder or God-killing.

Though all these things are not done by every sinful man, yet they are not only in the nature of sin, and that of every sin more or less, but are all of them in the heart of all sinners in their seed and root (Matthew 15. 19). So what is done by any man would be done by every man, if God did not restrain some men from it by his power, and constrain others to obedience by his love and power (2 Corinthians 5. 14; Psalm 110. 3). Here then is the desperately wicked nature of sin, that it is not only *crimen laesae Majestatis*, high treason against the Majesty of God, but it scorns to confess its crime. It is obstinate and will not that he reign over it. It is not only not subject, but it will not be subject, nor be reconciled to God; such is its enmity! But to show this more particularly:

1. *Sin is contrary to the nature of God.* God's name is holy, and as his name is, so is he and his nature, all holy; he is so, and cannot but be so. Therefore God takes it worse that men should think him wicked like themselves (Psalm 50. 16–22), than that they think him not to exist (Psalm 14. 1). It is said to weary him when men say that evil is good in his sight (Malachi 2. 17). This is the thing God glories in, that he is holy, even glorious in holiness (Exodus 15. 11).

Holiness is the attribute which frees God, not only from evil itself, but from all appearance or suspicion of evil. If God were not holy, many of the things which God does would look unlike him : his justice and judgments would look not only like severity, but tyranny, were not it and they holy; his love in its conduct and behaviour to some people would look like fondness and respect of persons, but that it is holy; his patience would look like a toleration, if not approbation of sin, but that it is holy patience. Thus many acts of God, were it not for holiness, would appear as seemingly evil as they are really good, and would be as much suspected by all, as they are unjustly censured by some.

God is holy, without spot or blemish, or any such thing, without any wrinkle, or anything like it, as they also that are in Christ shall one day be (Ephesians 5. 27). He is so holy, that he cannot sin himself, nor be the cause or author of sin in another. He does not command sin to be committed, for to do so would be to cross his nature and will. Nor does he approve of any man's sin, when it is committed, but hates it with a perfect hatred. He is without iniquity, and of purer eyes than to behold (i.e. approve) iniquity (Habakkuk 1. 13).

On the contrary, as God is holy, all holy, only holy, altogether holy, and always holy, so sin is sinful, all sinful, only sinful, altogether sinful, and always sinful (Genesis 6. 5). In my flesh, that is, in my sinful corrupt nature, there dwelleth no good thing (Romans 7. 18). As in God there is no evil, so in sin there is no good. God is the chiefest of goods and sin is the chiefest of evils. As no good can be compared with God for goodness, so no evil can be compared with sin for evil.

2. *Sin is contrary to all the names and attributes of God.* It sets itself in opposition to them all. (1) It deposes the *sovereignty* of God as much as in it lies. It will not that the King of kings should be on the throne, and govern this world which he has made. It was by this instinct that Pharaoh said, Who is the Lord, that I should obey his voice to let Israel go? I know no Lord above me; I will not let Israel go (Exodus 5. 2). The voice and language of sin is, 'Our lips are our own, who is Lord over us?' (Psalm 12. 4). It was from hence that the Jews of old said, 'We are lords, we will come no more to thee' (Jeremiah 2. 31). Thus it attempts to dethrone God.

(2) It denies God's *all-sufficiency*. As if there were not contentment and satisfaction enough to be had in the enjoyment of God, but that vanity and wickedness had more of pleasure and profit than he, whose ways are all pleasantness, and whose service is the health of man! Every prodigal who leaves the Father's house says in effect, It is better to be elsewhere.

(3) It challenges the *justice* of God, and dares God to do his worst (Malachi 2. 17). It provokes the Lord to jealousy, and tempts him to wrath.

(4) It disowns his *omniscience*. Pooh! they say, God does not see, nor does the most High regard.

(5) It despises the riches of God's *goodness* (Romans 2. 4).

(6) It turns his *grace* into wantonness (Jude 4). It will make bold with God, and sin because grace abounds.

In short, sin is the dare of God's justice, the rape of his mercy, the jeer of his patience, the slight of his power, the contempt of his love, as one writer prettily expresses this ugly thing. We may go on and say, it is the upbraiding of his providence (Psalm 50), the scoff of his promise (2 Peter 3. 3–4), the reproach of his wisdom (Isaiah 29. 16). And as is said of the Man of Sin (i.e. who is made up of sin) it opposes and exalts itself above all that is called God (and above all that God is called), so that it as God sitteth in the temple of God, showing itself as if it were God (2 Thessalonians 2. 4).

3. *Sin is contrary to the works of God*. It works contrary to God, and it is contrary to God's works, and is called the work of the devil (1 John 3. 8). All God's works were good exceedingly, beautiful even to admiration; but the works of sin are deformed and monstrously ugly, for it works disorder, confusion, and everything that is abominable. Sin may be arraigned for all the mischiefs and villainies that have been done in the world; it is the master of misrule, the author of sedition, the builder of Babel, the troubler of Israel and all mankind. So contrary is sin to the works of God, that it sought and still seeks to undo all that God does, that there might be no seed, nor name, nor root left him in the earth. Everything works according to its nature; as the root is, so is the fruit; and thus

[32]

every tree is known, whether it is a good tree or a bad (Matthew 7. 17–18). God is good, and does good (Psalm 119. 68). Sin is evil and does evil, indeed, it does nothing else. So sin and its works are contrary to God and his works.

4. *Sin is contrary to the law and will of God*, to all the rules and orders of his appointment. There is not one of his laws which it has not broken, and endeavoured to make void and of none effect. It is not only a transgression of, but also a contradiction to the will of God. When the Son of God came into the world to declare and do his Father's will, he was encountered by, and underwent the contradiction of sinners (Hebrews 12. 3) who would have made men believe that neither he nor his doctrine was of God.

Sin is an anti-will to God's will; it sets itself to oppose preaching, prayer, and all the institutions of God. And it does this, not only out of envy to man, that he should not be the better for them, but out of enmity to God, that he should not be worshipped in the world. Now to act contrary to the will and statutes of God is to act contrary to God himself, as may be seen by comparing Leviticus 26. 14–15 with verses 21, 23, and 27 of the same chapter, and many other places. David, in fulfilling the will of God, was said to be a man after God's own heart (Acts 13. 22); and they who obey the will of sin are said to walk after the heart of sin (Ezekiel 11. 21).

5. *Sin is contrary to the image of God, in which man was made.* God made man in his own likeness, viz. in righteousness and true holiness (Ephesians 4. 24). Now sin is clean contrary to this image, as much unlike it as deformity and ugliness is unlike handsomeness and beauty, as darkness is to light, as hell to heaven. Yes, and there is more too : sin is the Devil's image. When God made man, he made him in his own image; so when the Devil made man sin, he thereby made him his own image and likeness. In this sense I conceive the Devil meant that phrase, 'Ye shall be like gods', *Elohim* (Genesis 3. 5). He did not say or mean that he should be like the *Elohim*, the Creators, as the word is in Job 35. 10 and Ecclesiastes 12. 1, the God who made them; but like *Elohim*, gods, viz. such as I and my angels

are, who once knew good, but now know evil, both by doing it, and suffering the sad effects of it. The word *Elohim* is used not only of God and good angels, but of fallen angels or devils (1 Samuel 28. 13). And under the covert of this ambiguous word, he craftily abused our first parents; for he well knew that by sinning they could not become like *Elohim*, God above, but would become like *Elohim*, the gods below. And alas! are we not like *Elohim*-devils, knowing good by loss, and evil by its sad and dismal effects? Thus he that runs may read the picture, image, and likeness of the Devil in sin; sinners are as much like the Devil as anything. He that sinneth is of the Devil (1 John 3. 8), not only a servant but a child of the Devil: 'Ye are of your father the devil' said holy Jesus to the sinful Jews (John 8. 44). Never was child more like the father than a sinner is like the Devil; sin has the nature, the complexion, the air, the features, the very behaviour of the Devil.

6. *Sin is contrary to the people and children of God.* It is true, sin cannot hate them as much as God loves them, nor do them as much hurt as God can do them good. Yet, out of spite and envy, it will do its worst, and hate them because God loves them. God's children are his darlings and favourites, as dear to him as the apple of his eye. In all their afflictions he bears a part, and is afflicted, and looks upon it as if he himself were treated as they are in this world (Acts 9. 4–5; Matthew 25. 41–45). Now the nearer and dearer they are to God and the more God's heart is set upon them for good, the more sin sets its heart against them for evil. Sin is always warring against the seed of God in them, the flesh lusts against the spirit (Galatians 5. 17) and wars against their souls (1 Peter 2. 11). So, by sin's ill-will, God's people should neither enjoy nor do any good in this world. It is always provoking the serpentine race to make war upon, to imprison and persecute, even to destruction, the little flock and remnant of the holy seed. It will not, further than it is rebuked by grace, let them have one quiet day. It disturbs and interrupts them, so that they cannot attend upon God without distraction. When they would do good, evil is present with them, either to keep it undone, or to

[34]

make it ill done. It endeavours to spoil all they take in hand, and to turn their holy things into iniquity, by reason of which they cry out as greatly oppressed: 'Wretches that we are! Who shall deliver us from this body of death?' (Romans 7. 24).

This evil and envious sin is bent also on hindering, all it can, the comfort, welfare and happiness of the saints. Sin, like the Devil, has not such an evil eye or aching tooth at all the sinners in the world, as it has at the saints in the world. It is true, the Devil is a man-hater, but more a saint-hater. Watch! for your adversary the Devil seeks whom (of you) he may devour, as St Peter tells us (1 Peter 5. 8). And this he does to cross and thwart God and his design, who and which is set upon the happiness of his people.

7. *Sin is contrary to, and set against the glory of God*, and all that should and would give glory to him, or has any tendency to do so. Confession of sin and repentance gives glory to God (Joshua 7. 19), and sin endeavours to obstruct and hinder this. It began to practise upon Adam and Eve, and still carries on this trade among the children of men (Revelation 16. 9). Faith would give glory to God; so, in order that men may not believe, sin employs the Devil to blind their eyes (2 Corinthians 4. 4). Good men would do all they do to the glory of God, but sin will let them do nothing at all, and is ever throwing one dead fly or another into their most precious boxes of ointment. Sin is so malicious, that it will not only displease and dishonour God itself, but labours to defeat and frustrate the endeavours of all who attempt to do otherwise. If sin's desires might take place, there should not be a person or thing by whom and by which God should be pleased or glorified. It gives out false reports of God and goodness, lays prejudices and rocks of offence and stumbling in men's ways, that they may be out of love with all that is good. So desperately is it bent against the honour of God.

8. *Sin is contrary and opposite to the being and existence of God*. (This was hinted at before.) It makes the sinner wish and endeavour that there might be no God, for sinners are haters of God (Romans 1. 30). As he who hates his brother is a murderer

(1 John 3. 15), so, as much as in him lies, he who hates God is a murderer of God. Sin keeps garrisons and strongholds against God (2 Corinthians 10. 4, 5). It strives with and fights against God, and if its power were as great as its will is wicked, it would not suffer God to be. God is a troublesome thing to sinners, and therefore they say to him, Depart from us (Job 21. 14), and of Christ Jesus, Let us break his bands in sunder, and cast his cords far from us (Psalm 2. 3). And when the Holy Ghost comes to woo and entreat them to be reconciled, they resist and make war with the spirit of peace (Acts 7. 51). So that they are against every person in the Trinity, Father, Son and Spirit. In short, and for a conclusion, sin is contrary to God and all that is dear to him or has his name upon it; and though it is against all good, yet not so much against any good as against God, who is, and because he is the chiefest good.

Before we pass on, let me beseech you, whoever you are who read this, to pause a little and consider what is said. For what is said of sin is to be considered by the sinner, and is meant of your and my sin. Shall I not plead for God and your soul, and entreat you to be on God's side, and to depart from the tents of wickedness? Poor soul! Can you find it in your heart to hug and embrace such a monster as this? Will you love that which hates God, and which God hates? God forbid! Will you join yourself to that which is nothing but contrariety to God, and all that is good? Oh, say to this idol, this devil, get hence, what have I to do with you, you (*Elymas*) sorcerer, you full of all malignity and mischief; you child, yea father of the Devil, you who are the founder of Hell, an enemy to all righteousness, who ceases not to pervert the right ways of the Lord, and to reproach the living God! Away! away! Shall I be seduced by you to grieve the God of all my joy, to displease the God of all my comfort, to vex the God of all my contentment, to do evil against a good God, by whom I live, move, and have my being? Oh no!

Thus consider these things, and do not go on to provoke the Lord, lest a worse thing befall you than any hitherto. Do not contend with God who is stronger than you are, who is able

[36]

when he will (and he will one day be found both able and willing enough) to turn the wicked into hell, the element of sin and sinners, who shall go into it as into their own place, as Judas did (Acts 1. 25). Oh, learn to pity your own soul, for he who sins offends and wrongs God, but also wrongs and destroys his own soul, or, as some read the text, despises his own soul (Proverbs 8. 36). Oh, think of it! what! have you no value, no regard for your soul? Will you neglect and despise it, as if it were good for nothing, but to be damned, and go to Hell? Will you be *felo de se*, a self-soul-murderer? Shall your perdition be of yourself? Oh, look to yourself, for sin, notwithstanding all its flattering pretences, is against you, and seeks nothing less than your ruin and damnation. And this brings and leads me to the second thing to be treated of, which is, sin's contrariety to man.

## 2. SIN'S CONTRARIETY TO MAN

This is the thing which our text (Romans 7. 13) especially means and intends, and it must therefore be more copiously spoken of. Sin is contrary to the good of man, and nothing is properly and absolutely so but sin. This results and is evident from sin's contrariety to God: just as there is nothing contrary to God but sin (for devils are not so but by sin), so sin in being contrary to God, is and cannot but be contrary to man. Inevitably, that must be evil to man, which is evil against God, who is the chiefest good of man. Communion with, and conformity to God is man's felicity, his heaven upon earth and in heaven too, without which it would not be worth his while to have a being. Now since sin is a separation between God and man, an interruption of this communion and conformity, it must needs be prejudicial and hurtful to him.

Besides, the commandment of which sin is a transgression was given not only for God's sake, that he might have glory from man's obedience, but for man's sake, that man might enjoy the good and benefit of his obedience, and find that in keeping the commands of God there is great reward. These two were twisted together, and no sooner is the law transgressed but God and man are joint-sufferers, God in his glory and man in his good. Man's suffering follows at the heel of sin, indeed, as he suffers by sinning, so in sinning; suffering and sinning involve each other. No sooner did sin enter into the world, but death, which is a privation of good, entered by it, with it, and in it, for sin is the sting of death. So sin says, Here is death, and death says, Here is sin. No sooner did the angels sin, but they fell from their first estate and habitation, which they had with God in glory. There was not a moment between their sin and misery; as soon as man had sinned, his conscience told him that he was naked and destitute of righteousness and protection, and consequently an undone man, who could not endure God's presence or his own (Genesis 3. 7–8). So apparent is it that sin, in being contrary to God, is contrary to man, for what crosses God's glory is opposed to man's happiness.

To proceed more distinctly, and in detail, I shall show that sin is against man's good, both present and future, here in time and hereafter to eternity, in this life and world which now is and in that to come. It is against all and every good of man, and against the good of all and every man.

1. SIN IS AGAINST MAN'S PRESENT GOOD, IN THIS LIFE, against the good of his body and the good of his soul. For on both it has brought a curse and death.

(1) Against the good of man's body. It has corrupted man's blood, and made his body mortal, thereby rendering it a vile body. Our bodies, though made of dust, were more precious than the fine gold; but when we sinned, they became vile bodies. Before sin our bodies were immortal (for death and mortality came in by sin), but now alas they must return to dust. It is appointed to all men once to die, and it is well if they die but once, and the second death have no power over them. They must see corruption, or the equivalent of death, i.e. a change; for this flesh and blood cannot inherit the Kingdom of God, as that with which we were created might possibly have done (1 Corinthians 15. 50). Our body is sown in corruption, in dishonour, in weakness (1 Corinthians 15. 42,

43), and is therefore called vile (Philippians 3. 21). Before this body is laid in the grave, it is languishing, in a continual consumption, and dying daily, besides all the dangers that attend it from without.

(2) Against the good of man's soul. The soul is transcendently excellent beyond the body, and its good is beyond that of the body; so that a wrong done to the soul is much more to man's hurt than a wrong done to the body. Therefore our Saviour says, Fear not them that can kill the body, and do no more (which is little in comparison of what God can do to the soul, if it sins), but fear him that can destroy, i.e. damn, soul and body in hell (Matthew 10. 28). It is not very ill with a man if it is well with his soul. We can more easily and cheaply die than be damned, and may better venture our bodies to suffering than our souls to sinning, for he that sinneth wrongs his soul (Proverbs 8. 36). Nothing but sin wrongs a man's soul, and there is no sin which does not do so.

Thus we see in a general way that sin is against the good of man's body and soul. But in order to exhibit this more clearly and fully, I shall consider and speak of man (1) in a natural sense, (2) in a moral sense.

## (1) In a natural sense

If we consider man in a natural or physical state, we shall find sin to be (i) against the well-being, and (ii) against the very being of man. It will not suffer him to be well or long in the world, nor if possible to be at all.

(i) It is against man's well-being in this life. Well-being is the life of life, and sin bears us so much ill-will, that it deprives us of our livelihood, and of that which makes it worth our while to live. Man was born to a great estate, but by sin, which was and is treason against God, he forfeited all. Man came into the world as into a house ready furnished; he had all things prepared and ready to hand. All the creatures came to wait on him and pay him homage; but when man sinned, God turned him out of house and home, and all his lands, goods and chattels were taken from him. Paradise was man's inheritance, where he had everything pleasant to the eye and good for food (he needed no clothes while innocent). But when he sinned, God dispossessed him of all, and drove him out into the wide world, like a pilgrim or a beggar, to live by his own hands and to earn his meat by the sweat of his brow, as you may read at length in Genesis 3.

Thus, by sin, man, who was the Emperor of Eden, is banished from his native country, and must never see it again but in a new and living way; for the old is closed up, and besides that, it is kept against him with flaming swords. Ever since, it has been every man's lot to come into and go out of this world naked, to show that he has no right to anything, but lives on the alms of God's charity and grace. All we have or hold between our birth and death is clear gain and mere gift. God might choose whether he would allow us anything or not, and when he has given he may take back again, and none of us has cause to say anything but what Job did: 'Naked came I into the world, and naked shall I return; the Lord hath given, and the Lord hath taken away; blessed be the name of the Lord' (Job 1. 21). All we have, our food and raiment, is only lent to us. We are only tenants at will, and therefore, seeing we deserve nothing, we should be content with, and thankful for anything (1 Timothy 6. 7, 8).

To show that man by sin had lost all, when our Lord Jesus came into this world for the recovery of man, and stood as in the sinner's stead, he had not where to lay his head. 'Foxes have holes, and birds of the air have nests, but the Son of man hath not where to lay his head' (Luke 9. 58). This plainly shows that the sin of man had left the Son of man nothing. Though Christ were Lord of all, yet if he will come in the likeness of sinful flesh, he must not go like the Son of God, but the Son of man, and be a man of sorrows, destitute, forsaken and afflicted. Though we fare the better for his suffering, he fared the worse for our sin; and among the other miseries he underwent, he had not where to lay his head.

To add yet another evidence of the venomous nature of sin in this matter, it is not a little remarkable that God did not take the full forfeiture, nor strip us so naked and bare as he might have done, but allowed us a competent subsistence and accommodation. Also, as the first fruits of his goodness, he made the first suit of clothes which Adam and Eve wore. Yet sin is against that good which God left us, and fills it with vanity and vexation, with bitterness and a curse. God left Adam many acres of land to till and husband, but he has it with a curse, sweat and sorrow; many a grieving briar and pricking thorn stick fast to him (Genesis 3. 17–19). God left him ground enough (v. 23), but, alas, it is cursed ground! So sin is against man's temporal good, either in taking it from him, or cursing it to him. Sin is so envious, that it would leave man nothing; and if God is so good as to leave him anything, sin's eye is evil because God is good, and puts a sting in it, viz. a curse. To be more specific:

a. *Sin is against man's rest and ease,* of which man is a great lover; and, indeed, he needs it as a great part of the well-being of his life. It is a sore travail which the sons of men have under the sun. What hath man of all his labour, and the vexation of his heart wherein he laboured? for all his days are sorrows, and his travail grief (Ecclesiastes 1. 13; 2. 22, 23). This is so whether he increase wisdom and knowledge, or pleasure and riches. He takes no rest in the night, but is haunted with vain and extravagant, if not terrified by frightful dreams; and his fancies, which are waking dreams by day, are more troublesome than those of the night. Man's ground is overgrown with thorns, so that he has many an aching head and heart, many a sore hand and foot, before the next year comes round, to get a little livelihood out of this sin-cursed ground. Man's paradisical life was easy and pleasant, but now it is labour and pain, such as makes him sweat. Even his recreations fall short of his labour, for pain and sweat (Ecclesiastes 2. 1–2). The old world was very conscious of this, as may be gathered from Genesis 5. 29: 'He called his name Noah, saying, This same shall comfort us concerning our work, and toil of our hands, because of the ground which the Lord hath cursed.' Sin, curse and toil keep company.

b. *Sin is against man's comfort and joy.* In sorrow shalt thou eat all the days of thy life (Genesis 3. 17). Not one whole merry day! It would be some comfort to a man, after he had toiled and moiled all day, if he could eat his bread with joy, and drink his wine with a merry heart. But sin will not allow him to do so; if he laughs, sin turns it to madness (Ecclesiastes 2. 2), or else it is no better music than the crackling of thorns (Ecclesiastes 7. 6). In Paradise, the blessing of God on Adam's diligent hand made him rich, and there was no sorrow with it (to allude to Proverbs 10. 22); but now man's sweetmeats have sour sauces – 'in sorrow shalt thou eat' – and his bread is the bread of affliction.

The female, the woman, has a peculiar sort and share of sorrow, for the time of conception, breeding, bearing and birth are tedious. Yet, alas! many who feel the pain which sin brought are not sensible of the sin which brought the pain, though their sorrow and pain also is greatly multiplied, as we find it expressed in Genesis 3. 16, and the more so for the want of faith and sobriety (1 Timothy 2. 15).

c. *Sin is against man's health.* From it come all diseases and sicknesses; till sin there were no such things. For this cause, in general, many are weak and sickly among you. Let man take the best air he can, and eat the best food he can, let him eat and drink by rule, let him take ever so many antidotes, preservatives and cordials, still man is but a shaky, sickly thing for all this. Verily every man in his best estate is a frail and brittle thing, yea altogether vanity (Psalm 39. 5); this text is spoken with reference to diseases and sickness. Take him while his blood dances in his veins, and his marrow fills his bones; even then he is a brittle piece of mortality.

d. *Sin is against the quiet of a man's natural conscience.* It wounds the spirit and makes it intolerable: 'A wounded spirit who can bear?' (Proverbs 18. 14). While that is sound and whole, all infirmities are more easily borne, but when that is broken, the supports fail, which has a great influence on the body: 'A merry heart doeth good like a medicine (there is no cordial like it) but a broken spirit drieth the bones' (Proverbs

17. 22); it sucks away the marrow and radical moisture. 'Heaviness in the heart of man maketh it stoop' (Proverbs 12. 25). A good conscience is a continual feast, but sin mars all the mirth. When Cain had killed his brother, and his conscience felt the stroke of the curse, he was like a distracted man, and mad. When Judas had betrayed his Master, he was weary of his life.

e. *Sin is against the beauty of man.* It takes away the loveliness of men's very complexions; it alters the very air of their countenance. 'When thou with rebukes dost correct man for iniquity, thou makest his beauty (or, as it is in the margin, that which is to be desired in him) to consume (or melt) away like a moth: surely every man is vanity (his beauty vain)' (Psalm 39. 11). There was no such thing as vanity or deformity till sin entered; everything was lovely before, and man above anything in the inferior world.

f. *Sin is against the loving and conjugal co-habitation of soul and body.* They were happily married, and lived lovingly together for a while, till sin sowed discord between them, and made them jar. There is now many a falling out between body and soul, between sense and reason; they pull in different directions; there is a self-civil war. Even in this sense the flesh lusteth against the spirit; the poor man is dragged and pulled this way and that, tossed to and fro as with several winds. Man is full of contradictions: time was when the mind commanded the body, but now this servant rides on horseback, while that prince walks on foot. Man is inverted: his head is where his heels should be; his soul is become a prisoner to the body, rather than a free man, far too often. The beast is too hard for the man, and the horse rides the rider. Sense lords it, and domineers over reason.

g. *Sin is against man's relative good in this world.* Man's comfort or sorrow lies much in his relationships; the weal or woe of his life is as his relationships are. That which was made for a help proves only too often a hindrance. Sin has spoiled society, so that one man is a wolf, even a devil to another. Sin will not let husband and wife, parents and children live quietly, but sets them at variance, and many times a man's enemies are they of his own house and bosom; they who eat bread at our table lift up the heel against us, and familiar friends become enemies. Lust makes wars (James 4. 1), and from pride comes contention (Proverbs 13. 10). It breeds divisions and factions in Church and State, so that there is little union or order, harmony, society or friendship in the world.

Thus sin sets itself to oppose man's well-being.

(ii) *Sin is against the very being of man.* Sin aims not only that man should not be well, but that man should not be at all. How many it strangles in the womb! How many miscarriages and abortions it causes! How many it sends from the cradle to the grave, who have run their race before they can go! Others die in their full strength, beside the havoc it makes by war, and some always eat their bread in darkness (Job 21. 23, 25). Man no sooner begins to live, but he begins to die; and after a few days, which are but as a span, and pass away more swiftly than a weaver's shuttle, sin lays all in the dust, princes as well as beggars. Sin has reduced man's age to a very little pittance, from almost a thousand to a very uncertainty, not only to seventy, but to seven, for among men no man's life is valued at more. Man's time is short and uncertain: he that is born today is not sure to live a day. And what is our life but as a vapour, which soon passes away. I could enlarge here, but this may suffice, to show that sin is against all the good of man in this life, considered in a natural sense.

## (2) *Sin is also against the good of man in a moral sense*

(i) *It has degraded man*, by defiling him, and has almost unmanned him; for, as our text speaks of sin as a man, so the Holy Scripture speaks of man as if he were sin, and every man were a man of sin (i.e. a man made up of sin) whether we consider the outer or inner man. Man was a very noble thing, made little lower than the angels (Psalm 8. 5). But, alas, by sin he is made almost as low as devils. Man was once a companion for God himself, but sin has separated between God and him, and has robbed man of his primitive excellence. From being a lord he is become a servant, indeed, a slave to creatures, to devils, and lusts of all sorts. Now this debasement came by defilement, which cleaves

a. *To his body*, for the flesh is filthy (2 Corinthians 7. 1), and the body needs sanctifying and cleansing (1 Thessalonians 5. 23). The body is a body of sin, the members are servants to uncleanness and to iniquity (Romans 6. 19). Take him from head to foot, from the crown of the one to the sole of the other, there is no whole (because no holy) part of him; but all is filthy, and full of putrefactions and sores. If we dissect and anatomize man, we shall find this only too true, for without naming every sin that cleaves to the whole or every part, but speaking in a more general way, it is thus said of sinful men : their *mouth* is full of cursing and bitterness, with their *tongues* they use deceit, the poison of asps is under their *lips*, their *throat* is an open sepulchre (Romans 3. 13, 14); *eyes* full of adultery (2 Peter 2. 14); the *eye-lids* haughty (Proverbs 30. 13); *ears* dull of hearing (Hebrews 5. 11), yea, deaf as the adder (Psalm 58. 4); the *forehead* is as impudent as a brow of brass (Isaiah 48. 4); both *hands* are employed to work iniquity (Micah 7. 3); the *belly* is an idol-god (Philippians 3. 19); the *feet* are swift to shed blood (Romans 3. 15); and if we look within, their *inward part* is very wickedness – the Hebrew is 'wickednesses' (Psalm 5. 9); the *gall* is a gall of bitterness, in a moral, as well as in a spiritual sense; the *spleen* is affected, indeed infected with envy and malice. What part is there which is not the seat of one or other evil?

b. *This defilement also cleaves to the soul*, which is the principal subject of it. It is not only flesh, but spirit that is filthy (2 Corinthians 7. 1). God's image was more in and on the soul than the body of man, and sin's ambition and desire is to deprive the soul of this image. Righteousness and holiness were stamped on man's soul, but sin has blotted this image and superscription, which once told from whence it came, and to whom it belonged, so that man is fallen short of the glory of being God's. It must be new created or renewed ere God will own it for his, because till then his image is not legible, if, in

[45]

this sense, it is his at all, for there is none righteous, no not one (Romans 3. 10).

It is not any one faculty only that sin has defiled, but, like a strong poison, it soaks and eats through them all; so that whereas all was holy, and holiness to the Lord, it is now evil, and evil against the Lord: Every imagination (figment or creature) of the heart is only evil continually (Genesis 6. 5). Even the Flood, which washed away so many sinners, could not wash away sin; the same heart remains after the Flood as before (Genesis 8. 21), and as it was with the heart of man from his youth, so it has continued to be to this old and decrepit age of the world. For to this day, there proceed out of the heart the same evil thoughts, words and deeds that then did (Matthew 15. 19). From this unclean fountain issues forth all that defiles the man.

Sin has made the heart of man deceitful, and desperately wicked (Jeremiah 17. 9), and it is hardened in impenitence through the deceitfulness of sin (Hebrews 3. 12, 13), although thereby man does nothing but undo himself, and treasure up wrath against the day of wrath (Romans 2. 5). It makes man obstinate, that he will not be saved, but will be damned: 'Ye will not come to me, that ye might have life' (John 5. 40). As for the Word of the Lord, we will not hearken, 'but we will certainly do whatsoever thing goeth forth out of our own mouth' (Jeremiah 44. 16–17). It is out of the abundance of folly and madness that is in men's hearts and bound up there, that they thus speak; not only vain thoughts and words, but villainous ones bubble and break forth from this corrupt fountain, which sets the tongue on fire of hell, so that the Devil could not broach and belch out more horrid blasphemies against God, than do the tongues and hearts of sinful men. It has defiled and spoiled man's memory and conscience also. How treacherous is his memory as to good! but alas it is too tenacious as to evil! The conscience is become an evil conscience, and in many a seared conscience.

Thus all over, without and within, man is defiled and polluted. I may speak more of this later, but at present I will show a little more fully how sin has almost put out man's eyes, and even extinguished the candle of the Lord:

*The effects of sin on the understanding.* It has dimmed and benighted man's leading faculty, the understanding, which should show a man the difference between good and evil, and guide him in the way in which he should walk. Now it is too often an *ignis fatuus* (will-o'-the-wisp) which leads men into bogs and ditches, into errors and immoralities. Sin has blinded man's understanding, and made him ignorant. It has depraved his understanding, and made him a fool.

(ii) *Sin has darkened man's understanding.* Poor man is wise to do evil, but to do good he has no knowledge (Jeremiah 4. 22). There is none that understandeth, viz, as and what he ought (Romans 3. 11). All the workers of iniquity have no knowledge (Psalm 14. 4). Poor man is covered with Egyptian thick darkness; he is said to be not only dark, but darkness in the abstract (Ephesians 5. 8), and, sadly, he is in love with darkness (John 3. 19), and his light is darkness (Matthew 6. 23).

That man is in darkness by sin is as clear as the light of the sun by the light of Scripture truth, beside that of sad experience. For, in general, when men are converted, they are called out of, and turned from darkness to light (Acts 26. 18; 1 Peter 2. 9). Our Lord Jesus came to be, and to give light to them that sat in darkness (Luke 1. 76–79). Indeed, none but he can open the eyes of them that are born blind (John 9). He was the light of the world, which without him is a dark dungeon. It may be seen in various ways that man is dark:

a. *By his groping,* which, in the Scripture, is constantly attributed to blindness and darkness. Peruse Deuteronomy 28. 29; Job 5. 14, and 12. 25; and Isaiah 59. 10. Man, like Solomon's wise man, had his eyes in his head, and clearly saw his way before him. The door and way of peace and happiness lay wide open to him. But now, like the blind Sodomites, he gropes to find the door of hope, and wearies himself in vain pursuits. Man has lost his way, since he lost his eyes. Poor man catches at every straw, grasps every trifle, if he can only find out what is good for him. Oh, how did Solomon seek and search this and that, tiring and vexing himself, till the true light guided him into the true way! How he groped after happiness, but felt none, till he came to fear God (Ecclesiastes 12. 13)!

b. *Though the light shines, yet man's darkness comprehends it not* (John 1. 5). Ah, how blind is the man, who at mid-day, when the sun shines in full strength, cannot see it! It was no great wonder that the law was darkness to man, for Moses had a veil on his face. But that the Gospel, the clearest light that ever shone in the world, that Christ himself, the brightness of his Father's glory, should not be comprehended – oh, marvellous darkness!

In the innocent golden-age, man could have comprehended the least hint that came from God, and have seen day through a little hole or crevice. He could have looked on the sun, and his eyes not blink. But now the natural man receives not the things of the Spirit, nor can he discern them. No, the wisdom of God, the preaching of the Gospel is foolishness to him (1 Corinthians 2. 14). This Gospel, while revealed, continues a hidden thing to this blinded world (2 Corinthians 4. 3, 4). And to know Christ Jesus requires as great a power as was in the creation, when God commanded light to shine out of darkness, as the Apostle tells us in the same place (2 Corinthians 4. 6, 7).

c. *By his walking in all kinds of wickedness*, which are called the works of darkness (Ephesians 5. 11). Good and holy works are of the light, and give light, for they shine (Matthew 5. 16); but wicked works are from darkness. Who but blind men would walk in dirt up to the ears, indeed over head and ears? Solomon, speaking of wicked men, says they leave the paths of uprightness, and walk in the ways of darkness. This is a clear evidence of their darkness, especially when we consider the boldness of men in sinning. Who is more bold than the blind? They rush like horses into the battle, without fear or wit. Did men see the danger that attends sin and wickedness, would they follow it to destruction? Oh no! he goes after her as a fool to the stocks, till a dart strikes through his liver; as a bird hasteth to the snare, and knows not (or sees not) that it is

[48]

for his life (Proverbs 7. 22, 23). For in vain is the net spread in the sight of any bird (Proverbs 1. 17), or of a seeing man.

d. *Man knows not whither he goes* (John 12. 35; 1 John 2. 11). Men are busy in this world, like a company of ants, creeping up and down from one mole-hill to another; but they are not so wise, for the ants know, but poor blind men do not know whither they go. Whether forward or backward, from home or to home, they are in a maze and bewildered. They think they are going to pleasure and profit, honour and happiness, but, alas, they are mistaken, and are going to pain and loss, to disgrace and death. They are like the Syrians, who thought they were going to Dothan as conquerors, but were found in Samaria at the mercy of their enemies; they were hoodwinked with blindness (2 Kings 6). In the same way, men think they are going heavenwards, when alas, sin leads them to hell, while their eyes are shut and they do not know where they go.

e. *He stumbles, and does not know why* (John 11. 9, 10; Proverbs 4. 19). Sinners are ever and anon stumbling at Christ Jesus; they are offended at him, but cannot tell for what. They would complain of something, and find fault with it, if they knew what; but they seek faults where none are to be found. Yet rather than not be offended with Christ, this shall be his crime, that he is guilty of none. The reason why they find so much fault with God is because he finds out their faults, and finds fault with them. Man's waspishness and touchiness, his being so captious and ready to take offence at God and godliness, are clear manifestations of his darkness. Did they know him, they would never crucify, nor be offended with the Lord of life, light and glory. Blessed is he that is not offended with Christ.

f. *Man knows not his time*, nor how to order his thoughts, words and actions. He does not know how to order any of his affairs in season, which is the beauty of all. Thus it is evident that, ever since the Fall, his intellect is bruised, and he has a soft place in his head. Man, like Job, could have said, 'His candle shined upon my head . . . by his light I walked through darkness . . . the secret of God was upon my tabernacle' (Job 29. 3–4). But, alas, now he must say, 'Because to every purpose there is time and judgment, therefore the misery of man is great upon him. For he knoweth not that which shall be: for who can tell him when it shall be?' (Ecclesiastes 8. 6, 7). Man knows not his time; it is not in man to direct his way (Ecclesiastes 9. 12; Jeremiah 10. 23). We cannot order our speech by reason of darkness (Job 37. 19). We know not what to pray for as we ought (Romans 8. 26). Ah! what a poor, silly thing sin has made man!

g. *He can be content to be led, even by a dog.* This is our last evidence that sin has blinded man. A half-eyed man may reign among the blind. Would a man be led by a dog if he were not blind? he would scorn it. Our Saviour tells us that the blind lead the blind (Matthew 15. 14); and if men were not blind, they would never be led by blind guides. But, being in the dark, they are best pleased by suitable guides: 'Like people, like priest', as God complains (Hosea 4. 9). 'The prophets prophesy falsely, and the priests bear rule by their means; and my people love to have it so' (Jeremiah 5. 31). Falsehood and flattery was their business, and the people's choice and pleasure. God and godliness, righteousness and holiness were troublesome; they must have smooth things and soft pillows. And alas, they were fitted to a hair, this suited their tooth and pleased their palate. But all this argues undeniably that men are dark and blind, who can be content with such dogs to lead them; and not only dumb dogs, but blind guides, yes, and false prophets too, who lead them into the ditch of sin and dungeon of Hell. What does all this prove but man's darkness? and what does that infer but sin's sinfulness in darkening the understanding of man? Is not light good? God who made it saw that it was so. But now, that the soul be without knowledge, it is not good (Proverbs 19. 2).

So sin is against the good of man in that it has put out the sight of his eyes, which, in a spiritual sense, is worse than if it had put out the eyes of his body. Man's eyes are very dear to him. God expresses the tenderness he has for his people by this, that they are to him as the apple of his eye (Zechariah 2. 8). And the Apostle sets out the love of the Galatians by this, that they would have pulled out their eyes for him (Galatians 4. 15). To show our love to God, we are to pull out our right eye, if it offend (Matthew 5. 29). Israel took great indignation at Nahash the Ammonite, when he would have put out their eyes (1 Samuel 11). Herein then lies the malignity of sin, that it has so darkened the eyes of man's understanding, and left him in this condition for a reproach.

(iii) *Sin has depraved man's understanding, and made him a fool*, a sot, a very brute; ignorant, foolish and beast are joined together in Psalm 73. 22. Folly is the common name of sin, and so is fools the name of sinners in the Scripture: 'Ye fools, when will ye be wise?' (Psalm 94. 8), i.e. O ye sinners, when will ye fear God? The fear of God is the beginning of wisdom, indeed, it is wisdom (Job 28. 28), the height of wisdom (Proverbs 1. 7). Till a man fears God, he only plays the fool. Indeed, he is unmanned, and beside himself, for when the prodigal, the representative of sinners and converts, repented, and was converted, it is said that he came to himself, and then quickly went to his father. In the recovery of man, our Lord Jesus Christ is made of God to us not only righteousness, but light and wisdom (1 Corinthians 1. 30). We were without that ourselves which Christ is made to us.

That this is the common case of Jew and Gentile, i.e. all men, the Apostle assures us (Romans 3. 9–11); indeed, men themselves declare it to be so. I may say of man as Solomon does of the fool: 'When he walketh by the way . . . he saith to every one that he is a fool' (Ecclesiastes 10. 3); the way and course he takes, his carriage and behaviour show him to be a fool. Like a child, a man is known by his doings (Proverbs 20. 11). As he that doeth righteousness is righteous, so he that doeth folly is a fool.

Man's folly is shown to be great in three ways:

a. *In relation to his chief and ultimate end, the* summum bonum. Man should seek greatly for happiness, in what to place it as well as how to obtain it. Oh the variety of opinions

[51]

that men have had about happiness! Varro tells us of a great many, but who can tell us of all? So many men, so many minds, for when man goes from unity, he falls into multitude. He has found out many inventions. Time was when man had light and wisdom enough to know that God was the *kuriotaton agathon*, the supreme and chief good, and that his happiness lay in knowing and enjoying God. But since sin, man has become such a fool as to say, in his heart, There is no God, at least no happiness in knowing God; for if sin does not make men such atheists as to believe there is no God, yet it makes them such as to wish that there were no God, and to say that it is no happiness to know him, or profit to serve him. Let us eat and drink, is the voice of men rather than, Let us seek and serve God. Who will show us any good, viz. corn, wine and oil, is the voice of man (Psalm 4. 6), indeed of all till regenerate.

Man has become so sottish and brutish that he lives by sense. Now sense will never look to God who is invisible – that is for faith – but to the creatures, which are visible, and the objects of sense. How Solomon has set this out to the life, in his Ecclesiastes, viz. that sense seeks for happiness below God; man is fond of toys and trifles, and seeks contentment where there is nothing but vexation, as if he could find ease in the place and element of torment, viz. in hell! He sets his eyes and heart upon that which is not (Proverbs 23. 5). The lust of the eye, the lust of the flesh, the pride of life is the trinity, the god of this world, and excludes the love of God (1 John 2. 15, 16).

All things of sense are only for one, and that the worse half, of man, viz. the body. Now when all a man's labour is for this, with neglect of the soul, which is the principal man of the man, what folly is it! To mind the less, and neglect the greater, to be troubled about these many things, and neglect the one thing necessary is folly with a witness, and will be followed with a vengeance. What is it, to labour for the back and belly, as if it were God, to mind earthly things and neglect, even despise heavenly, but folly in the extreme! it is to glory in shame (Philippians 3. 19). He who bade his soul take ease, in eating, drinking, and being merry, was called a fool, and so is every one that lays up treasure for himself, his sensual self, and is not rich toward God, as our Saviour tells us (Luke 12. 16–21). I have discoursed elsewhere on this text, to show the folly of such men, and, if God please, it may in due time come to view. Therefore, I shall wholly waive, and omit to speak of it here, though I did treat of it when I preached these sermons on the sinfulness of sin.

But before I proceed to the other manifestations of man's folly, in relation to the ways and means that lead to happiness, let me briefly show by three things, among many others that might be named, that man's happiness cannot be made up of any or all creature-enjoyments, of having the world for a portion, even all of it. For, beside what has just been said:

(1) *It was not so when man was in paradise.* Not only man, but all the creatures were in a better condition then, and not subject to vanity, as they are now. All that God made was very good, and Adam had all that God made—yet that was not his happiness. Now if the creatures in their best estate were not man's happiness, much less are they so in this their worst estate. So our sin, in placing happiness in creature-enjoyment now, is worse than Adam's sin was; for the creatures were then far more alluring, attractive and taking than they are now. A worthy person expresses it as follows: Though the old walls and ruinous palace of the world stand to this day, yet the beauty, gloss and glory of the hangings is soiled and marred, with many imperfections cast on every creature. What is only outside us cannot be our happiness.

(2) *That cannot be our happiness which is below us.* God's design in making the creatures was that they should serve us, and not that they should be served by us. God put Adam *colere*,* to till the earth, not *colere*,* to worship the earth and make a god of it, as earthly-minded men do, for covetousness is idolatry. Not only did God place them below man, but man reckons them below himself; for skin for skin, or skin after skin, yea, all that a man hath will he give for his life—which

* The same word (in Latin) bears both meanings.

is a great truth, though spoken by the Father of lies. By this it is evident that man reckons all below himself. Though old Jacob's life was bound up in the life of young Benjamin, yet he would part with him rather than starve. Now, without further amplification, it is as clear as the sun, that what is inferior to us cannot be our happiness.

(3) *That cannot be our happiness which is not so much as a token of the love of God.* If you had all the cattle on a thousand hills, and never so many thousand bags of gold in your chest, though all the beauty and honour in the world centred in you, yet I must tell you what a very wise man has told me: Man knows not love by prosperity, any more than hatred by adversity (Ecclesiastes 9. 1). Indeed, the world, great and good as it is, or was, is not good enough for a love-token. God sent his Son, and nothing else but him, and what is in him, for a love-token.

Well then, from all this we conclude, that seeing happiness is of a higher nature than the creation, and is not in less than God himself, man is a fool in seeking it elsewhere, and sin is very pernicious to man, in making him such a fool.

b. *Man's folly appears to be great in relation to the means and way leading to happiness,* as well as in relation to his end and happiness; he mistakes them both. The enjoyment of God is our happiness, and religion, viz. rightly serving and worshipping God, the means of enjoying God, and therefore of our happiness. Alas! here man is a very fool. Though in general men acknowledge that there is a God, and that God is to be worshipped and obeyed, yet who this God is, and how he is to be worshipped – man is full of darkness, doubt and perplexity about it. Hence we have expressions in the Scripture concerning sinners, such as: 'Ye worship ye know not what' (John 4. 22). Surely they who worship they know not what, worship also they know not how, as there follows. The Athenian altar had this inscription, To the unknown God (Acts 17. 23), and the world by wisdom knew not God, viz. God manifest in the flesh (1 Corinthians 1. 21). Though nothing is more knowable, yet nothing is more unknown than God. It is visible to all the

[54]

creation, by the creation, that there is a God (Romans 1. 20); but who and what he is, and what his will is, who hath known the mind of God? (1 Corinthians 2. 16).

Sin has made men worship either (1) a false God, which is idolatry; or (2) God falsely, which is superstition. Man has become such a fool that his worship, till enlightened and converted, is either a breach of the First or Second Commandment. He fails as to the object or the manner of worship, and both speak man's folly, that his religion is either idolatry or superstition.

(1) *Idolatry* is man's folly. To worship no God, or that which is not a God, but an idol, is folly. Therefore the Gentiles are called not only atheists, but a foolish people, and with this the Apostle upbraids them (Galatians 4. 8; Romans 1. 21, 25). Man is such a fool that he neglects to serve the God who made him, and serves gods of his own making, though the fact that they are made proves that they are not as their name is, but gods (like their knowledge) falsely so called, as is in detail imputed to them of old (Isaiah 44. 14–16).

The world has been guilty of most abominable idolatry. The Romans made diseases gods, such as the fever. And sinners make not only creatures, like gold and their belly, their God, but sins – this was the case among the aforementioned Romans. Even the Devil himself has been made a God and sacrificed to. He is called the god of this world (2 Corinthians 4. 4), and the Apostle says, the Gentiles sacrificed to devils (1 Corinthians 10. 20; cf. Deuteronomy 32. 17), and sacrificed not only their children (Psalm 106. 37) but their souls, for in all services, the soul is the sacrifice. Oh, sinful sin!

(2) *Superstition* is man's folly, also, as to religion. This is the younger brother to idolatry; it is of the same womb with idolatry. Superstition is not worshipping a false God, but worshipping the true God falsely, in a way not commanded by God. It teaches and practises for doctrines the devices and commandments of men; that is to say, it worships, not according to the will of God, but to the will of man. This is called the sacrifice of fools (Ecclesiastes 5. 1). They mind the matter

more than the manner, and are taken up with the work done, though it is not well done. They mind the outside more than the inside, yes, and worship God more because they fear him, than because they love him.

This must suffice to show man's folly, and how sin has duped man, as to his end, happiness, and the means to it, religion. I now proceed to show

c. *Man's folly as to the non-improvement or mis-improvement of means, when made known in truth and clearness.* Though the will of God as to worship is revealed, yet sin makes men fools still, either in that they do not use, or in that they make a bad use of the revelations of God. A treasure is put into their hand, but they are such fools as not to know how to use it (Proverbs 17. 16).

God has been pleased in and by Christ Jesus to declare his mind to us (1 Corinthians 2. 16). His Gospel and grace have appeared, teaching us (Titus 2. 11, 12). But alas! how men pervert the Gospel, turn grace into wantonness (Jude 4), and sin abundantly because grace abounds! What strivings and strugglings, reluctances and oppositions against the Gospel! How men stumble, and kick at and against Christ Jesus, instead of building on him as the corner-stone, as a rock and sure foundation! How angry they are when Jesus Christ comes by his Word and Spirit to bless them, in turning them away from their iniquity! When God comes in Christ Jesus and the ministry of his Gospel to reconcile them, and make them happy, they take up arms and make war against him. When the Gospel comes with the weapons of its warfare, to pull down the strongholds, and to reduce men to obedience, how they fortify themselves! When God stands at the door and knocks, and woos men for entertainment, how they lock themselves up, bar and bolt up their hearts against him, that the King of grace and glory may not enter in! It is no less a power than that which raised Christ from the dead, that makes men willing to believe and obey the Gospel (Psalm 110. 3; Ephesians 1. 19).

Christ's messengers make glorious reports, but who believes

them? (Romans 10. 16): They stretch out their hands, but to whom is the arm of the Lord revealed? They beseech and entreat, but men harden their hearts. And among the many who seem to profess the Gospel, how few practise it! In words they confess God, but in works deny him. They are lovers of pleasure, and themselves, more than of God; and though they have a form of godliness, they deny the power thereof. All these ways of theirs of not improving or mis-improving the means which God has vouchsafed, I say, all these their ways are folly .

It would be almost endless – if it were possible – to enumerate the follies of man. He thinks like a fool, unsteadily and rolling, independently and broken, inconsistently, and to no purpose, at random and rovers; many run waste, like waters beside the mill. He builds castles in the air; his imaginations are like vagabonds, and his contrivances romantic. This is not to mention the more wicked and sinful thoughts, which, if they were known, would make one man ashamed and afraid to converse with another. For not only vain, but vile, injurious, adulterous, murderous thoughts lodge in the hearts of men. Thus when anyone comes to be awakened, and made sensible of the sinfulness of his heart, it makes him say, as St Paul says of himself, I am the chief of sinners. Never was any heart such a shop of vanity, such a den of thieves, such a cage of unclean birds, such a Newgate of murderers, such an inn and thoroughfare of travelling lusts, such a court of flattery, ambition, pride and envy, such a sink and common draught of filthiness, such a hell of blasphemy as mine is!

As man thinks, he often speaks, *quicquid in buccam* (anything that comes into his head), foolishly, idly, and proudly, and as he speaks he acts; out of the abundance or fulness of the heart the mouth speaks, and out of the heart are all the issues of life. All the follies of his life are just the untying and letting loose of that folly which is bound and bundled up in his heart. They are there in gross, and are retailed out as he meets with customers, occasions and opportunities in the course of his life and conversation.

Let us consider some examples, and only some, of man's folly:

(1) *Man is so heady, hasty and rash in his undertakings.* Nothing more becomes a man than deliberation and consideration. This is his pre-eminence above the beasts; they act but do not consider. And herein is a great part of man's foolishness, that he does not consider the end of his actions. 'O that they were wise, that they understood this, that they would consider their latter end!' (Deuteronomy 32. 29). People often say, I never thought of this, and it is the property of a fool to say, I had not thought of this, in something which, maybe, it most concerned him to think of. 'The simple believeth every word (which he would not do but that he is simple and a fool) but the prudent man looketh well to his going. A wise man feareth, and departeth from evil: but the fool rageth, and is confident' (Proverbs 14. 15, 16). Did men consider what they are doing when they sin, they would abhor it; for who would rush to his own ruin? Who would drink poison? None but fools or madmen! Did men consider that the wages of sin is death, that wrath and hell attend sin, they would surely be more wary. Men go on and on, and never consider what the end of these things will be; will it not be bitterness in the latter end? His lack of consideration is a proof as great as it is clear that man is foolish.

(2) *Man laughs at, and sports himself in his sin and misery.* It is a sport to a fool to do evil (Proverbs 10. 23), and this sporting and jesting at sin shows him to be a fool in earnest. Fools will laugh at the shrewd turns and mischiefs which they do, and sinners are such fools that they make sin their trade (they are sin-makers) and their recreation too. It is their pastime to pass away, to spend and lose their time and souls in sinning. 'Fools make a mock at sin' (Proverbs 14. 9). When they have cheated others, they laugh at them as fools, though they themselves are the greater fools for cheating others. They sport themselves in their own deceivings (2 Peter 2. 13). Though they know that they who do such things are liable to the judgment of God, yet not only do they do the same, but have

pleasure in them that do them (Romans 1. 32). But they are fools for so doing, for professing themselves to be wise they became fools (v. 22), and they were without understanding (v. 31). But when God shall laugh and mock at these mockers, then it will appear what fools they were, who sported at that which should have been their greatest sorrow and grief.

(3) *Man says, It is vain to serve God*. What greater folly can there be than to call religion and the wisdom of God foolishness, vanity and unprofitableness, when beside them there is no profit under the sun? This is the whole of man; all the rest is vanity and vexation of spirit. The author of the seventy-third Psalm concludes himself a fool for having almost said this: foolish, ignorant, and as a beast (v. 22); so much a fool that he could not emphasize it enough. What fools, then, are they who say it openly? Because Job merely hinted at such a thing, Elihu reckons him among the foolish; 'Hearken to me, ye men of understanding (for fools will not); far be it from God that he should do wickedness' (Job 34. 9, 10). Oh no! the work of man will he render to him. There is a day coming in which a difference will be put between them that fear God and them that fear him not (which is spoken in connection with this very matter, Malachi 3. 14, 18) and then it shall appear that no man's labour is in vain in the Lord. I speak to wise men; let them judge what I say and I know they will conclude that it is egregious folly to say that it is vain to serve the Lord.

(4) *Man is so ungrateful to God, who has put him under an infinite obligation*. No matter how many courtesies you do a fool, it is like throwing pearls before swine, who return evil for all the good turns which are done to them. Moses upbraids Israel with this: 'Do ye thus requite the Lord, O foolish people and unwise?' (Deuteronomy 32. 6). None but fools would do so. And men are like swine in this, that they gather up the fruit that falls and never look up. 'Were there not ten cleansed? where are the nine?' said our Saviour. Scarcely one of ten proves thankful! Men take God's corn and wine and oil to make a feast for Baal, for their Bel and the Dragon, for their belly and lusts. Instead of giving God thanks and glory, they

[59]

return him sins. They kick with the heel when fat and full, and say, Who is the Lord? as if they were not beholden to him and did not owe him any acknowledgements. What fools!

(5) *If God corrects man, or afflicts him for his sin and folly, he soon grows angry with God.* Such is the nature of fools that they cannot endure those who chastise them. Though man is punished only for his iniquities, yet he complains (Lamentations 3. 39). Though God's judgment is just, yet the foolishness of man perverteth his way, and he fretteth against the Lord (Proverbs 19. 3). Man's sin brings God's judgment, and then, when God hedges up his way with thorns which prick him, he frets and fumes. When Job was sorely afflicted, his wife said, Curse God and die – which was a cursed speech. But Job said, Thou speakest like one of the foolish women. Men and women never speak more foolishly than when they speak against God. They are fools who quarrel with God and charge him with folly.

(6) *Man's folly is apparent in that he is unteachable.* One may better deal with seven men of reason than with one fool who is not only ignorant but conceited and stubborn. Fools despise wisdom and instruction (Proverbs 1. 7). They scorn to be instructed. They are in love with folly. 'How long, ye simple ones, will ye love simplicity?' (Proverbs 1. 22). A fool will not hearken to counsel (Proverbs 12. 15). Even though instruction comes from a father, yet a fool despises it (Proverbs 15. 5). Though you add correction to instruction, yet one 'reproof entereth more into a wise man, then an hundred stripes into a fool' (Proverbs 17. 10). Though you bray a fool in a mortar, yet will not his foolishness depart from him (Proverbs 27. 22). Thus it is that though Christ's messengers labour so much, they profit so little, for sin has made men such fools that they will not receive instruction.

(7) *Some men are such fools as to apostatize,* even after they have received the truth and have gone far in the profession of it, which is no small folly. 'As a dog returneth to his vomit, so a fool returneth to his folly' (Proverbs 26. 11 compared with 2 Peter 2. 20–22). The Word of God works on some

men like a medicine: it makes them vomit, makes them confess their sin, which one of the old writers calls *vomitus
animae*, as if it lay hard and heavy on their stomachs and they
were sick of it; but after a while they lick it up again. They
repent, and sin again as if they repented of their repentance.
For this reason the Apostle calls the Galatians fools: 'O foolish
Galatians, who hath bewitched you, that ye should not obey
(that is, go on to obey) the truth?' They had begun to obey,
and so he adds: 'Are ye so foolish? having begun in the Spirit,
are ye now made perfect by the flesh?' (Galatians 3. 1–3).
This is folly with a witness! An apostate is a double fool, a tree
twice dead. His latter end is worse than his beginning. Thus we
see how sin has duped men. But this is not all:

(iv) *Sin has degraded man and made him a beast.* It is true,
he has the shape of a man, but, alas! he is degenerated into a
bestial and beastly nature. I may begin, as Ovid began his
*Metamorphoses*: '*In nova fert animus*' (Strange things come to
mind). I must show you a monster, indeed, many monsters in
one: a dog-man, a goat-man, a wolf-man, a fox-man and so on.
It would be better to be a beast than to be like a beast, living
and dying like one. It would be better to be Balaam's ass than
such an ass as Balaam himself was. But to set this degeneration
and degradation of man by sin before you more clearly and
fully, I shall deal with it under three headings: Sin has made
man (a) like a beast, (b) like the worst of beasts, (c) worse than
the beasts.

a. *Sin has made man like a beast*, and not only like one, but,
indeed, a very beast! The Man of Sin, the great Antichrist, is
called a beast, and the great ones that Daniel saw in his vision
are called beasts. In Scripture, sinners are ten or eleven times
called brutish; and what some men are all would be if left to
themselves, if common or special, restraining or renewing
grace did not interpose and prevent. Three things will indicate
this likeness:

(1) Sinful man is like the beasts *in ignorance and stupidity*.
'So foolish was I, and ignorant: I was as a beast before thee'
(Psalm 73. 22). Man, though a man in honour, that

understandeth not, is like the beast that perishes (Psalm 49. 20); he is of no more value or honour, though he sits at the upper end of the world as the Antichristian beast does. O ye brutish, when will ye understand? O ye fools, when will ye be wise? (Psalm 94. 8). Brutish and foolish are synonymous and parallel expressions, as was hinted before. A heart void of understanding is the heart of a beast, as is clear from Daniel 4. 16 with 34–36.

(2) Sinful man is like the beasts *in sensuality*, as if he were only belly-wise, and had no soul to mind, or a soul only to mind his body. He places his happiness only in sensual and bodily enjoyments and satisfactions. In this sense some understand that saying: 'I said in mine heart concerning the estate of the sons of men, that God might manifest them, and that they might see that they themselves are beasts' (Ecclesiastes 3. 18). Solomon does not use a gentle or courtly compliment, but calls them (in downright and plain English) beasts. They live and die like beasts, make no provision for eternity, and have no mind for the world to come, which is the world of eternal good or evil.

(3) Sinful man's likeness to the beasts consists in, and is apparent from *his unfitness and unsuitableness for society and communion with God and man*. The sinner's society is but *societas belluina*, the society of beasts, and good men are as shy of it as of conversing with beasts. In the state of innocence among all the beasts there was not found a meet help, anyone for man to associate himself to and keep company with; and ever since, sinful man is as unfit for pleasing and profitable converse as the beasts were then. Job's friends took it as great scorn and disdain that they should be counted as beasts and reputed vile in his sight, that is, not fit or worthy of his conversation. God and sinful men do not walk together; they are not agreed. And good men are enjoined by God himself not to be unequally yoked, for 'what communion hath light with darkness?' (2 Corinthians 6. 14). Thus by their ignorance, sensuality and unfitness for society sinful men have become like beasts.

[62]

b. *Sinners are like the worst of beasts.* They are not only like beasts in general, but such as are called in Scripture, evil and hurtful beasts. Sinners are not likened to the dove or the sheep, the harmless creatures, but to lions, tigers, boars and bears, the ill-qualitied and ill-conditioned creatures. If at any time they are likened to a creature that is harmless, it is not for that good quality but for some bad one in the creature. For example, Ephraim is likened to a dove, not for innocence but silliness (Hosea 7. 11). So when sinners are likened to serpents it is not for their wisdom but their venomous and poisonous nature, or the enmity that is in them against mankind. But usually sinners are set out and painted like the worst of animals; like a dog, an angry dog, a creeping dog, a howling dog, a back-biting dog, a greedy dog, a dumb dog; by lions, devouring lions, roaring lions; by a raging bear; by a deceitful fox. So man is like the evil and hurtful beasts, for as one lion will devour many beasts and one wolf will devour many sheep, so one sinner devours much good (Ecclesiastes 9. 18) and his tender mercies are cruel (Proverbs 12. 10).

c. *Sin has made men worse than the beasts*; more beasts than the beasts themselves and worse than the worst of beasts. Sinful man is not only as ignorant as, but more ignorant than the beasts. He is more sensual and more unsociable than the sensual and unsociable beasts. This is apparent in several ways:

(1) The beasts do not transgress the law of their nature, but man has done and does so over and over again. The instinct of these creatures is their law, and they constantly observe it. The characteristic of a beast, which is condemnable in man, is not condemnable in the beast: ignorance and stupidity is no crime in an ox or ass, but it is in man. It is no fault in a lion to be devouring, but it is sin in man to be like a devouring lion. The beasts fulfil the law of nature, but men transgress it when they act like beasts. So sinful man is worse than the beasts.

(2) *Sinful man is worse than the beasts in the very quality for which he is likened to them.* The ox and ass have no understanding, and sinful man is compared to them for ignorance

and stupidity; but they are more knowing than he (Isaiah 1. 3). The same is spoken of the stork, crane and swallow, by way of rebuke to man (Jeremiah 8. 7). These foolish creatures have more understanding than sinful man. And as to sensuality man is worse than the beasts. Things of sense are the proper objects of an animal's appetite, but not of the natural appetite and inclination of man. It is no sin in an animal to be sensual, but it is so in a man, who though created to higher ends and purposes, is so degenerated as to be in many things more sensual and carnal than the animals are. Sin has made man so unsociable and cruel that bears are more kind to one another than men are; it were better for a man to meet a bear in her rage, when robbed of her whelps, than to meet a fool in his folly (Proverbs 17. 12). Man is more hurtful to man than the animals are to man.

I could give a long list or catalogue of the animals sinners are likened to, showing where the parallel or similarity holds. The wicked tyrannical rulers of the world are compared to a roaring lion and a ranging bear (Proverbs 28. 15): they have no pity, but make a prey of all to whom they come near. Hypocrites are like vipers (Matthew 23. 33). Herod was called a fox, not only for his craft and cunning, but for hunting after the life of the Lamb, Christ Jesus. Thus some sinners are like some animals and some like others, but there are two animals to which all sinners are likened: the goat and the dog.

a. Sinners are called *goats* (Matthew 25. 32, 33): He shall set the sheep, that is, the godly on his right hand, and the goats, that is, the wicked on his left. There are two or three things which naturalists observe concerning goats, in which the wicked are like them.

(1) Goats are very lascivious, wanton and lustful. Sinners are so too: the lust of the flesh, and the lust of the eye are the things they are taken with (1 John 2. 16). To these they give themselves up. The Apostle says, Among whom we all had our conversation in the lusts of the flesh (Ephesians 2. 3), and served divers lusts (Titus 3. 3). In this they are like goats.

(2) Goats are stinking animals. A goatish smell is a stinking smell, and to smell of or like the goat is to have a very strong, unsavoury and stinking scent. Likewise the wicked are in abomination to the Lord, a very stink in his nostrils.

(3) Goats are very bold and adventurous animals. They climb rocks and precipices to browse and feed on what they can get with hazard. In this sinners are like them too; they run risks and many dangerous adventures for a little, indeed, no satisfaction. They venture peace, conscience, life, soul and all, to get that which is not bread (Isaiah 55. 2).

b. Sinners are likened to *dogs*. I shall not make divisions in this nor pursue the metaphor into details, of which a little was said before. I will only show that though it was more usual with the Jews to call the Gentiles *dogs*, and our Saviour spoke in their language when he told the woman that it was not meet to take the children's bread and cast it to dogs (Matthew 15. 26), yet it is a common name for sinners, whether Jews or Gentiles, to all without God and Christ; for without are dogs (Revelation 22. 15).

All in all then, it is only too clear and evident what mischief sin has done man in thus degrading him, by making him a fool, an animal and a monster. And still this is not all.

(v) *Sin has separated man from God in a moral sense.* Though by nature we are his offspring and 'in him we live, and move, and have our being' (Acts 17. 28), yet morally and spiritually sinners are separated from God and are without God. This is a great injury; indeed, it is the greatest. For since God is man's chiefest good, to be separated from him must be his greatest evil and loss. There was always a very great disproportion and distance between God and man, God the Creator and man the creature, God Infinite and man finite, but this was no misery to man. It is sin, only sin that has made a difference and separation between God and man. Therefore sinners are said to be afar off (Ephesians 2. 13) for they depart from God and like the prodigal go into a far country (Luke 15. 13). In particular, sin has separated man

a. *From the sight of God.* Man could talk with God face to face, as a man converses with his friend, but alas! man cannot see his face and live. One of the first evidences of man's sinfulness and misery by it, was that he could not endure, but hid himself from the sight and the voice of God (Genesis 3. 8). Our happiness lies so much in the sight of God that it has the name of 'beatific vision', a sight which passes all sights. When our Saviour prays for the happiness of his own, he not only prays that they may be where he is but that they may see his glory (John 17. 24). And this is the glory which doth not yet appear, that we shall be like him, for we shall see him as he is (1 John 3. 2).

They who are regenerate and enlightened from above, and who are refined and clarified, have some glimpses and gradual sights of God, and yet it is, comparatively, called darkness: we see but darkly (as it were, his back-parts) through a glass, which is short of seeing face to face (1 Corinthians 13. 12). We live by faith now rather than by sight, as the Apostle expresses it in 2 Corinthians 5. 7. It is true, faith is to us instead of our eyes, for it is the evidence of things not seen (Hebrews 11. 1), and by it we look, as Moses did, to him who is and to his things which are invisible (2 Corinthians 4. 18). Seeing then that man's happiness lies so much in seeing God, what a great mischief has sin done to man in separating him from the sight of God! Man cannot see God and live, whereas the best life is in seeing God.

b. *From the life of God.* Sin has separated man not only from living to God and with God but from living the life of God, that is, such a life as God lives, which is a life of holiness and perfection. Therefore it is said of sinners that they are alienated from the life of God (Ephesians 4. 18). Indeed, they are dead in sins and trespasses (Ephesians 2. 1). They are so far from living that they are dead; so far from living to God that they live against God; so far from living the life of God that they live the life of devils. They live according to the prince of the power of the air, that is, the Devil (Ephesians 2. 2). What an injury sin has done in separating man from the divine life and nature and sinking him into the dregs and death of sin! It has made him dead in sin.

c. *From the love of God.* I am not speaking now of the love and goodwill which is in God towards man, but of that love and the actual communication thereof which man once had and enjoyed. Now sin has not only deprived him of this but made him the object of his wrath, for God is angry with the wicked every day (Psalm 7. 11), and they are by nature the children of wrath (Ephesians 2. 3, 4), and therefore are said not to be loved (Romans 9. 25). Man was once the object of his love and delight: when man came into the world in the likeness of God, God looked on him with delight and was enamoured of this his image. But sin has made him the object of his wrath. Oh, injurious sin!

d. *From communion with God.* While man and holiness kept company God and man kept company, but when man and holiness parted, God and man parted, and the restoration of any to this relationship is on a new basis. They could not walk together because of this disagreement (Amos 3. 3). When man left walking in the light of holiness and walked in the darkness of sin, fellowship ceased (1 John 1. 6, 7). It is true, there is reconciliation and recovery by Jesus Christ, but sin did what in it lay to cut man off from all communion with God for ever. Oh this spiteful and pernicious sin!

e. *From the covenant relationship in which he stood to God.* As a result God had no obligation upon him to own man or look after him or to have anything to do with him except to sentence him. And what sin did at first, if not repented of and pardoned, it will do to this day. Therefore sinners are called 'Lo-ammi', not my people, which is worse than not to be a people (1 Peter 2. 10). They are without God, promise and covenant (Ephesians 2. 12). Man can claim nothing of God as of right, having sinned; and therefore men are said also to be without hope that is, hope in themselves. What a separation sin has made! When it robs man of God it robs him of all things, for all things are ours only so far as God is ours (1 Corinthians 3. 21).

Arising out of this separation from God two great miseries come upon sinners as judgments upon it:

a. *God hides his face.* This follows on the separation, as is expressly stated in Isaiah 59. 2: 'Your iniquities have separated between you and your God, and your sins have hid his face from you, or, as the margin reads it, have made him hide his face from you. It is his face which makes heaven, and a smile of it or the lifting up of the light of his countenance upon us refreshes us more than corn, wine and oil (Psalm 4. 6–7). His loving kindness is better than life – we would have done better to have parted with life than with that! Man's sin is expressed by this, that he turns his back to God and not his face. His punishment is expressed by God turning his back to him and not his face. God behaves not like a friend but a stranger. Indeed, this hiding of his face signifies many more miseries than I can now stay to mention in detail.

b. Another and no less misery is that *God does not hear his prayers.* This follows in the aforementioned text (Isaiah 59. 2) and it accompanies the hiding of God's face (Isaiah 1. 15). God is a God hearing prayers, but sin shuts out our shouting, and the prayers of the wicked are an abomination unto the Lord who calls them no better than howlings (Hosea 7. 14).

There are two or three further miseries, not to name many more that result from this separation, which continually attend poor sinful man.

c. *Man is without strength.* Man's great strength is in union with God. Separation weakens him, for without God, apart from him, out of him, and separated from him we can do nothing. To be a sinner is to be without strength (Romans 5. 6, 8). Man was once a Samson for strength, but having parted with his locks, his strength is departed from him, so that of himself he is not sufficient to think one good thought (2 Corinthians 3. 5). He was strong while in the Lord and in the power of his might, but now his hands are weak, his knees feeble, and his legs cannot bear him up; he has got the spiritual rickets.

d. *Man becomes afraid of God and ashamed to come before*

*him*. While he was innocent, though naked, man was not afraid or ashamed to approach God, or of God's approaching him. But when he had sinned he was ashamed to show his face and afraid to see God's face or to hear his voice (Genesis 3. 9, 10). When righteous he was as bold as a lion, but now he runs into a bush.

e. *This separation and departure hardens his heart against God.* When God comes to talk with man about his sinning, he will lay it anywhere, even at God's own door as Adam did, rather than confess it. It is three times said in one chapter: 'Harden not your hearts', 'lest any of you be hardened', 'harden not your hearts' (Hebrews 3. 8, 13, 15). All this is in relation to hearing the voice of God. For when God comes to convict man he cannot hear of it but hardens his heart. And as it was in the beginning, so it is now among the sinful children of men.

## 2. SIN IS AGAINST THE GOOD OF MAN IN THE LIFE TO COME

It has brought on man that eternal death, damnation. In this life, man, by reason of sin, is in deaths often, but in the life to come he is in death for ever. If sin had only wronged man in this life, which is but for a moment, it would not have been so serious. But sin's miserable effects are everlasting: if mercy does not prevent, the wicked will die and rise to die again, the second and a worse death. There is a resurrection to life for the righteous, the children of the resurrection; and for the wicked a resurrection to condemnation or to death – for this is opposed to life (John 5. 29).

But before I show what damnation is and thus what mischief and misery sin has brought on man, I shall first state a few things which will make our passage smooth and easy:

### (1) *God damns no man except for sin*

Damnation is a punishment (Matthew 25. 46), and all punishment presupposes guilt and transgression. God, the Judge of all the earth, will do right and he lays not upon man more than is right, that man may not enter into judgment with God (Job 34. 23) or quarrel and find fault with him, which man would quickly do if God's judgment were not just, for even sinners themselves are judges. Death is but sin's wages (Romans 6. 23); that which sin has merited. Man's undoing is only the fruit of his own doing. Man's perdition is of himself (Hosea 13. 9). His own wickedness corrects him (Jeremiah 2. 19), and that not only in this life, but in the life to come (Matthew 7. 23; 25).

## (2) By sin all men are liable to condemnation

We were all of us children of wrath by nature (Ephesians 2. 3), and the wrath of God cometh upon the children of disobedience (Ephesians 5. 6). He that believeth not is condemned already (John 3. 18); he is in a state of condemnation beside that which unbelief will bring upon him. And he that believeth not, the wrath of God abideth on him (John 3. 36). He was a child of wrath by nature and continued so in unbelief; the wrath of God seizes on him as its habitation and abode. Every mouth must be stopped for all the world has become guilty; all have sinned and come short of the glory, and are obnoxious to the judgment of God (Romans 3. 19–23).

## (3) Some men have been, are, and will be damned for sin,

all but those who have condemned, do condemn and shall condemn sin and themselves for sin. If we judge ourselves we shall not be condemned of the Lord; otherwise woe be to us! When our Saviour sent his disciples to preach, he said, 'Go, preach the Gospel; he that believes shall be saved' (Mark 16. 16). Yes, but what if they will not believe? What shall we say then? Why in that case tell them, 'He that believes not shall be damned'. Now this is as great a truth of the Gospel, that he who believes not will be damned, as this is, that he who believes shall be saved. Heaven and salvation is not more surely promised to the one than Hell and damnation is threatened to, and shall be executed on the other. Broad is the way that leads to this destruction; there are as many paths to it as there are sins, but impenitence and unbelief are the highroad, the beaten path in which multitudes go to Hell.

*(4) Damnation is the greatest evil of suffering which can be-
fall a man*

It is the greatest punishment which God inflicts. This is the
wrath of God to the uttermost; it is his vengeance. Who knows
the power of his wrath? None but damned ones. To be damned
is misery, altogether misery and always misery. This will be
more evident when we examine what damnation is. It may be
considered in two ways: 1. Privatively as a punishment of loss
(*poena damni*). 2. Positively as a punishment of sense (*poena
sensus*). We have an instance of both of these in Matthew 25.
41: 'Then shall he say to them on the left hand, Depart from
me' – there is privative damnation – 'into everlasting fire' –
there is positive damnation. As sin is negatively not doing
good and positively the doing of evil, so damnation is a denial
of good to, and an inflicting of evil upon, sinners. Salvation is
*ademptio mali*, the taking away of evil, and *adeptio boni*, the
obtaining and enjoying of good. It is expressed in both ways in
John 3. 16: 'God so loved the world that he gave his Son that
whosoever believeth in him should not perish' – there is negative salvation – 'but have everlasting life' – there is positive
salvation. Similarly the damnation of sinners is negative and
positive.

From the above text (Matthew 25. 41) we may observe:

1. *Who are to hear and undergo this doom*, that is those on
his left hand, the goats, the sinners or the workers of iniquity
as it is in Matthew 7. 23.

2. *The sentence or doom itself:* 'Depart from me.' Woe unto
you, says God, when I depart from you (Hosea 9. 12); but it
will be woe, woe, woe when sinners must depart from God.
It is worthy of comment that the punishment answers to and
is called by the name of sin. What is sin but a departure from
God? And what is the doom of sinners but departure from
God? It is as if God should say to them, You liked departing
while you lived; now depart from me. You would none of me
nor my company; now I will none of you or yours. Depart
from us, is the cry of sinners to God (Job 21. 14). Depart from
me, will be the cry of God to sinners.

[71]

3. *The state in which sinners will be when they receive this doom* — 'cursed'. God will not send them away in peace or bless them before they go, but away they must go with a vengeance and a curse at their backs. They loved cursing, and cursing shall be unto them. All the curses in the Book of God shall light on them.

4. *The torment they are to undergo:* 'fire'. Indeed it is everlasting fire, kindled and maintained by the wrath of God.

5. *The company they are to have.* This will be none but 'the Devil and his angels'.

To comment on this briefly, it is as if sinners should say to God in the day of judgment, Lord have mercy upon us! Have mercy upon you! says God. No, I will have no mercy on you. There was a time when you might have had mercy without judgment, but now you will have judgment without mercy. Depart! Depart! If they should then beg and say, Lord, if we must depart, let it be from thy throne of judgment but not from thee. No, says the Lord, depart from me; depart from my presence in which is joy. Depart and go to Hell. Lord, they say, seeing we must be gone, bless us before we go so that thy blessing may be upon us. Oh no, says God, go with a curse; depart, ye cursed. Oh Lord, if we must go from thee, let us not go into the place of torment, but appoint some place, if not of pleasure, then of ease. No, depart into fire, burning and tormenting flames. Oh Lord, if into fire, let it be only for a little while; let the fire soon be out or us soon out of it, for who can dwell in everlasting burnings? No, neither you nor the fire shall know an end; be gone into everlasting fire. Lord, then let it be long before we go there. No, depart immediately; the sentence shall be immediately put in execution. Ah! Lord! let us at least have good company who will pity us though they cannot help us. No, you shall have none but tormenting devils; those whom you obeyed when they were tempters you shall be with as tormentors. What misery sin has brought on man! to bring him to hear this dreadful doom!

I come now to consider in detail privative and positive damnation.

1. *Privative damnation*. This penalty of loss will not be the least plague of the sinner's Hell. He shall be deprived of all good, never to enjoy a good day or a good thing more. When once a man is damned he may bid adieu to all good (Luke 16. 25). But we will go on by degrees, step by step.

a. *Damned sinners will be stripped naked and deprived of all the good things they have had in this life*. Wicked men are called the men of this world (Psalm 17. 14); they have their portion and consolation in this life (Luke 6. 24; 16. 25). Many of them fare well and prosper in this world. They have stately houses, lavish tables, full cups, soft beds, pleasant walks, and delightful gardens filled with fragrant fruits and flowers. They sit at the upper end and they have the grandeur and finery of this world. But when they come to be damned, neither riches nor honours nor pleasures will go with them. Wicked men would be content with the good they have if they could have it always. If, like Dives, they might be clothed with purple and fine linen and fare deliciously for ever, they would say 'Happy is that people, that is in such a case' (Psalm 144. 15). But this vain petty happiness, such as it is, they must part with for ever, and bid adieu for good and all to all their good. When devils carry away their soul, whose shall all these things be (Luke 12. 20)? None of theirs, for all must be left behind. They cannot carry with them a drop of water to cool their tongues. To have a portion of this world may be a mercy, but to have the world for a portion is a misery. To have all good things in this life and only for this life is a misery indeed! You shall be clothed with silks no more. You shall eat the fat and drink the sweet no more.

*Objection:* Saints themselves must part with these things too.

*Answer:* This is true, but they shall have better things in lieu of them. The impenitent sinner goes from all his good to all evil, but the saint goes from all his evil (and a little good) to all good. Who would not part with counters for gold? or with a world for Heaven? This a saint does and it is a good exchange, I think. But when a man must part with all his jewels, all his fine things, his wine and music and the delights of the

[73]

sons of men, and have no good thing left him, how sad is his condition!

b. *Sinners must part not only with these things but with the joy, pleasure and delight they had from them.* These good things of which they will be deprived are most valuable for the use and comfort of them. The rich man in Luke 12 did not cheer himself in having much goods but because he expected ease and mirth from them. The wicked spend their days in mirth (Job 21. 12), and have a fine time of it, as they think. They sing care away all the day long and refresh themselves with *requiems* and *placebo* songs;* they chant to the viol. And though this frolic and joy is a misery in itself (for what truer misery is there than false joy?) yet it is the best they have in this world.

But even this must be parted with. This crackling of thorns will go out and their mirth will end in woe, their joy in sorrow and their light in darkness. It will add to their grief in Hell that they were so merry on earth. When this evil day comes they will say that there is no pleasure in remembering their old days. It seems Dives was loath to think of this, and so Abraham said, 'Son, remember'; but it was a sad remembrance to remember good things as being lost and gone for ever! They will say then as Adrian did, Oh my poor soul! Thou wilt laugh and joke and jest no more.

c. *They must suffer the loss of all their peace.* It is true, the wicked have no real and solid peace here, for there is no peace to the wicked, saith my God (Isaiah 48. 22; 57. 21). But they have that which they call peace, and which is to them instead of peace, that is, security and stupidity, a seared and benumbed conscience; because of this they think that they are in peace. But when they come to Hell all will be different. Conscience which was seared as with a red-hot iron here will feel the flames there and be alarmed by it. They who met with no trouble here will be consumed with terrors there. There are no seared consciences in Hell; they are all tender and sensitive there. Conscience will awake and rise up like a lion or gnaw

* *Placebo* songs=songs that please.

like a worm. They shall no longer have the small comfort of concealing their pain as they used to do here.

d. *Sinners then must lose the hopes they had of Heaven.* Wicked men have no reason to hope for Heaven and yet they will hope, though against hope, as Abraham and good men hope against hope when they have God's promise. Notwithstanding God's threatenings the wicked will build their hopes as high as Heaven even though they build on the sand and without a foundation. But their fall will be great (Matthew 7. 22–27), from the hopes of Heaven into Hell. The hope of God's people keeps their heart from breaking and it shall never be ashamed, but this hope of sinners will break their heart in Hell, for there it will be ashamed. When the wicked dies, his expectation shall perish and the hope of unjust men perishes (Proverbs 11. 7). Their hope shall be as the giving up of the ghost (Job 11. 20). The hypocrite's hope shall perish and his trust is but as a spider's web. He shall lean upon his house but it shall not stand. He shall hold it fast but it shall not endure (Job 8. 13–15). Where will the hope of the hypocrite be when God takes away his soul? Will God hear his cry when trouble comes upon him? (Job 27. 8 and 9). No, he will not.

e. *They must suffer the loss of all good company.* They shall no longer have the company of a single good man. In this world the wicked fare the better for God's people being among them. Though they despise and scoff at them and think them not worthy to live, yet God assures us that the world is not worthy of them (Hebrews 11. 38). Truly they are too good for this world. Now though the wicked count good and holy men's lives to be folly and madness, when they come to die they would be glad with all their hearts if their souls were in as good a condition as those of the righteous after death. Balaam, that wicked wretch, who loved the wages of unrighteousness and lived in unrighteousness all his days, even he could wish to die the death of the righteous and that his latter end – the Hebrew is his *afterward* or *after state* – might be as theirs (Numbers 23. 10).

At that time the wicked would be glad to take hold of the

skirt of a Jew, that is, one who is so inwardly (Romans 2. 28 and 29), and say, 'We will go with you, for God is with you' (Zechariah 8. 23). But they will find a great gulf fixed between them. Heaven will not hold any of the wicked, nor shall Hell have any of the righteous to hold. 'The ungodly shall not stand in the judgment, nor sinners in the congregation of the righteous' (Psalm 1. 5). Here below they may throng in, the bad among the good, but hereafter God will find them out and separate them. Though now many a sinner may separate from the world to join with saints, then God will separate them from saints and join them with sinners and devils. They shall be excommunicated from the society of saints and be delivered up to Satan, the executioner of God's wrath and vengeance, and have no company but the damned crew.

f. *They must be without Heaven which they hoped for*; not only without their hopes of Heaven. To have parted with their hopes for possession of Heaven would have been no loss, but gain; but to part with their hopes and with Heaven as well is a double loss. Whatever shall be the portion of the saints, they must go without it and not share in it in the least degree. And though perhaps, as some think, the wicked may be permitted to look into Heaven, as Dives saw Lazarus in Abraham's bosom, it will only be to heighten the depth of their misery by letting them see what they have deprived themselves of by their sin. To lose Heaven is to lose a kingdom and glory, more worthy and more glorious than all the kingdoms of this world, and their several glories put together. It is to part with rest, or *Sabbatism* as it is called: Sabbaths they cared not for while they live, and Sabbatism or rest they will have none when they die. They gloried in their shame in this world and in the world to come they shall have shame enough, but no glory. The thought that they were happy, though only in imagination, and that others are really happy for ever while they themselves are excluded from any share in any happiness – this will cut them to the heart.

g. *They must suffer the loss of God himself*, who is the Heaven of Heaven. All good things are like a drop in the ocean

[76]

in comparison with him. 'Whom have I in Heaven but thee' (Psalm 73. 25) — as if all the rest were nothing. If a saint went to Heaven this very day he would say like Absalom: 'Why am I come up from Geshur if I may not see the King's face' (2 Samuel 14. 32). This will be the misery of miseries for the damned, that they must depart from God, in whose presence only there is joy and pleasures for evermore. They must see his face no more except as they shall see it frowning upon them for ever. The good people sorrowed most for the words that Paul spake, that they should see his face no more (Acts 20. 38). This will prick and wound sinners to the heart that they must see God's face no more, no more of his goodness, no more of his patience, no more of his mercy. When Cain, who is a type of this, was turned out of and banished from the presence of the Lord, he cried out that his punishment was intolerable (Genesis 4. 13).

h. *They shall continue utterly incapable of any alteration for the better.* This makes Heaven so much Heaven, that it is always so, and likewise what makes Hell so much Hell is that it is always so. In this world there is a door of hope, a day, an offer, and means of grace, space for repentance, a Mediator in Heaven, a patient God, and a possibility of being blessed. But once damned, the door is shut and it is in vain to knock. The day, offers, and means of grace are at an end. No room is left for repentance. God's longsuffering will suffer no longer. The mediation of Christ Jesus is over. There is no possibility of mending one's condition. We should hear the words of the wise: 'Whatsoever thy hand findeth to do, do it with thy might; for there is no work (no working out salvation) in the grave, whither thou goest' (Ecclesiastes 9. 10). Think of it, poor sinner, think of it in time before it is too late; for if you die in your sins, though you should weep out your eyes in Hell it will do you no good. God will not know you nor hear your cry, but will laugh at your calamity and mock you in the midst of your torments (Proverbs 1. 25 and 26).

I have now briefly shown you the privative part of damnation, that wicked men must part with all their goods, joys, peace, hopes, and good company, all of which stood them in good stead in this world, and with Heaven. And what is more and worst of all, they must part with God himself and be utterly incapable of ever being in a better condition. And what do you think now? Is not sin exceeding sinful, which separates man from all good, past, present and to come? If it were only from past good, what Adam enjoyed in Paradise, or only from present good, such as men have in this world, it could be better endured. If the future and eternity were secured it would be well. But sinful sin has cut off Paradise, so that none of us were ever in Eden since we came into the world; it has spoiled, embittered and poisoned with a curse all present temporal enjoyments so that they prove satisfactions to none but vexations to all. Yet of so spiteful and malignant a nature is sin that it reserves its worst until last, namely Hell and damnation. And it will be worse to us in eternity than it was in time. In order to make this still more evident I proceed to consider the second part of damnation.

2. *Positive damnation.* This the schools justly call *poena sensus,* the punishment of sense. If it were not for this, that men will then feel both their loss and their gain – the pain which they have gained by their sins – damnation would seem to be but a dream or an imagination. But their senses as well as their understanding, feeling as well as fancy, will tell them what a dreadful thing it is to be damned. It is a thing which I wish with all my soul that none of you may ever know save by hearing of it, and I wish that hearing of it may be a means to prevent your feeling it. But what shall I do? Who that has not been in Hell can tell what Hell is? Who would go there to find out what it is? Surely eye hath not seen nor ear heard, neither hath it entered into the heart of man to conceive what God hath prepared for them that love him, and likewise for them that hate him, that is for impenitent sinners.

It is the design and work of sin to make man eternally miserable, and to undo him, soul and body, for ever. The better to represent this doleful state and woeful misery I shall search the Scriptures and endeavour to fathom the depth of expressions used there. Thus we may learn what damnation is, and from that the sinfulness of sin. I will first lay down three propositions:

a. The punishment that sinners must undergo will be such a state of misery that *all the miseries of this life are not to be compared with it*. They are nothing to it. If you take the dregs of all the miseries of this life and extract from them an essence, the very spirit of miseries, as men take the essence from the lees and dregs of wine and beer, it will fall infinitely short of this misery which is damnation. The gripings and grindings of all the diseases and torments that men do or can suffer in this life are like flea-bites to it. To pluck out a right eye or to cut off a right hand would be a pleasure and recreation in comparison with being damned in Hell (Matthew 5. 30). A burning fever is nothing to burning in Hell. Indeed – to make a sweeping but true statement—if all the miseries which have been undergone by all men in the world were united and centred in one man, it would be nothing to Hell. Hell would be a kind of paradise if it were no worse than the worst of this world.

b. It will be *a state quite contrary to that which the saints shall enjoy in eternity*. Their different states are expressed in different terms: 'He that believeth shall be saved, but he that believeth not shall be damned' (Mark 16. 16). Damnation and salvation are contrary states. One is a state all of evil and of all evil; the other all of good and of all good. 'The wicked shall go into everlasting punishment, but the righteous into life eternal' (Matthew 25. 46). The life which saints obtain, sinners go without; and the misery the saints are delivered from, sinners are delivered to. As different as grief is from joy, as torment is from rest, as terror is from peace; so different is the state of sinners from that of saints in the world to come (Romans 2. 6–10).

c. *This damnation-state of sinners will admit of no relief.* It will be punishment without pity, misery without mercy, sorrow without succour, crying without comfort, torment without ease. The sinner can look for no relief from God, for God judges and condemns him; none from conscience, for that accuses and upbraids him; none from the devils, for they torment him; none from hope, for that is departed from him; none from time, for this state is for ever. It is a state of all misery and it has no consolation, not so much as a little drop of water to cool the tongue. It is misery, more misery, nothing but misery, just as sin is all sin, and nothing but sin.

I will consider the damnation-state of sinners in detail under six heads: (1) The torments themselves and the kinds of them. (2) The quantity and quality of them. (3) The duration of them. (4) The tormentors or inflictors of them. (5) The aggravations of them. (6) The effects of them. By the time that I have set these before you, I expect you will conclude and cry out, oh sinful sin! What a thing is sin! And who would sin at this rate, and go to such great expense to damn himself!

1. *The torments of Hell*. Under this heading I shall consider the place with its names, and the thing itself.

a. *The place with its names*. In general, and most frequently, it is called Hell, the place and element of torment (Luke 16). This is the general rendezvous for the wicked after the day of judgment. It is common to express the dreadfulness of any condition or thing by joining the name of Hell to it, just as to signify excellence of a thing the name of God and Heaven is joined to it. For example, the cedars of God.

(1) Hell is a place and state of sorrow. The greatest sorrows are called 'the sorrows of hell' (2 Samuel 22. 6). Just as the joys of heaven are the greatest joys so the sorrows of hell are the greatest sorrows.

(2) It is a place and state of pains and pangs far beyond those of a woman in travail. 'The pains of hell gat hold upon me' (Psalm 116. 3). There is no ease in hell.

(3) Destruction is joined with it. To be in hell is to be destroyed. 'Hell and destruction are before the Lord' (Proverbs 15. 11). He can destroy body and soul in hell (Matthew 10. 28).

(4) It is a place and state of fire, of fiery indignation. He that calls his brother fool without cause and in rash anger is in danger of hell fire (Matthew 5. 22), the worst of flames (Luke 16).

(5) There is damnation in it and ascribed to it: 'How can ye escape the damnation of hell?' (Matthew 23. 33).

(6) Torment is attributed to it. It is called the place of torment (Luke 16. 28).

Thus you see what kind of a place and condition hell is. It is all these and much more than these words can express or than you can conceive from these expressions.

Let us now consider the names given to the place hell:

(i) Hell is called *a prison*. Heaven is set out by attractive and delectable things and similarly hell is set out by what is distasteful and loathsome. A prison is one such thing and so hell is called a prison (Matthew 5. 25; 1 Peter 3. 19). Prisons and common jails are the worst places to live in, but hell is worse than the worst of prisons.

(ii) Hell is called *'the bottomless pit'* (Revelation 9. 11). The devil is the angel of the bottomless pit. This is a pit into which sinners must fall and be ever-falling, for there is no bottom.

(iii) Hell is called *a furnace of fire*. That is a terrible thing: Nebuchadnezzar's furnace was terrible, especially when heated seven times more than usually, yet hell is a worse furnace of fire (Matthew 13. 41–42). Those who do iniquity (who are sin makers by trade) shall be cast into a furnace of fire which shall not devour them but shall torment them and make them wail and gnash their teeth.

(iv) It is called *a lake which burneth with fire and brimstone* (Revelation 21. 8). Certain people there named shall have their part and portion in the lake which burneth with fire and brimstone. They shall always be over head and ears in this lake, yet never drowned; always burning but never burnt to ashes. They will in this be like the burning bush which was burnt with fire but was not consumed. As the church was on earth so will sinners be in hell.

(v) It is called *utter and outer darkness*; even though it burns with fire and brimstone, those flames will administer the heat of wrath but not the light of consolation. Darkness is a dreadful thing, but to be in the fire in darkness, to be tormented in flames and still in darkness, how dismal must this be? 'Bind him hand and foot and cast him into outer darkness' (Matthew 22. 13). Thus it will be in vain to think of making resistance, for you will be bound hand and foot and be in darkness too. Indeed it is called chains of darkness (2 Peter 2. 4), and blackness of darkness for ever (Jude 6, 13).

b. The thing itself, Hell. We shall consider the thing itself with its names, for as its name is so is it. The most common and usual name of this punishment is damnation, which is a dreadful word. Who knows how much it means? It will make the stoutest heart tremble, the most confident countenance to fall, the most daring courage to fail, when they feel it. If His wrath be kindled but a little, it is terrible; how much more is it so, then, when it shall be wrath to the uttermost? For it is contrary to being saved to the uttermost. In particular it is called

(i) *Destruction.* That is to say, it is a moral destruction, not of man's being but of his well-being. They shall be taken, destroyed and utterly perish (2 Peter 2. 12). And they shall be punished with everlasting destruction from the presence of the Lord (2 Thessalonians 1. 8, 9). It would have been better for them that they had never been born, or if born, that they had never died, or if died, that they had never risen again, than to be thus destroyed. To be banished from God and the Divine Life is the worst death (Hierocles).

(ii) *It is a curse.* It is to be in an accursed state, under the curse of God. God not only says, 'Depart from me', but 'Depart, ye cursed' (Matthew 25. 41). There is not the least dram of blessing or blessedness in this state. If so many curses hung over the Jews while on earth when they continued in their impenitence (Deuteronomy 28. 16–20), how full of curses is this state of damnation! This valley of Gehinnom is a Mount Ebal, the Mount of Curses (Deuteronomy 27. 13).

(iii) Damnation is called the *second death* (Revelation 21. 8). It will be a strange and miraculous kind of death, a living death, a death which never dies, an immortal mortality. They whose portion this death is will live, and death will be their portion all their life.

(iv) It is a state of *shame and contempt*. There is scarcely anything in this world that we are less willing to undergo than shame. Although a thief is not afraid to steal, when he is arrested he is ashamed. Shame and confusion and contempt will be their lot. 'Many of them that sleep in the dust of the earth shall awake, some to everlasting life and some to shame and everlasting contempt' (Daniel 12. 2, 3).

2. *The quantity and the quality of the torments of hell and damnation*. These will be exceedingly great and terrible; they will be universal; and they will be without intermission.

a. *They will be exceedingly great and terrible*. They are such as will make the stoutest hearts to quake and tremble. If the writing on the wall caused a change in Belshazzar's countenance, and trouble in his thoughts, so that the joints of his loins were loosed, and his knees smote one against the other (Daniel 5. 6), what a commotion and heartquake will the day of God's wrath and vengeance produce! You will find an instance of this in Revelation 6. 15–17, where not only bondmen, that is, persons of little and puny souls, but great and mighty men, chief captains and kings of the earth, that is, persons with great souls who have made the earth to tremble, shall hide themselves in dens and rocks and say to the mountains, Fall on us and hide us from the face of him that sits on the throne and from the wrath of the Lamb, for the great day of his wrath is come and who shall be able to stand? For bondmen to be faint hearted and flee is no great wonder, but for men of might and power to run away and hide, that is strange! but you see it is from wrath, even though only the wrath of a Lamb. So what will they do when he shall rise up and roar like the Lion of the tribe of Judah?

It is the day of wrath, which is the terrible day of the Lord. It is the day of vengeance which is implacable. For God who is now hearing prayer will not then spare for their crying; not even though they cry, Lord, Lord. God always acts like himself, like a God. When he shows mercy it is like the God of all grace who is rich in mercy and loves with a great love; so when he executes wrath and vengeance, he makes bare his arm and strikes like a God. Who knows the power of his anger? None but damned ones! The sense of it here, the fearful reception of judgment (as it is in the Greek, Hebrews 10. 27) and fiery indignation, make a kind of hell; so fearful a thing is it to fall into the hands of the living God when he acts like a God of vengeance, as the apostle speaks in verses 30 and 31. How dreadful a thing then would it be to be in hell itself under the tortures of his executed wrath for ever?

As the man is so is his strength. It is only a game to be whipped by a child. But to be whipped and lashed by a man or a giant whose little finger is heavier than another's loins, how painful must it be! The rod is for the back of fools, but when it shall be turned into scorpions and God himself shall lay on strokes without mercy or pity, how tormenting will it be! A stone thrown from a weak arm will not hit very hard, but when the hand and arm of God shall throw down that wrath from heaven which is now only threatened against ungodly men, and turn them into hell as a mighty man throws one over his shoulders, how will it sink them deep into hell!

b. *The torments of hell will be universal.*

(i) *The torments themselves* will be universal. It will not be merely one or two torments but all torments united. Hell is the place of torment itself (Luke 16. 28). It is the centre of all punishments, sorrow and pain, wrath and vengeance, fire and darkness; they are all there as we have already shown. If a man goes through so much with one disease, what would a complication of diseases mean? If one punishment, the rack or some other torture, is so tormenting, what would all be at once? What then will Hell be?

(ii) *The persons* on whom these torments will be inflicted *will be universally tormented.* Not merely one or two parts of the person, but all over. The whole man has sinned and the whole man will be tormented; not the soul alone, or only the body, but the soul and the body, after the resurrection and the judgment. All the members of the body have been instruments of unrighteousness, and therefore all the members will be punished. As man is defiled from the crown of his head to the sole of his foot, so will he be plagued. The senses which men have indulged and gratified will be filled with pain and torment. This will be clean contrary to those pleasures with which they were gratified in this world. The eye which took so much pleasure in and was enamoured of beauty shall then see nothing but ugly devils and deformed hags of damned wretches. And the ear that was delighted with music and lovesongs, what shall it hear but hideous cries and gnashing of teeth, the howlings of damned fiends. The smell that was gratified with rosebuds and sweet perfumes shall have no pleasing scents but unsavoury brimstone and a stink. The taste that refreshed itself with eating the fat and drinking the sweet must have nothing but the dregs of the cup of God's wrath. The touch and feeling shall then be sensible, not of fine and silken things, but of burning flames and scorching fiery indignation.

The soul and all its faculties will fare no better. The mind will be tormented by understanding the truth with terrible force. That which it laughed at as foolishness it will then find true by the loss of it, that is, gospel happiness. The conscience will be like a stinging adder, a gnawing worm. The will will be vexed because it has had its own way for so long. Here men think it is a princely thing to have their wills, but there they will find it a devilish thing.

c. *These torments will be without intermission.* They shall be tormented day and night (Revelation 14. 11). They shall have no rest. In this life our sleep is only a parenthesis to care and sorrow and pain, but there, there will be no sleeping. The God who executes wrath and those upon whom wrath is executed neither slumber nor sleep. Here they may have some intermission and some sane moments in their madness, but there, there will be night continually for vexations of heart.

I cannot go any further without pleading with you, whoever you are, who are reading this. Do you need anything more to dissuade you from going on in sin which is the way to damnation than the thought of damnation, and what a damnation, which is at the end of the way of sin? For your soul's sake hear and fear and do no more wickedly. What! Will you be damned?

[85]

Can you think calmly of going to hell? Have you no pity on your precious soul? If you were to go from reading of hell, into hell, you would surely say, There was a prophet, and I would not believe it, but now I feel it. Think of this and also of what follows.

3. *The duration of these torments.* They will be for ever. Even though they were great, universal and for a time without a break, yet if you knew that they were to have an end, that would be some comfort. But here lies the misery of it, they will be today as they were yesterday, and for ever. As they were in the beginning so they will be all along and for ever; always the same, if not increasing. This is the world's woe, the hell of hells, that it is woe and hell for ever. After the sinners have been in hell millions and millions of years, hell will be as much hell as it was at first. The fire that burns will never go out and the worm that gnaws will never die—these things are three times repeated by our Lord and Saviour in one chapter (Mark 9. 44, 46, 48). It will be a lasting, indeed an everlasting misery. It is everlasting punishment and everlasting fire (Matthew 25. 41, 46).

4. We must now consider the *tormentors* or inflictors of these torments. These are the Devil, conscience, and God himself who will torment the damned.

a. *The Devil.* The tempter will be the tormentor; they will not only be tormented with devils but by devils. They will be delivered to the jailors, the tormentors: 'So likewise shall my Heavenly Father do also unto you' (Matthew 18. 34, 35); that is, deliver you to the tormentors. When the church excommunicates, which is a symbol of this, it delivers to Satan; and when God excommunicates he gives up to the Devil, saying, Take him, jailor, and torment him, tormentor. The apostle thought it a great misery to fall into the hands of unreasonable men and therefore he prays and begs the prayers of others against it. But if the tender mercies of wicked men are cruelties, what are the cruelties of the Devil and his angels, especially when God delivers men up into their hands? What a misery it is to fall into the clutches of the Devil! To be tormented by the Devil! If he does so much now by permission, what will he then do by commission, when he shall be under no restraint! By what he now does we may very well guess what he is likely to do, and will do then.

There are many instances of his malice, rage and power; let us take one or two. We read of one possessed of a dumb spirit; 'Wheresoever this spirit taketh him, he teareth him that he foameth, gnasheth with the teeth and pineth away' (Mark 9. 17–22). When he came into the presence of Christ Jesus he tore him, that he fell on the ground and wallowed foaming. Oftentimes he cast him into the fire and the water to destroy him. You know also how the Devil dealt with Job and went to the utmost extent of his commission, and almost prevailed, for he brought him to curse the day of his birth, though he did not curse God. If now while he is still in chains and under restraint the Devil can do so much to torment a man, how sad is it likely to be with men when the Devil shall have them in his hands by commission from God! When God shall say, Take him, Devil, Take him, jailor! Into the fire with him! Do your worst with him! Who can stand before the Devil's rage and envy when it has been whetted by a commission from God! Sinful sin which thus gives a man up to the Devil!

b. *Conscience* is the second tormentor. I mean a reflecting, an accusing, and an upbraiding conscience. In some ways this is a greater torment than any the Devil can inflict, because conscience is within us whereas the Devil is outside of us. What is within has the greatest influence upon us, whether for comfort (1 John 4. 4) or for torment (Mark 9. 44). The worm that never dies is within a man. It would be a dreadful thing to be eaten up of worms, to be continually fretted and vexed with the gnawing of worms, but this worm gnaws the spirit, which is more tender than the apple of one's eye. A wounded spirit who can bear? Judas sank under the weight and burden of it and so have many more. But if conscience is so terrible when awakened here, what will it be when a man shall be fully convinced and have all his sins set in order before his face (Psalm 50. 21)? How will conscience lash men then? It will be as when schoolmasters reckon up their boys' crimes: first for this, and then a lash; next for that, and then another lash, and so on. So conscience will say, salvation was held forth, grace was offered, and then it will lash you for neglecting so great a salvation and turning grace into wantonness. Then follows the next charge. Says conscience: You knew that the wages of sin was death and that the judgment of God is just, and yet you would do such things; and then conscience pricks and torments, whips and lashes. The next point: after you had vomited up your pollution and had been washed from your filthiness, you returned like the dog to your vomit and like the sow to your wallowing in the mire. And then it lashes you again. If a man were falsely imprisoned, that would be some mitigation, some relief, but when a man is self-condemned and finds that his perdition is of himself, and that his own wickedness comes home to him, this will be the sting of death and damnation.

c. *God will torment them*; not only the Devil and conscience, but God himself. Though in this life God allows himself to be pressed with their sins just as a haycart is pressed down with sheaves, yet at the last he will show his power in avenging himself upon all wicked men. Now he seems to have leaden feet and to be slow to wrath; but then he will be found to have iron hands. Here God is patient, and if he does judge, yet in the midst of judgment he remembers mercy; he does not deal with men as their wickedness deserves. But then he will be extreme in punishing; the Lord himself will rain upon wicked sinners fire and brimstone and an horrible tempest (Psalm 11. 5, 6). This shall be the portion of their cup from the Lord. They shall drink of the wine of the wrath of God which is poured out without mixture in the cup of his indignation. They shall be tormented with fire and brimstone in the presence of the holy angels and of the Lamb (Revelation 14. 10, 11). Sometimes when judges suspect that their officers will not execute the judgment properly, they will have it done in their presence, with the whole court and company looking on. So it shall be with the sinner, 'and the smoke of their torment ascendeth up for ever and ever, and they have no rest day nor night.'

5. *The aggravations of these torments* must now be considered. Sin has been aggravated and so will the torments be. There will be degrees of torment. Though it will be intolerable for all, yet it will be more tolerable for some than others (Matthew 11. 21–24). In certain cases the torments will be aggravated:

a. *Those who have lived long in sin.* The longer men have lived in sin on earth the greater will their torments be in hell. 'The sinner being an hundred years old shall be accursed' (Isaiah 65. 20). He has for a long time been treasuring up wrath against the day of wrath. He has a greater count to pay for all the patience and forbearance of God. Some people grow rich by having other men's goods; men leave their money in their hands and do not call it in, and so they grow rich by it. In the same way wicked men grow rich in wrath by abusing the goodness and patience of God. God forbears them and does not enter into judgment with them and so they grow rich. But alas, they are rich in wrath.

b. *Men who have had more means.* The more expense God has been put to and the more pains he has taken with men, if they still continue impenitent, the more severe will their judgment be. If Christ had not come they had had no such sin. This is the condemnation, that light is come into the world and men love darkness. Capernaum that was exalted to heaven, that is, in terms of the means of grace it enjoyed, will be thrown to hell in the end (Matthew 11. 23). To fall from earth to hell will be a great fall, but to fall from heaven to hell will be a greater. To go from Turkey to hell will be sad, but to go from England to hell, and from London to hell, ah, how ruefully sad!

c. *The more convictions men have had, the greater will their condemnation be*; that is, the more knowledge they have attained to without practice and improvement (Luke 12. 47). That servant which knew the Lord's will and did not according to his will shall be beaten with many stripes. And it were better they had never known the way of righteousness than, having walked in it, to depart from it (2 Peter 2. 21). To him that knows to do good and does not do it, to him it is sin, that is, great sin or sin with a witness and condemnation with a vengeance. How can they escape the great condemnation who neglect the great salvation? Such people will become inexcusable under the judgment of God (Romans 1. 32 compared with Romans 2. 1, 2, 3).

d. *The further men have gone in the profession of a religion the greater will their condemnation be!* They have gone far but without the power of godliness. Formalists and hypocrites will know the worst of hell: 'how can ye escape the damnation of hell' (Matthew 23. 33)? Not only hell but the damnation of hell, the hell of hells! The form of Godliness and the power of ungodliness will fare alike at that day (Matthew 24. 51 compared with Luke 12. 46).

e. *Apostates will meet with aggravated torments in hell.* The back slider will be filled with his own ways; his latter end will be worse than his beginning (2 Peter 2. 20). It would have been better for them had they died in their sins at first than to be twice dead as they are now (Jude 12).

6. So much for the aggravations of torment. We must now consider *the effect of these torments.*

a. *Inexpressible sorrow.* There will be sighing and groaning that cannot be uttered, weeping and wailing and gnashing of teeth (Matthew 8. 12). Anger, indignation and vexation, even to madness and rage, will be the effects of this torment.

b. *Intolerable sorrow and pain.* If thunder, lightning and earthquakes make men afraid and shrink together, what will hell do! If the throbbing of toothache or the gnawing of gout puts men to such excruciating pains, what will hell do! If sickness makes us fear death, and the fear of death is so dreadful, what will hell be! If you, like Felix, tremble to hear of this judgment to come, what would you do if you were to undergo it! If to see ugly and devilish shapes frightens us, what will it do to be with the Devil and his angels!

c. *Final and eternal impenitence.* This will be the sad effect of these torments and despair, even to cursing and blaspheming. He who dies impenitent continues so for ever; and impenitence brings with it blasphemy. 'They shall pass through it hardly bestead and hungry, and it shall come to pass that when they shall be hungry, they shall fret themselves and curse their king and their God' (Isaiah 8. 21). I quote this to show what a fretting and vexing heart is like under torments. This is very common with people who are despairing and therefore desperate. When men are scorched with great heat, they blaspheme the name of God and repent not to give him glory. 'And they gnawed their tongues for pain and blasphemed the God of heaven because of their pains and their sores' (Revelation 16. 10, 11). When the plagues of God are on impenitent sinners, there are cursings. Though they may be sorry for the plagues, yet they are not sorry for the cause of them, which is their sins. And so many infer that if these plagues, which are far inferior to those in hell, provoke men so much, the plagues of hell will do so much more. Thus we see what a dismal and miserable condition it is to be damned and what a sinful thing sin is which brings this damnation.

I have now dealt with the way in which sin is contrary to the good of man in this life and in the life to come. But before I go on, to bring in the witnesses to prove this charge against sin to be true, let me urge you, Reader, to consider what has been said. I do this so that you may be more afraid of sin than of hell; for had it not been for sin, hell should not have been, and you will never be in hell if you repent and believe the gospel, for righteousness is not by repentance but by faith. So believe and love faith as you love your souls and heaven. Hate sin and avoid it as you would hell and damnation. Sin no more, lest a worse thing come unto you, lest the rod be turned into a scorpion, lest the next loss be the loss of heaven, lest the next sickness be unto death, and death unto damnation. For if you die in sin you are damned irrecoverably. It would be sad to die in a hospital or a prison or a ditch; but it is worse to die in sin, just as it is worse to live in sin. If you go on in sin, this book will witness against you as much, if not more so, than if one had risen from the dead. If two or three devils or damned wretches should come from hell and cry Fire, Fire, it might startle you, but if you do not believe Moses and the prophets and Christ and his apostles, it will do you no good.

Therefore, mind the good of your soul and do not bring on yourself this great, universal, intolerable and eternal damnation. Take heed lest, when your flesh and body are consumed and your soul damned, you should say too late: 'How have I hated instruction and my heart despised reproof; and have not obeyed the voice of my teachers nor inclined my ear to them that instructed me!' (Proverbs 5. 11–13). You will say, how I have rewarded my own soul with evil by doing evil against God! I scorned these things and mocked at sin, but now when I would hear, and when I would return, hope is perished. Such will be the terrible cry of sinners one day. Take heed therefore, for if you have not the wedding garment on, you will be cast out (Matthew 22. 11). And if you are found a worker of iniquity, you must depart accursed.

# SECTION THREE

# THE WITNESSES AGAINST SIN

———

If sin is so exceeding sinful that it is extremely and notoriously guilty of contrariety to God and man, I have a cloud of witnesses to produce. These include God himself, angels and men both good and bad, the law and the gospel, the whole creation, sins' names and actions. Even sin's own confessions bear witness to this charge that sin is an exceeding sinful thing. From heaven, from earth, even from hell, will we bring witnesses against sin.

## I. GOD HIMSELF BEARS WITNESS AGAINST SIN

He does not leave us without witness that he is good and neither does he leave us without witness that sin is sinful, that it is against him and that it is against the good of man.

### (1) *God has forbidden sin and made a law against it*

All the laws and every command of God are his witnesses against sin. He who does not believe the testimony God bears of his Son makes God a liar, who is true and cannot lie, and so does he who does not believe God's testimony against sin. The law written in man's own heart, the law written in tables of stone and the gospel also (1 John 2. 1) which is the law of faith, are written as witnesses against sin.

Now surely God would not have prohibited sin had it not been an abominable thing, abominated by him and to be abominated by us. God has given man room and scope enough, a very large allowance. Of all the trees of the garden man might eat, only one being excepted. Whatsoever things are true, honest, just, pure, lovely; whatsoever is of good report, if there be any virtue, any praise, these things think on and do (Philippians 4. 8). Now sin comes under none of these names but is contrary to them all and therefore it is forbidden. God has not forbidden man honours or riches, nor any pleasures except the pleasures of sin. Surely then, seeing God does not delight to grieve the children of men but rejoices over them to do them good with all his heart and all his soul, as he is pleased to express it (Jeremiah 32. 41), he would never have forbidden anything to man but what was prejudicial to him, as well as being displeasing to himself. But I shall speak more of this when I show how the Lord God witnesses against sin.

## (2) *God will not allow us to do evil that good may come*

Thus God witnesses against sin. As pleasing a thing as good is to God, yet he will not allow us to do the least evil for the greatest good. We see how angrily and with what indignation the apostle speaks against those who said the contrary (Romans 3. 8). Indeed, it is a damnable doctrine to teach that we may do evil for a good end, or that good may come of it. This doctrine was first broached by the Devil and ushered in the first sin (Genesis 3. 1–6).

1. *We may not do evil that good may come to ourselves.* God allows man to love himself, and he has made self-love the rule and measure of our love to others: 'Thou shalt love thy neighbour as thyself'. God is not against man being rich, only he will not let men grow rich by sin (Jeremiah 17. 11). God is not against man's pleasure so long as it is not attained by displeasing or dishonouring him. God well knows that good gained by evil will do man no good but only hurt. To gain the world and lose a man's soul has more of loss in it than of gain; and there is not a single sin which does not wrong and hazard the loss of a man's soul. God would not allow Adam and Eve to eat of the forbidden tree, even though it was good for food, pleasant to the eye and to be desired to make one wise (Genesis 3).

[96]

2. *We may not do evil that good may come to others.* God indeed has commanded us to do good to all, but he forbids us to do evil to that end. He that provides not for his family is worse than an infidel, but so is he that provides for it by a sinful way, by covetousness, lying, cheating or oppressing (Habakkuk 2. 9–12). Paul, like Moses before him, could wish himself dead and anathematised to save the Jews, but he did not dare to sin for their sakes. When someone asked St Augustine whether he might tell a lie for his neighbour's good, Oh no, he said, you must not tell a lie to save the world. There is such a malignity in sin and it is so contrary to God, that it must not be done for any good. It is our duty to honour our father and mother, but this must be in the Lord; though it may be a duty to disobey, if not to hate father and mother, rather than obey them if to obey them will be disobedience to God. 'Whether it be better to obey God or man, judge you.' So God will not allow us to sin to gratify the greatest persons or our nearest and dearest relations.

3. *God will not allow us to sin even though we should professedly do it for his glory.* Sin can never directly glorify God, and though he knows how to bring good out of evil, yet he does not wish that we should sin for him. He does not need us, much less our sin. God will take vengeance and is righteous in doing so, even though our unrighteousness commend and enhance the righteousness of God (Romans 3. 5). Though the truth of God has more abounded through your lie, yet you will be found a sinner (Romans 3. 7). So for this good, evil must not be done (verse 8).

Those who cast out their brethren, saying, Let God be glorified, God will put them to shame (Isaiah 66. 5). Though they thought in putting them to death that they should do God good service, yet God reckons it as their serving the Devil (John 16. 2 with Revelation 2. 10). When Saul excused his sin under a pretence of sacrifice, it was called rebellion and reputed as witchcraft, a most abominable thing (1 Samuel 15). Job upbraids his friends with this irreligious piety: 'Will ye speak wickedly for God? And talk deceitfully for Him? . . . He will surely reprove you' (Job 13. 7, 10). Sin is so much the worse for being committed in the name of the Lord. Men thereby make God serve the Devil's designs.

It will be no excuse that men like Herod, Pilate and Judas fulfil the counsel and secret will of God (the determination of God as to what eventually shall be), if they sin against his revealed will, which is the rule by which men are to walk and to which they are to be obedient. So by all this it plainly appears that God witnesses against sin, that we may not sin for the good of any, nor for any good, not even for God.

### (3) God witnesses against sin by threatening man

In case men sin he makes penal statutes against sin. If thou eatest the forbidden fruit thou shalt surely die. If sin were not an abominable thing, surely God would not have forbidden it on such peril, on pain of death. More will be said of this when we consider the execution of these threatenings and the just judgment of God on sinners.

### (4) God is angry with the wicked

God is angry with the wicked every day (Psalm 7. 11) and that proves that God is angered by them; for he is displeased with none save those who displease him, and nothing displeases him but sin. Is that not an evil thing then that tempts God, provokes him to jealousy, to anger, to wrath, and even sometimes to swear in his wrath (Hebrews 3)? Though judgment does not come every day, yet God is angry every day. David prayed that God would not rebuke him in anger (Psalm 6. 1) for who knows the power of his anger (Psalm 90. 11)? If his anger and wrath be kindled but a little, how happy are those who trust in them (Psalm 2. 12)! 'If God will not withdraw his anger, the proud helpers do stoop under him' (Job 9. 13), all the helpers of pride, as it reads, for man is apt to be very proud and has helpers of pride. Now it is noticeable that the word which we read as 'pride' signifies strength also, to denote that man is very apt to be proud of his strength. But all the strong helpers of pride must stoop if God does not withdraw his anger. The strength of riches (Proverbs 10. 15), the strength of friends and family (Psalm 49. 7), strength and stoutness of spirit, must all stoop if his anger break forth, if he take but one of his arrows and discharge it against a sinner, if he strike him with only one blow of his sword (Psalm 7. 11–14). 'Kiss the Son, lest he be angry and ye perish from the way' (Psalm 2. 12). Perishing is at the heels of his anger. 'The fear of a king is as the roaring of a lion; whoso provoketh him to anger sinneth against his own soul' (Proverbs 20. 2). How dreadful then is the anger of the King of kings! When God sets our iniquities before him, we are consumed by his anger and troubled by his wrath (Psalm 90. 7). We know therefore that if God's anger is so terrible and that it is sin which makes God angry, then certainly sin is extremely sinful and contrary to God. Otherwise the God of all grace, the God of patience, whose name is love, would never be so angry at it and for it.

## (5) *Sin alone made God repent that he had made man* (Genesis 6. 5, 6)

God saw that the wickedness of man was great on the earth and that every imagination of the thoughts of his heart was only evil continually, and it repented the Lord that he had made man on the earth, and it grieved him at his heart. And so in verse 7, God says, It repenteth me that I have made them. Now the repentance of God argues a very great dislike of and displeasure against the wickedness of man. There was a time, although it lasted only a little while, when there was no sin, and when God looked on what he had made, he was very far from repenting, and was infinitely pleased. But when sin had spoiled the fashion and beauty of his work, then indeed, speaking after the manner of men, he grieves and repents. So it is not the work of his own hand but the work of man's heart that makes God repent. Is God man that he should repent? What a horrible thing must that be which makes the unchangeable God change! For such a thing is repentance, a change. It repented the Lord that he set up Saul to be king (1 Samuel 15). When men do wickedly God repents that he has done them good (Jeremiah 18. 7–10). If men do evil against God, God repents of the good he has done men. But such is his goodness that if men repent of their evil God will repent of the evil he thought to do to them. Now just as anything which makes God repent of the evil must be very good, so undoubtedly anything which makes God repent of the good he has done to man must be very evil.

## (6) *God witnesses against sin by many great and severe judgments*

He has threatened judgments to sinners and will in all ages execute them on many. On some sinners he will do so to all eternity. For what God has done shows what God will do, as the Apostle Peter infers (2 Peter 2. 3–6). Sinners greatly mistake God when they say that evil is good in his sight, or Where is the God of Judgment? (Malachi 2. 17). They no less forget themselves and what God has done when they say, All things continue as they were, and so go on to scoff, Where is the promise of his coming?, that is, his coming to judgment (2 Peter 3. 3–4). It is true, if God were to judge as fast as men sin, the world would soon be depopulated and at an end. But his patience now is an argument of his judgment to come (2 Peter 3. 9, 10). At that time when God sends men to hell and damns them, they will know and acknowledge what an evil thing sin was and what bitterness it brings in the latter end.

Since damnation is such a dreadful thing, no less than the pouring out of God's wrath for ever on sinners, we must conclude that sin is extremely displeasing to God because it is contrary to him. That can be no little matter for which God brings on men such grave damnation. The next judgment to this consists in being left alone or given up to a reprobate judgment and a hardened heart. But that, though a present judgment, is invisible, and eternal damnation is future and so I shall not further speak of them, but will show that God has visibly judged this world for sin from age to age.

He is a God that judges in the earth, as he is a God who will judge the earth. 'The Lord is known by the judgment which he executeth: the wicked is snared in the work of his own hands' (Psalm 9. 16); he is known to be against sin. So notable a text is this that it has a double note added to it – Higgaion, Selah. I do not remember any other text where this happens.

God has testified his displeasure against sin by executing judgment on sinners, saints, and his Son.

1. *God has executed judgment on sinners.* Usually the first person to commit any particular sin has been punished with eminent and remarkable punishment. Not to mention Adam who was all men in one, and who underwent a punishment and a curse for his sin, Cain, the first murderer, was as it were hung up in chains as a terrible warning to others. Judas, the first apostate, was made an example under the law, as were Nadab and Abihu, the first breakers of the ceremonial law after the establishment of Aaron's priesthood. Ananias and Sapphira, the first who lied to God in the beginning of the Christian church, were miraculously punished. God has made heaps of witnesses this way. God has set up monuments for pillars of salt, like Lot's wife. The flood that drowned the old world, the fire which burnt up Sodom and Gomorrah, and the many things that befell Israel for an example, were all types, as the Apostle says in 1 Corinthians 10. 11. God has punished all sinners more or less. He spared not the angels that sinned; they were all doomed to darkness. He consumed almost a whole world at once; only eight persons were saved. He has cut off cities and nations not a few, as well as the things that have happened to individuals. Therefore men cannot say that all things continue as they were, and that God is not a God of judgment or that he is an allower of the evil of sin.

There is no age in which God does not really and actually judge sinners. Perhaps this may not be so clear to prejudiced and partial observers, who think that nothing is a punishment except what is miraculous or extraordinary. As if the earth must always swallow men up, or God strike men down with thunderbolts continually, and nothing less be called a punishment! How often is God's hand lifted up but men will not see, indeed, felt yet not acknowledged! God has his deputy in men's bosoms, their own conscience which often accuses and condemns them so that they cannot stand before its judgment. When their hearts smite them they sink, and their countenance and courage falls, as was the case with Cain and Judas and Spira. If men were only honest and would only tell what stings of conscience they feel, there would be witness enough how God lashes man within, and executes judgment upon their spirits. But God often inflicts corporal punishment visibly and before the eyes of others. Before the flood this was most commonly done directly and in person. But it may also be through an intermediary, sometimes by angels, and sometimes by magistrates who are human and mortal gods, deputies to the God above. You could say that by these God rides circuit and holds assizes very frequently. Judgment is now a strange work and does not seem so appropriate to this day of patience as to the day of wrath which is to come. Yet even so, God often makes examples and though he does not make as yet a full end of all nations, yet he leaves none altogether unpunished.

2. *God has executed judgment on his own people* when they have sinned, to show how hateful sin is, even in those he so dearly loves. One would think that if God would spare any, he would spare his own; and indeed, he pities them and spares them as a father pities and spares the son who serves him. But though he forgives them, yet he takes vengeance on their iniquity (Psalm 99. 8). God forgives many a sinner, as to punishment, in this life, who will not be forgiven in the world to come; but since God fully resolves to forgive his people for ever, he will not wholly forgive them, that is, he will not leave them altogether unpunished here in time. God has been very severe with his people when they have sinned; it has cost them dear. King David's adultery and murder cost him broken bones: 'Heal the bones that thou hast broken', he says in a penitential psalm (Psalm 51. 8). When Peter had sinned it cost him a bitter weeping. Repentance is a costly thing. It is disgrace, sorrow and pain to a man, even though it is a grace and duty.

If God's children go astray and play truant they must feel the rod. It is the rod of the Covenant, for chastening and correction of wantonness are in the Covenant as well as the supply of wants, threatening of judgment as well as promises of mercy. Sometimes sin brings such sorrow on the very members of the Church that they are in danger of being swallowed up with overmuch sorrow, if not of despairing altogether and giving up hope of mercy (2 Corinthians 2. 7). God is gracious and merciful, yet he is a God visiting iniquity, and will sometimes punish those whom he has known and loved above all the people of the earth. Though he will not take his loving kindness from them, yet he will visit their transgressions with the rod and their iniquity with stripes (Psalm 89. 30–33).

3. *God did not spare his Son*, when he came in the likeness of sinful flesh. He was no sinner except by imputation and representation. God was ever well pleased with his Son, yet when he stood in the place of sinners it pleased the Lord to bruise him. It was as if no one else could strike a stroke hard enough, and though he cried with strong cries, yet his Father would not take the cup out of his hand. He did not suffer for sinning himself, for though he was tempted to sin yet he was without sin, but he suffered for the sin of others. In the glass of his suffering we may clearly see the sinfulness of sin. This leads me to the last and great testimony of God against sin.

## (7) *God sent his Son into the world to condemn sin and to destroy it* (Romans 8. 3; 1 John 3. 8)

God did not spare his Son but delivered him up for us all, which clearly witnesses for God how odious sin is to him. It ought also to be odious to man for whom Christ suffered and died that sin might die, and man might live; indeed, that he might live to him who died for us, for his love constrains us to no less (2 Corinthians 5. 14, 15).

To prove this more clearly and fully I shall show that Christ's sufferings were for sinners, that they were exceedingly great, and that the greatness of his suffering is a full witness on God's part of sin's sinfulness against God and man.

1. *Christ's sufferings were for sinners.* Jesus Christ himself suffered but he did not suffer for himself, for he was without sin (Hebrews 4. 15, and 7. 26). Neither was guile found in his mouth, nor any unbecoming word, when he suffered, although this was a most provoking time (1 Peter 2. 22, 23). It is a faithful saying that Christ came into the world to save sinners (1 Timothy 1. 15). This was the errand and the business upon which he came. He had his name Jesus because he was to save his people from their sins (Matthew 1. 21). And he himself confesses that he came to seek and to save that which was lost (Luke 19. 10). Now dead and lost is the sinner's motto (Luke 15. 32). Accordingly, when Christ was in the world he suffered and died that He might save sinners. He died for our sakes and so loved his church that he gave himself for it (Ephesians 5. 25). It is not only often said that he died for us but that he died for our sins (Romans 5. 8; 8. 32). He died not only for our good as a final cause, but for our sins as the procuring cause of His death. He was delivered for our offences (Romans 4. 25). Christ died for our sins according to the Scripture (1 Corinthians 15. 3); that is according to what was typified, prophesied and promised in the Scripture. One remarkable passage, not to mention many others, is : 'He was wounded for our transgressions, he was bruised for our iniquities, the chastisement of our peace was upon him, and with his stripes we are healed' (Isaiah 53. 5). To this the Apostles bear witness in the New Testament. He gave himself for our sins (Galatians 1. 4); who his own self bare our sins (1 Peter 2. 24). Now this dying for us and our sins signifies several things :

a. That he died and gave himself *as a ransom* for us. I came to give my life a ransom for many, said our sweet and blessed Saviour (Matthew 20. 28). He gave himself a ransom for all (1 Timothy 2. 6). Christ's dying was the paying of a price, a ransom price. Hence we are said to be bought, redeemed, and purchased : 'Ye are not your own, for ye are bought with a price' (1 Corinthians 6. 20), that is, the price of his blood. 'Ye were redeemed with the precious blood of Christ' (1 Peter 1. 18, 19). And the church is purchased with his own blood (Acts

20. 28). He gave himself as the redemption price, and we are a purchased people (1 Peter 2. 9).

b. He died for us *as a sacrifice* for our sins. He became sin for us (2 Corinthians 5. 21). In the Old Testament the sin offering is called sin; so here Christ Jesus, as an offering for sin, is said to be made sin for us. It is said in the Holy Scripture that Christ offered his body, his soul, himself. 'We are sanctified through the offering of the body of Jesus Christ once for all' (Hebrews 10. 10) – there is the offering of his body. He made his soul an offering for sin (Isaiah 53. 10). 'And he has given himself for us an offering and a sacrifice to God' (Hebrews 9. 14). He offered himself without spot to God, and he put away sin by the sacrifice of himself (verse 26). Now just as we were redeemed by the price, so we are reconciled by the sacrifice of his death. For we are reconciled by the death of his Son (Romans 5. 9, 10).

c. Christ laid down his life for us, *bearing the curse and punishment* due to our sins. Therefore it is said, 'He was made a curse for us', which was the punishment of our sin (Galatians 3. 13). He bore our sins, that is, the curse due to our sins. The punishment of sin is often called sin in Scripture, and to bear iniquity is to be punished. As redemption came by the price, and reconciliation by the sacrifice, so justification came by his bearing the curse and punishment. He shall justify many, for he shall bear their sins (Isaiah 53. 11, 12). He became a curse for us that the blessing of Abraham might come upon us, and that is justification by faith as you may see from the context (Galatians 3. 13, 14 with verses 8 and 9).

2. *The sufferings of Jesus Christ were exceedingly great.* I shall omit what might be gathered from the types under the law, and what is spoken by the prophets concerning the suffering of Christ, though many things might be collected thence. But they are all fulfilled in him, and I shall therefore confine myself especially to what is related in the New Testament. He was a man of sorrows, as if to say that he was a man made up of sorrows and nothing else, just as the man of sin is as it were made up of sin. He knew more sorrow than any man, indeed,

more than all men ever did. For the iniquity, and therefore the sorrows of all men, met in him as if he had been their centre. He was acquainted with grief – indeed, he was acquainted with little else. Grief was his familiar acquaintance. He had no acquaintance with laughter: we never read that he laughed at all when he was in the world. His other acquaintance stood afar off, but grief followed him to his Cross. From his birth to his death, from his cradle to the Cross, from the womb to the tomb he was a man of sorrows, and never were sorrows like his. He might say, Never was grief or sorrow like my sorrow. Indeed, it is impossible to express the sufferings and sorrows of Christ, and so the Greek Christians used to beg of God that for the unknown sufferings of Christ he would have mercy on them.

Though Christ's sufferings are abundantly made known, yet they are but little known. Eye has not seen, nor ear heard, nor has it nor can it enter into the heart of man to conceive what Christ suffered. Who has known the power of God's wrath? Christ Jesus knew it, for he underwent it. Though it is impossible to declare all Christ's sufferings, it is useful to take a view of what we can. I shall therefore consider Christ's sufferings under three heads: (a) He underwent all kinds of sufferings, (b) He suffered by all kinds of persons, (c) All kinds of aggravating circumstances met in his sufferings.

(a) Jesus Christ suffered *all kinds of sufferings*. It is said that he was tempted in all things like unto us (Hebrews 4. 15), and among other things meant by temptations, sufferings are not the least. He suffered being tempted – he suffered while he lived, but especially a little before and when he died. All his life was a suffering, not to mention his self-denials which were voluntary. He was no sooner born but suffering came upon him. He was born in an inn, even a stable; he had only a manger for his cradle. As soon as his birth was noised abroad, Herod sought his life, so that his supposed father was forced to flee into Egypt. He was persecuted before he could, after the manner of men, be aware of it, and have understanding of his sufferings. When he returned his sufferings grew up with him.

Hunger and thirst, travel and weariness, scorn and reproaches, false accusations and contradictions waited on him, and he had not where to lay his head. But his special sufferings took place just before and at his death. Then he suffered in his body and in his soul.

1. *In his body*, which was wounded and crucified, he suffered in bearing his cross, as Isaac, who typified him, did. And he suffered in his body on the cross (1 Peter 2. 24). He not only suffered unto death but in the manner of his dying: it was a shameful, a painful and an accursed death; indeed, he bled to death. Christ Jesus lost blood several times: at his circumcision, in his agony when he sweat drops and clots of blood, when he was whipped and scourged, when he was nailed to the cross, and probably when they plaited a crown of thorns (the earth's curse) on his head. And lastly when they thrust the spear into his side, with which he bled out his life and gave up the ghost.

He suffered in every part and member of his body from head to foot. His head, which deserved a better crown than the best in the world, was crowned with thorns, and they smote him on the head. His face suffered being spat upon. His back was turned to the smiters, was stripped and whipped; indeed they even ploughed upon his back and made deep and long furrows. His hands and feet were pierced and nailed to the cross. Indeed, he says through the prophet: 'All my bones are out of joint', as if he had been on the rack (Psalm 22. 14). He suffered also in his senses, his feeling; could he be smitten, wounded, nailed and pierced without feeling? His taste suffered, for instead of strong drink and wine of consolation, which was usual for men ready to die (Proverbs 31. 6), they gave him vinegar and gall to drink. His sight suffered, and among other things the sight of his mother and other grieving friends could not but affect his heart (Luke 23. 27). It was a grief to him to see them grieve for him. Did it not afflict him to see his enemies wag their heads? His hearing suffered many a scoff and jeer, many an ill word and blasphemy. His smell could not but suffer when he came to Golgotha, the place of

[107]

skulls, where filthiness and putrefaction lodged, the very stinking sink of the city. But this is not all.

2. Christ Jesus suffered *in his soul*. We read of his sighing and groaning, but let us consider him especially in his agony and upon the cross. In his agony he began to be sorrowful and very heavy (Matthew 26. 37), for these were but the beginnings of sorrows. Sorrow is a thing that drinks up our spirits. And he was heavy as if feeling a heavy load upon him. And he is exceeding sorrowful unto death (Matthew 26. 38). Sorrowful! Exceeding sorrowful! And unto death! It was such an extremity that it made him cry out, Father, if it be possible, let this cup pass. And this was with strong cryings and tears (Hebrews 5. 7). When he was upon the cross he was under a desertion which made him cry again, My God, my God, why, or how, hast thou forsaken me? Now to cry, and to cry with a loud voice, argues an extremity of suffering. And after this he gave up the ghost, he poured out his soul an offering for sin. And so he suffered all kinds of sufferings both in soul and body.

(b) *He suffered from all kinds of persons*. Christ Jesus suffered from the Devil, for though Christ bruised his head yet he bruised Christ's heel. No sooner had Christ the testimony from heaven that he was the Son of God, but he was immediately carried into the wilderness to be tempted of the Devil. The thing which was questioned and disputed about was whether he was the Son of God or not, and though Christ worsted him and beat him out of the field, yet he departed but for a season. So when Christ was about to suffer, the Prince of this world mustered up all his forces again and came upon him with much violence. He made men of all types his agents to add to the sufferings of Christ. For as is stated in Scripture (Acts 4. 26) he did not suffer from bad men only, which was a fulfilment of prophecy (Psalm 22). He was often tempted by the Pharisees, and he endured the contradiction of sinners. Yet this was not all, for he suffered from his own disciples and his nearest relations. Peter was once a Satan to him, and denied him thrice. The rest grieved him with their slowness and littleness of faith. Judas betrayed him. His brethren did not believe on him. And the heaviest of all was that he suffered from his Father: he put the cup into his hands and took pleasure to bruise him, and he laid upon him the iniquities of us all. God did not spare him nor abate him anything, but hid his face from him as if he had been angry with his only and most beloved Son.

(c) *He had all kinds of aggravating circumstances united in his sufferings*. He was made of a woman; now, that he who made the woman should be made of a woman, and become and be made a son to the work of his own hands, was a degree of suffering. He who made the law was made under the law (Galatians 4. 4). He who was Lord of all was made in the form of a servant, and though equal to God, came in sinful flesh and so obeyed as a servant. It is this that is referred to as Dr. Jackson points out, when he says: I came not to do my own will but the will of him that sent me. He also suffered as a sinner, for so he was judged and as such put to death, though his judge confessed he found no fault in him. Indeed, more than this, he became a curse (Galatians 3. 13) and which is the worst of words, he became sin for us (2 Corinthians 5. 21).

There are still more circumstances which added to his sorrow and suffering. He came to his own and they received him not, he had least honour among his own in his own country. Indeed, he was wounded in the house of his friends, and one of his own betrayed him, devil that he was (John 6. 70). He did good to many but had little thanks from any. Of ten lepers cleansed only one returned to give him thanks. What insincerity and ingratitude! And what aggravating circumstances there were at the end! He was taken and apprehended as a sinner. They came against him with swords and staves, as they would to take a thief. They charged him with blasphemy for speaking the truth. They preferred Barabbas, the son of their father the Devil, before him. The disciples left him and his Father forsook him, as was mentioned before. Who can reckon up the aggravating circumstances of his sufferings? He was crucified between two thieves and upbraided by one of them.

His death was painful and shameful. There is much more, but I will pass on.

3. *The greatness of Christ's sufferings is a full witness against the sinfulness of sin.* What an odious thing sin must be to God! He will pardon none without blood (Hebrews 9. 22). God would accept no blood but the blood of his Son; not that of bulls and goats (Hebrews 9. 13), but that of his Son (1 Peter 1. 18, 19). God would not abate one drop of his blood, but he must pour out his life. His very heart-blood must be spilt and spent for sinners. And, wonder of wonders, all this was a pleasure to God, for it pleased the Lord to bruise him. That it should please the Lord to bruise the Son in whom he was well pleased is to us men an inconceivable mystery. Thus God has borne great witness against sin in that he sent his Son to die for sinners.

What a hell of wickedness that must be which none but God can expiate and purge! God does not do it except by taking human nature. The God-man could not do it without suffering. No suffering will serve but death. And no death but an accursed one. What an evil odious evil is sin that must have blood, the blood of God, to take it away!

So we conclude the witness of God against sin.

## 2. ANGELS BEAR WITNESS AGAINST SIN

Both good angels and bad angels do so.

### (1) *Good angels*

The angels of God and heaven, as they are often called, bear witness against sin as an exceedingly sinful thing.

a. *Their very title as holy angels* shows that they have an antipathy against sin and are at enmity with it. That which is meat and drink to wicked men – to do the will of the devil – is poison to holy angels whose meat and drink it is to do the will of God. They are all holiness to the Lord and cannot endure iniquity. They often contend and fight with evil angels and so witness against sin (Jude 9). In that they are holy, love holiness, and contend against the Devil, they witness against sin.

b. *In being God's heralds*, to proclaim the law which is against sin. It is the aggravation of the sin of the Jews that they did not receive the law which was given by the disposition of angels (Acts 7. 53). The law which was added because of transgressions was ordained by angels (Galatians 3. 19). Every transgression of this law received a just recompense of reward, for the word spoken by angels was steadfast (Hebrews 2. 2). So angels, in proclaiming the law, have openly declared against sin as being exceedingly sinful.

c. *They will not sin even to be revenged on the Devil himself*. They will not rail at a devil because railing is sin; it is said of Michael that he dare not bring a railing accusation (Jude 9). One would have thought that he would have answered the Devil back and told him plainly, but he durst not bring a railing accusation, nor give the Devil bad language. We hotspurs and hotheads that we are, are apt to render evil for evil and railing for railing, to pay men in their own coin; but angels dare not do so for it is a sin. Railing is language that holy angels cannot speak.

d. *They will not allow men to sin who would do it to honour them*. When John fell at the feet of one of them to worship him, the angel said: 'See thou do it not' (Revelation 19. 10); Do not that to me which is to be done to God alone. And again, John said: 'I fell down to worship before the feet of the angel which showed me these things, but he said unto me, "See thou do it not, but worship God"' (Revelation 22. 8, 9). The angels are so holy that they cannot endure the least reflection being cast on God or the least duty neglected towards God.

e. *They rebuke sin when they find it in God's own people, and that sharply and severely*. Though the hard treatment that she had received made Hagar run away, yet the angel said to her, 'Return to thy mistress and submit thyself to her' (Genesis 16. 8, 9). It is as if he had said, 'Hagar, Hagar, it is better to suffer than to sin.' When Sarah laughed at the news of a son, and then being afraid denied having done so, the angel said:

'Nay, but thou didst laugh'; he told her her fault bluntly (Genesis 18. 12–15). When Zacharias believed not the angel, he was made dumb (Luke 1. 13–20). Thus the angels rebuked for sin.

f. *They rejoice at the conversion of sinners.* To be converted is the recovery of a soul from a dead and lost condition; and then the angels rejoice (Luke 15. 7–10). There is a kind of joy in hell among the devils when one who is converted sins and when sinners are not converted; and so there is joy in heaven at the conversion of a sinner. The Rabbis say of this, While sinners rejoice in their sins, the angels are grieving for them; when and while men live in sin they dishonour their and the angels' God. But when they are converted they give glory to God which is the angels' work and joy. This is their song: Glory to God on high. And when men bear a part with them in this song, it is their joy.

g. *They constantly oppose wicked angels and wicked men.* Good and holy men are committed to the charge of good angels. He gives his angels charge to keep them in all their ways (Psalm 91. 11); and the angels are ministering spirits for the good of them that shall be heirs of salvation (Hebrews 1. 14). They encamp round about them that fear the Lord (Psalm 34. 7). And when wicked men or devils would hurt this charge, they rise up in their might. Gabriel and Michael join against the Prince of Persia (Daniel 10. 20). Michael and his angels fought against the dragon and his angels and overcame them (Revelation 12. 7). When Balaam hankered after the wages of unrighteousness to curse Israel, the angel of the Lord withstood him (Numbers 22. 32). Thus by their protection of the good the angels show their detestation of sin in them that would touch God's anointed or do his prophets harm.

h. *They are ready to execute God's judgment and vengeance on sinners.* The angel that was merciful to Balaam's ass was ready to slay Balaam; but he was reserved to fall by other hands. When Herod was wicked enough to assume glory to himself which of right is God's, the angel of the Lord smote him because he gave not glory to God (Acts 12. 23). When

God judges men, the angels will execute the judgment spoken by him. The angels executed destruction from the Lord against Sodom and Gomorrah because their sin was great (Genesis 19. 13). When Israel sinned, God sent destroying angels among them. They made great havoc among the armies of the aliens. They pour out the vials of God's wrath upon the earth and praise God as they go about their work because God is just in judging ungodly men (Revelation 16. 1, 5). At the end of the world the angels will be the reapers and will gather out all that doth offend (Matthew 13. 39–41). The Lord will come with his holy and mighty angels and take vengeance on them that know not God and that obey not the gospel of our Lord Jesus Christ (2 Thessalonians 1. 7, 8).

I could give other examples of how the angels bear testimony against sin. They are present at our worship and observe us, which is a great obligation to reverence and a witness against immodesty (1 Corinthians 11. 10). They take account of our vows: it is better that you should not vow, than vow and not pay, because it is before the angel (Ecclesiastes 5. 5, 6). The Apostle charges Timothy not only before God but before the elect angels, to be strictly conscientious (1 Timothy 5. 21). They are witnesses of what we do, and shall be witnesses of what God will do; for he who confesses Christ shall be owned by him, and he who denies Christ shall be denied by him and that before the angels (Luke 12. 8, 9). It will be one part of glory hereafter to be like angels; then let us be like them here in witnessing against sin, and doing the will of God on earth as they do it in heaven.

## (2) Evil angels witness that sin is sinful

Evil angels, that is, the Devil and his angels. They do this not only in being devils by sin and suffering for it, but in many other ways as I shall show. We have a saying that virtues confessed by foes, and vices confessed by friends, are true. Surely then, by the Devil we shall find that vice and sin is as we have declared it to be. And if such a friend of sin as the Devil is will confess it to be sinful we may believe him. For though he is the father of lies, yet in this he speaks truth, a great and clear truth.

a. *The Devil witnesses against sin by his trembling.* A devil trembles that there is a God (James 2. 19). Now God was never terrible to the angels until they sinned; then they saw and trembled at the terror of God. Sin brought judgment on the devils (2 Peter 2. 4); judgment is what they tremble at. So sin is the first cause of the devils' trembling. So I conclude that whatever makes devils tremble at the belief of a God, who will be a God of Judgment, is exceedingly sinful.

b. *However great that judgment, they acknowledge it to be just and so, by consequence, sin to be unjust and sinful.* The justness of judgment confessed is a confession of the vileness of the sin which brings the judgment. The devils say 'Art thou come to torment us before the time'? (Matthew 8. 29). They confess that the Son of God was to consign them to torment and they had no exception to make against their being tormented except as to the time. They are reserved in chains to judgment (2 Peter 2. 4; Jude 6) and they say 'Art thou come to torment us before the time?' that is, before the Judgment of the great day to which we are reserved. And they do not deny that they are worthy of this death or that their damnation is just, and therefore they confess the ugliness and filthiness of sin.

c. *They tempt men to sin.* In so doing they witness that sin is sinful. It used to be said that surely they must be good men whom Nero hated and persecuted. In the same way we may say, that that must be evil which the Evil One tempts men to, just as that is good which he hates and persecutes. I ask you, can that be good which the Evil One tempts us to? Can any good come out of this Nazareth? Can any good come from hell? It is enough to prove sin to be sinful, that it is of the Devil, and it is a clear proof of the evil of sin that the Devil tempts us to it.

d. *The Devil turns himself into an angel of light that he may more effectually lead us into darkness.* In this way he tells us that sin is an ugly thing. If he were to come like a devil, like an enemy, everyone would be shy of him, but he comes disguised and puts on the face of a friend and so tricks and cheats us. Indeed, he prevails more by his wily subtleties than by his power. If the Devil had come to Eve and spoken to her as follows: 'I was once a glorious angel and lived above in the Court of Heaven, but I have sinned and am cast down to hell. Eat the forbidden fruit and you will be like me.' Would this have succeeded? Surely not! Thus if he came and tempted men to sin, telling them that this is a ready way to hell, would this prevail with them, to swear and fornicate? No! The Devil is subtle and an old serpent; he covers and paints sin; he covers his hook with a bait and draws men in before they are aware of it. He is a deceiver, but lest he should be known, he puts on a good garb and clothes himself with false light (2 Corinthians 11. 13, 14). Now this disguise and subtle transformation proves that sin is an ugly and monstrous thing. Why otherwise does the Devil paint it up? Why does he pretend good when he intends evil? This proves the sinfulness of sin that the Devil does not tempt in his own name or shape. He dare not say, I am the Devil, I am a deceiver, I will lead you to hell, for that would spoil his project.

e. *All the affliction and misery which the Devil brings upon men is to make them sin more.* So in the Devil's account, sin is worse than suffering. God brings evil upon us to do and make us good, and cure us of the evil of sin by the evil of suffering, and this proves the goodness of God. In the same way it proves the sinfulness of the Devil and of sin too, that he brings evil on us to make us worse. He takes care not to afflict us too much for our sins, lest we sin no more. The end of the Devil in persecuting Job was not only to make him smart but to make him sin, that he might curse God. In bringing suffering the Devil aims at something beyond suffering, and worse than suffering, and that is sin.

f. *When anyone is awakened to see his own vileness, the Devil tries everything he can to drive him to despair.* At first he wishes that the man should presume to sin, and afterwards that he should not hope for but despair of pardon. He belittles sin or makes nothing of it before commission, and aggravates it afterwards. When sin revived the apostle died (Romans 7. 9). It wrought in him apprehensions of death and hell. When Christ Jesus convinced him of his sin of persecution it made him tremble and struck him almost dead (Acts 9). Conviction of sin pricks men to the heart and makes them cry out like undone men: what shall we do? what will become of us? is there any pardon? is there any hope? Now is the time when the Devil strikes in and tells them that their sin is greater than can be forgiven. When the poor penitent was sorrowful, the Devil made use of his devices that he might be swallowed up and drowned in sorrow (2 Corinthians 2. 7 with 11). It is as if he told him, If these do not forgive you, much less will God; the church has cast you off and so will God. His great design is to persuade men that the mercy of God and merit of Christ is not enough to save them, and so the Devil speaks out fully that sin is exceedingly sinful.

g. *He is the accuser of the brethren* (Revelation 12. 10). What stories he tells God about the brethren, how sinful they are! And so doing he confesses to God himself the ugliness of sin, for on this alone does he base the arguments of his accusation. Christ ever liveth to make intercession for us, and so the Devil lives to make accusations against us day and night. When God asks the Devil if he has considered his servant Job, Yes, he says, I have, and I accuse him as a hired servant, one who serves you merely for wages, and would, if but touched by you, curse you to your face. When Satan accused Joshua, it was for his filthy garments, his iniquity (Zechariah 3. 1–4). He is always tale-telling, and sometimes true stories of the miscarriages of believers. He registers their pride and wantonness, their vanity and folly, all their unworthy walkings, and accuses them to God for these things, and even moves God to destroy them for their sinfulness (Job 2. 3). Sometimes as in Job's case it is without a cause, but whatever he says, surely he says to God that sin is an exceeding and out of measure sinful thing, when he accuses the brethren. So much for the witness of the Devil.

### 3. THE WITNESS OF MEN

#### (1) *Good men bear witness against sin*

To which of the saints shall we turn? They all with one consent, as one man, with one voice, and one mouth cry out against sin as a sinful thing. And they all say that even if there were no other hell it would be damnation to be a sinner. Another says that it would be better to be in hell with Christ than in heaven with sin. Another says that sin is more ugly than the Devil. They all subscribe to this, that sin is the most odious of all evils. Hell itself is not more odious, for it would not have been had not sin made it. Good men bear witness both against other men's sins and against their own.

a. *Against other men's sins.* Indeed, if it is possible they seek to prevent them; if not, then to convince men of their sinfulness.

(i) *They give advice and counsel to men against sin.* This proves that sin is an abominable thing in their esteem. The sum of what is spoken by way of commendation of Abraham amounts to this, that he would advise and charge his posterity not to sin (Genesis 18. 19). Samuel did the same to Israel (1 Samuel 12. 24, 25) and David to Solomon (1 Kings 2. 1–3); indeed to all his children; therefore he says, 'Come, I will teach you the fear of the Lord' (Psalm 34. 11) and it is by the fear of the Lord that men depart from evil. Similarly in the New Testament this is the general advice that good men give to everyone – Do not sin (1 Thessalonians 2. 11, 12; 1 Peter 2. 11; 1 John 2. 1).

(ii) *They reprove sin*, if they find that their advice is not being followed, and that men have sinned. Reproofs are arguments of sinfulness, for men do not reprove anyone for what is good. Were it not that sin is odious to them, good men would not go to the expense or run the hazard of reproving others for it. Reproving others is a thankless office and an unwelcome work for the most part; men take reproofs for reproaches, yet since God has laid it on good men as their duty to rebuke and not suffer sin to lie upon their brother (Leviticus 19. 17), they dare not omit it. Though Eli reproved his sons for their sins, yet he is sharply reproved for not reproving them more sharply (1 Samuel 2. 27–36). We find Samuel reproving King Saul. Elihu may say, Is it right to say to a king, you are wicked? (Job 34. 18); yet the prophet says to the king 'Thou hast done foolishly and wickedly' (1 Samuel 13. 13), and he calls his sin rebellion and stubbornness (1 Samuel 15. 22, 23). Thus Samuel touchingly reproved King Saul. John was not afraid to tell Herod of his wickedness, and to his face too (Luke 3. 19). St. Paul would not spare St. Peter when he found him erring and dissembling, but withstood him to the face (Galatians 2. 11). What does all this teach but that sin is an odious thing to good men and that they judge it extremely sinful against God and man.

(iii) *They withdraw from sinners and their company*. They must have no more to do with them. Now this separation from their persons is only because of their sins. If good men are forced to converse with them, yet they cry out, 'Woe is me that I dwell in Mesech, in the tents of Kedar' (Psalm 120. 5). The society of the wicked is very burdensome to the godly. Lot was in a kind of hell when he was in Sodom, for their wickedness was continually vexing his soul (2 Peter 2. 7, 8). By withdrawing from or groaning under the company of the wicked, good men testify against sin and do so in obedience to the command of God (2 Corinthians 6. 14).

(iv) *They mourn over other men's sins*. This shows that in their eyes sin is an abominable thing, though only the sin of others. 'Rivers of waters run down mine eyes' – why? 'because they keep not thy law' (Psalm 119. 136). Thus we see how dear is the law of God, and how vile is the sin of men, to holy David. The prophet Jeremiah expresses this same zeal for God, 'Hear ye, and give ear, be not proud, give glory to the Lord . . . but if ye will not hear, my soul shall weep in secret places for your pride, mine eyes shall weep sore and run down with tears' (Jeremiah 13. 15–17). When the apostle Paul speaks of the sins of men, he does so weeping (Philippians 3. 18). Other men's sins cost good men many a tear and an aching

heart because sin is so contrary to God and to the good of
men.

(v) *They pray and endeavour to get pardon for the sins of
those who hardly seek it for themselves.* Sinners little think
how much they are beholden to good men who pray for their
salvation even when the wicked seek their destruction. Thus
Stephen asked God to forgive them: 'Lord, lay not this sin to
their charge' (Acts 7. 60). How earnestly did Abraham pray for
mercy on behalf of Sodom, that if possible it might not be
destroyed! When Israel had sinned a great sin and provoked
the Lord, Moses mediates and intercedes for them and offers to
die that they might live (Exodus 32. 30–32). Now if they did
not know that sin was a sinful thing, offensive to God and
destructive to man, would they interpose in such a way? No,
they would not. Thus good men witness against sin as the
worst of evils.

b. *Good men witness against their own sin,* as well as
against other men's sins. They do not only wish for the reformation of others, but they endeavour their own. If possible,
they would be so innocent as not to sin at all. It is their ambition and prayer that their thoughts, words and deeds may be
all acceptable to God (Psalm 19. 14). If they could avoid it
they would not even dream extravagantly or allow a vain
thought to lodge within them. It is indeed possible that some
men may declaim bitterly against other men's sins and yet
indulge their own, as if they would rather see other men reform
than themselves, and as if virtue were a more pleasant thing
to talk of than to be possessed of. But godly men dare not do
so; they are against sin in others and against sinning themselves. This is apparent in several ways:

(i) *They will not sin even when they have opportunity.*
Though they might do so with pleasure, honour and profit as
the world counts these things, they dare not. Some men are
kept back from sin for lack of opportunity; if they had it they
would sin. They do not lack the heart but the occasion, not the
inclination but the opportunity. If tempted to sin they would
sin. Others avoid sins that would bring disgrace, but they can

easily embrace pleasant, fashionable and profitable sins. But godly men dare not sin; on this point they all concur. Take for example Joseph: when he was courted into pleasure, even then he said, How, how can I find it in my heart? can I do this? how shall I do this wickedness and sin against God! (Genesis 39. 7–9). It is, he said, sin against my master, sin against you, sin against my own soul, but the worst is, it is sin against God; how shall I do this wickedness and sin against God! There is another instance in relation to his brethren: what evil they deserved from him and what opportunity he had to be revenged is well known; yet he generously forgave them and provided for them, and this was the reason: I fear God, he said (Genesis 42. 18). Job too, in his defence gives a full account of how odious a thing sin of all sorts was to him, even in his prosperity when he might, according to the course of this world, have done whatever seemed good in his own eyes, and none should have said to him, What doest thou, or why are you doing thus? On the other hand you find Balaam after the manner of hypocrites talking and pretending like an angel but acting and intending like a devil; it was a kind of trouble to him that he could not sin. 'I cannot go beyond the word of the Lord' (Numbers 22. 18), but it seems he would have done if he could. A saint, however, would say, Neither can I, nor will I go against or beyond or short of the word of the Lord, if I can help it.

(ii) *They will rather suffer than sin.* Many men make a bad choice such as Elihu charged on Job, 'This (that is to say, sin) hast thou chosen rather than affliction' (Job 36. 21). But godly men make Moses' choice who chose affliction rather than the pleasures of sin (Hebrews 11. 24–28). As precious a thing as life is, a godly man would not willingly sin to save his life. Though the mouth of a fiery furnace heated seven times was open to devour the three children, as we call them, yet they would not sin (Daniel 3. 18). Daniel would rather adventure on the lions than neglect a duty to his God (Daniel 6. 10). Though bonds waited on St. Paul everywhere, yet he could not be restrained by fear of them from preaching the faith of Jesus

(Acts 20. 23–24 with 21. 11–15). You find in Hebrews 11 a long catalogue, a little book of martyrs who chose all manner of deaths before any kind of manner of sin. They would not accept deliverance on ignoble terms but would rather die holily than live sinfully. These all declare that it is better to suffer to avoid sinning, than to sin to avoid suffering.

(iii) *They will not sin though grace abound or that grace may abound* (Romans 6. 1, 2). No! God forbid! Though they have an advocate with the Father, Jesus Christ the righteous, who is the propitiation for their sins (1 John 2. 1, 2) they will not do so. The very doctrine of grace and their interest in the death of Christ is the great obligation upon them not to sin (Romans 6; 2 Corinthians 5. 15; Titus 2. 11, 12). The assurance of glory is a reason for mortification : 'When Christ who is our life shall appear, then shall ye appear with him in glory' (Colossians 3. 4, 5). What then? May we therefore gratify corruption and live as we list? No! 'Mortify therefore your members which are upon the earth.' Though there are promises of forgiveness to him who confesses his sin, a godly man dare not sin and buy repentance at so dear a rate. After St. John had said that if we confess our sin, God is faithful and not only merciful but just to forgive us our sin, and that the blood of Jesus Christ shall cleanse us from all sin, yet he adds, 'these things are written that you sin not' (1 John 1. 9 with 1 John 2. 1). They dare not sin that good may come of it, nor tell a lie that the truth of God may thereby abound unto God's glory (Romans 3. 7, 8).

(iv) *They take care and use means to prevent sin.*

(a) They maintain a continual war against the Devil, world and the flesh because they would not sin. As much as they love peace they live in war. Indeed, they must live in war to preserve their peace, on which sin would make a breach. Godly men would not hate the Devil except that he is a sinner and tempts them to sin. They would not hate their own flesh or father and mother except to prevent sinning. You may read of this war in Scripture (Romans 7; Galatians 5. 17). They have to fight their way to heaven from day to day and duty to duty and are at great expense and pains to keep this war on foot; and all this, that they might not sin.

(b) *They are always praying that they may not sin.* 'Lead us not into temptation' they pray, 'but deliver us from evil.' Temptations are not sins but they are the way to sins, and therefore they pray that if possible they might not be tempted. 'Let not any iniquity have dominion over me' said good king David (Psalm 119. 133), and keep me from presumption that I may be upright (Psalm 19. 13). Indeed at the same time they make this supplication: 'Thy will be done on earth as it is in heaven.'

(c) *They hide the word of God in their heart as an antidote that they might not sin* (Psalm 119. 11). When princes persecuted David without a cause, yet he dared not meditate revenge, but his heart stood in awe of the word which he had hid there (Psalm 119. 161).

(d) *They abstain from the appearances and occasions of evil.* Job made a covenant with his eyes (Job 31. 1). King David said that he would take heed to his ways that he might not sin with his tongue (Psalm 39. 1); that is to say, that he might be perfectly holy in the sense of the Apostle James: 'If any man offend not in word the same is a perfect man and able also to bridle the whole body' (James 3. 2); this is the very expression used in the Psalm we have just quoted. When Joseph met with a tempting mistress, it is said of him that he hearkened not unto her, not only not to lie with her but not to be with her, and fled as from a plague or a devil (Genesis 39. 10, 12).

From all these things, to mention no more, it is quite clear that in these records of good men, sin is an exceedingly odious and pernicious thing. But I am aware that two objections will be made against the witness of these men. (1) From what may be. Sin and sinners will say it is true these men reprove sin, condemn it in others and endeavour to prevent it in themselves. But is this because of the ugliness of sin or of some inconvenience that might befall them? Is it because sin is sinful or for some other reason? (2) From what is. You would make us believe that godly men are such ermines,* so nice and tender that they cannot endure any uncleanness. You make them so shy and strict that they would not come near a sin. Yet it is apparent that they have sinned; even the very men whose examples you delight in, and whom you make patterns for everyone else!

Before we can proceed, these objections must be removed out of the way. To remove the first, I answer that though good men make use of all kinds of arguments to keep themselves and others from sin, yet it is sin as sin that they abhor as ugly and abominable. Even though there were no afflictions, no hell or no wrath, they cannot abide it, and newborn men would exclaim against and hate sin. This is seen in several ways:

(a) *The main thing which keeps them from committing sin, or for which they repent when they have committed it, is that it is against God.* When Joseph had mustered many arguments, this was the one that prevailed with him: 'How can I do this wickedness and sin against God' (Genesis 39. 9), that is, sin against the will and glory of God. Job tells us he dare not sin; and why not? Because it was against God as well as against himself (Job 31. 1–4). In their repentance after a sin, this goes most to the heart of godly men, that they have sinned against God: 'Against thee, thee only have I sinned' (Psalm 51. 4). How is this so? Surely David had sinned against Uriah and against Bathsheba and against himself – his bones as well as his conscience felt it! Yes, but this goes most to his heart, that it was against God; it grieves him more that God was displeased by him, then that God was displeased with him. He puts in twice as much of that as of any other ingredient. And as to others, his tears run down like rivers, not so much because men did not keep his laws as because they kept not God's laws.

(b) *They abhor all sin*, all kinds and all degrees of sin. Surely we may conclude that they who hate all sin hate sin as sin. This godly men do, and only godly men do it, and godly men

* Men of purity.

[123]

always do it, in so far as godliness acts in power in them. Their prayer is, 'Order my steps (all and every one of my steps) in thy word and let not any (that is none) iniquity have dominion over me' (Psalm 119. 133). From the greatest to the least, from the highest to the lowest, let not any one iniquity have dominion over me! Some men abhor certain sins such as atheism, blasphemy, idolatry and murder, but pride and wantonness are as pleasant to them as meat and drink. This is the proof that they do not hate sin as sin. He who hates sin as sin hates all sin, and I think it may be inverted with truth, he who hates all sin hates sin as sin.

(c) *They abhor all their secret sins.* They hate sins which no one knows but themselves, even such as they do not know by themselves, that only God knows of. They hate that which no one can accuse them for or lay to their charge as being guilty of. Lord, who knows the error of his way (Psalm 19. 12). St. Paul confessed 'I know nothing by myself' (1 Corinthians 4. 4). The heart of man is such a maze that man himself cannot find out all its windings; such a deep that man himself cannot fathom it; so deceitful that man himself does not know it; only God searches it.

If this is so, Lord, cleanse me from my secret errors undiscerned and unknown, from errors and extravagances unknowable by me. We should say to God, 'That which I see not (that is, in what I have done amiss) teach thou me' (Job 34. 32). A man does many things amiss which escape his own notice as well as that of others, and a good man would be cleansed even of these. They create no trouble to his conscience and are only against God, but he would therefore be rid of them that they might not lodge in his heart, although strangers and unknown.

(d) *They are against all inclinations to sin,* against the very conception of sin. They do all that they can, not only that sin may not bring forth, or breed, but that it might not even conceive (James 1. 14, 15). Such is the burden of the body of death and the law of the members, that though St. Paul can say that it is not he that sins but sin that dwelleth in him, yet he would be rid of this indwelling sin that it might not so much as incline him to evil.

(e) *They cannot content themselves not to do evil, unless they also do good.* This is the final proof that they oppose sin as sin. They do not think it enough that they do not displease God, unless they please God. It is not enough for them to be negatively good, unless they are positively good. They will not only not commit evil, but they will not omit good. Many men will do no hurt, but neither will they do any good; the charge against some is not that they defrauded or oppressed or were cruel to the members of Christ but that they did not actually do them good by clothing, feeding and visiting them. Good men, however, are for being good and for doing good. Not only do they say, Cleanse me from secret sins, or Keep me from presumption, but O that the thought of my heart, the words of my mouth, and consequently the works of my life, may be acceptable to thee, O Lord (Psalm 19. 14). In the name of all the household of faith the apostle speaks thus: 'Wherefore we labour (the word is, we are ambitious or we affect this honour like heavenly courtiers), that whether present or absent (that is living or dying) we may be accepted of him (2 Corinthians 5. 9). The end of this verse may be read (and the Greek will well bear it), 'that we may be acceptable to him', even to all well pleasing.

The second objection we mentioned is as follows: It is matter of fact that godly men have sinned. Now if sin was as odious to them as you said, would they sin? But before I answer this objection, let me first make one or two things clear.

(a) I concede and confess that they do sin. Who is he that lives and sins not? If any man say he has not sinned, he makes God a liar for he has concluded all men under sin. And if we say we have no sin we both deceive and yet confuse ourselves, for we sin in saying so (1 John 1. 8–10).

(b) There is this to be said, that the sins of good men are more usually sins of captivity than sins of activity. Thus the apostle says that they are rather led into sin by temptation than that they go into it by choice and inclination; it is against the law of their mind (Romans 7. 23). It is indeed possible that a good man may plot and contrive a sin, as David did the death of Uriah. We may notice, however, that this is the only thing of which God himself says that David sinned (1 Kings 15. 5).

God covers all his other sins as being those of the man overtaken by temptation rather than as sins committed of deliberate purpose. So for the most part, good men are captivated rather than active as to sin. And David himself could say that he had not wickedly departed from God (Psalm 18. 21); that is, he had not departed after the manner of the wicked (Jude 15).

(c) God may sometimes lead a good man to this saddest of trials, to know all that is in his heart, as he left the good King Hezekiah (2 Chronicles 32. 31). We are not over-forward or over-willing to believe ourselves to be so bad as we really are in our hearts. We do not know what seeds of evil are sown there. 'Is thy servant a dog', said Hazael when his sin was foretold. St. Peter himself could not believe it possible that he should deny Christ his master; yet when left to himself he did it.

Now notwithstanding all that we have said, we still maintain that godly men hate sin. Indeed they hate it the more for having sinned. For several reasons then, the witness of the godly man against sin is still true, good and firm :

(a) *He abhors sin committed, and himself for committing it.* (Job 40. 4 and 42. 6). Sin is the burden of every good man's soul. When the author of Psalm 73 had sinned, he was so angry with himself that he could not forgive and pardon himself (though God did so), but calls himself fool and beast. Good men condemn not only their sin but themselves; and sin is the more hateful to them for having been done by them.

(b) *They are restless until sin is purged as well as pardoned.* King David could not content himself to have sin blotted out by a pardon unless it was washed and cleansed away (Psalm 51. 1, 2). The mending of his heart without it being made new by creation would not content him (verse 10).

(c) *They justify God when he chastises them and afflicts*

them for having sinned. Whoever justifies a punishing God condemns sin, for if the sentence is just the sin is unjust. They speak in this way continually: 'I will bear the indignation of the Lord because I have sinned against him' (Micah 7. 9). I make this confession in prayer, they say, that Thou, O Lord, mightiest be justified when thou judgest (Psalm 51. 3, 4). This also testifies against sin.

(d) *They take a holy revenge on themselves and become more zealous for God.* St. Peter not only wept bitterly but was made willing to feed sheep and lambs, to do any and every service for Christ. The penitent says: 'Restore to me the joy of thy salvation and I will teach the transgressors thy ways' (Psalm 51. 12, 13). So too, when the apostle had made the Corinthians sorry with his sharp epistle, he did not repent of it, because it wrought such sorrow in them as wrought repentance to salvation not to be repented of (2 Corinthians 7). This appeared in their indignation against sin, their revenge upon themselves, and their zeal for God.

(e) *They desire to die only to be rid of sin.* They do not wish to die for any other reason than that they may sin no more, but be holy as he who has called them is holy. They groan for a change for this reason (2 Corinthians 5. 4); mortality and corruption are joined together (1 Corinthians 15. 53, 54), and one is not laid aside without the other. Therefore they desire not only to be in Christ where there is no condemnation (Romans 8. 1), but to be with Christ (Philippians 1. 23), which is best of all, for in his presence there is no sin nor even temptation to it. There was never a temptation to sin in heaven since the Devil was cast out, and there never will be, for the Devil shall never be there, neither shall corruption, for that shall cease when mortality is swallowed up of life.

So then, all in all, the witness of godly men is unexceptionable, notwithstanding their having sinned.

(2) *The witness of wicked men*

Wicked men themselves are witnesses of and against the sinfulness of sin. They say that it is an ugly, shameful and an abominable thing which they are ashamed to own. Let us hear some of the heathens give their opinion of it. Cicero tells us that he did not think that man worthy of the name of a man who spent one day in the pleasures of the flesh. Indeed, he goes on to say that, after death, he thinks that there are no greater torments than sin. Another thought it one of the greatest torments that men should have in another life to be bound to the sins they most delighted in in this life. Socrates preferred to die rather than to consent to a sin of injustice, and one writer says, Socrates was not unhappy in being put to death, but they were unhappy who put him to death; he suffered but they sinned. Another says of men living in pleasure, very much like St. Paul says concerning the wanton widow: 'she that lives in pleasure is dead while she lives' (1 Timothy 5. 6).

Now the reasons why they said these things concerning sin was because sin degraded man and was a degeneration. Men who delight in sin live the life of a beast and not of a man, which is a life of reason and virtue. Thus Plotinus says, 'The pleasures of the body do so interrupt the happiness of the soul that it is the soul's happiness to despise the body's pleasures.' Sin, say the Stoics, is the worst kind of suffering, and he who is wicked is the only miserable man; the greatest punishment of sinners is sin (Seneca). I could produce many more sayings to this effect, but I shall not only take in the witness of these and other brave, magnanimous and well-bred heathens. The herd of wicked men, the very dregs of them, shall give a testimony (whether they will or not) by their thoughts, words or deeds and sad experiences that sin is an ugly, because a sinful thing. They are ashamed of sin when and before they commit it and after they have committed it.

a. *Sinners are ashamed of sin before they commit it and when they commit it.*

(i) Though they are sufficiently daring and impudent as to sin, they have not got the courage to consider what they are doing or at least to speak openly what they think concerning sin. They know that when they sin their conscience will accuse them, and that they will find regrets which they are loath to feel, much more to utter and declare. Therefore they dare not ask themselves what it is they are about to do, or are doing; they dare not catechize themselves and say, 'Is there not a lie in my right hand?' (Isaiah 44. 20). When men are loath to give themselves the benefit of a few forethoughts, and rush like horses into the battle, it suggests that they are afraid they shall find what they have no desire to find. The Scripture speaks as though it were impossible for men to be as wicked as they are, if they only considered; failing this they do not act like men. If they think of it and still sin, they dare not speak out their thoughts but would rather conceal their shame and pain as well as they can, than tell anybody what fools they have been and how foolishly they have acted. If sin had anything noble or honourable in it, why do they not proclaim its virtues and thereby their own in loving it? If they think it good, why do they not call it by its name? If they think it evil, why do they think it so? It is surely because they are ashamed of it and ashamed that anybody should know what they think. 'The fool hath said in his heart, there is no God' (Psalm 14. 1). It seems he did not have the hardiness nor the heart to say it with his mouth; he whispered and muttered or wished, but was loath to be heard. When they speak thus within, then it speaks out this, that they are ashamed of what they think and dare not utter it.

(ii) *Sinners dare not commit sin until they have given it a new name*. They do not sin under the name and notion of sin. Now, woe unto them! Just as they call good evil, so they call evil good (Isaiah 5. 20). Revenge they will not own; they term it a vindication of their honour, a doing right to their reputation. Covetousness, they say, is a sordid thing; theirs is only frugality and good husbandry. Drunkenness is unmanly, it is bestial, they confess; but theirs is only good fellowship in the liberal use of the creature. Pride must be called decency and being in the fashion. Fornication is only a trick of youth, or gratifying nature. Thus men disguise sin, for surely, were they to call it by its own name and look it in the face, they know they should find it such an ugly hag as was not fit for the embraces of men, no, not even of devils. This practice of giving new names to sin condemns it.

(iii) *They do what they do as much as possible in the dark.* Indeed, as they foolishly think, they do it in the dark from God's sight also. Thereby they implicitly confess that if men or God saw them they should be ashamed of what they do. The time was when they that were drunk were drunk in the night, it being a business of shame. The apostle tells us that it is a shame to speak of what is done by some in secret (Ephesians 5. 11, 12); and therefore it seems that they themselves do it secretly because they are ashamed lest it be known and talked of. Indeed, it is a general rule given by Christ himself that he who does evil hates the light; because his deeds are evil, and he cannot endure that they should be manifested, for then they would be reproved by the light (John 3. 19, 20). The abominations of the ancient people of Israel were so abominable that they did them in the dark and they thought that that hid them from God himself (Ezekiel 8. 5–12).

(iv) *They are tormented while taking their pleasure.* It is clear that sinners find sin a painful thing and are ashamed of it. They are stung with eating the honey; their conscience accuses them when it takes them in the very act (Romans 2. 15). 'Even in laughter the heart is sorrowful' (Proverbs 14. 13) —it is not only at the end of laughter, but in it, while at it. While men are taking the pleasures of sin they hear, 'But remember thou must die and go to judgment', which chills and cools their heat (Ecclesiastes 11. 9). We little think what secret sighs and groans are within, when wicked men are merry or seem at least to be so from the teeth outwards.

In 2 Samuel 13 you will find no less a person than a King's son vexed and tormented with his own passion. He was in a burning fever with lust; it made him sick and lean, even to being consumptive. But it may be said, This was because he could not have his will; was he the same when he had it? Yes, and worse too by his own confession, for the hatred wherewith he hated her was more than the love wherewith he had loved her. This is as much as to say, that he was more tormented now than he had been before. Sin disappoints men; they have false joys but true miseries, and they suffer rather than enjoy any pleasure from sin. They are vexed to see how they are cheated. Thus Amnon, to whom we have just referred, was one moment in a hot fit, the next in a cold one; he was as one tossed from a fever to an ague, cast into the fire and into the water, sick of love and sick of loathing, sick for want of her company and sick of having it, discontented at not having his will and then at having it. Sin does not please men whether they are full or fasting.

How sinners are tormented! Their desires are great and their enjoyments little, indeed, contradictions to what they had thought of. They expected pleasure and find pain, they sought joy and met with grief. Hence sinners are so weary of time, and not only of business but of recreations. But that they change so often proves that they have no satisfaction. Hence the Pythagoreans place the wicked on a rolling pin to show they have no quiet or peace, but as the prophet says, they are like the raging sea (Isaiah 48. 22 and 57. 20–21). The soul, says Tacitus, is lashed with guilt as the body is with stripes. Even Tiberius, impudent as he was, could not protect himself from those inward scourges which are such horrid and hideous furies and torments that hell has no worse.

(v) *Sinners must sin under a form of godliness*. They paint it and seek to make it look well, although it is so much the more ugly for being coloured and complexioned with a form of godliness, the thing itself and those who do it being witnesses. Though sinners are like devils yet they would be thought saints. Saul's sin must needs concern sacrifice, and so God must be the patron of the sin that was committed against himself (1 Samuel 15). Absalom covers his rebellion and treason with the devotion of a vow (2 Samuel 15. 7–8). Herod smooths over his murderous intentions with the pretence of worship; he will murder John the Baptist lest he should be perjured, as if forsooth he dares not sin unless he does it conscientiously.

This shall suffice to show that wicked men are ashamed of sin, that is, ashamed to own it as such. They are ashamed of it before and when they commit it.

b. *Sinners are ashamed of sin after they have committed it.* Good men are ashamed of what only looks like a sin, and of what may be interpreted to be meant for a sin, although not so, as when David cut off the skirt of Saul's garment. This proves that they are loath to and averse from sin. We shall find also that wicked men, when they have done evil, are ashamed that they have done it, which is a witness what an ugly because a sinful thing sin is.

(i) *Sinners dare not own their sin.* This clearly shows that they are ashamed of it and are not satisfied with what they have done, although, as I shall soon show, they may excuse it. When the thief, bold and sturdy sinner as he may be, is taken, he is ashamed. So the house of Israel is ashamed (Jeremiah 2. 26); they cannot plead sin's cause to justify it.

(a) *They cannot endure to be called by the name of the sin which they have committed and which they practise.* No drunkard likes to be so called, but takes it for a disgrace. No liar will receive the lie given him but as an affront. No adulterer will own that name. Now whoever follows a lawful and honest trade or calling is not ashamed of its name though it is never so mean, as for example a shoemaker. But sin is such an ugly base employment, that those who commit sin will not endure being called sin-makers, though that is their trade. Sinners charge God with slandering them when he complains of their sin (Malachi 1. 6; 2. 17; and 3. 8, 13). When God accuses them they put him to the proof and say, when and where? So impatient are sinners of being called sinners!

(b) *They palliate, excuse and disavow sin.* This shows that they are ashamed of their sin and dare not own it. When sin was but young, yet Adam and Eve were ashamed of this their firstborn, just as lewd women are ashamed of their base-born children; they cloaked and hid their sin (Job 31. 33). If they do well what need is there of excuses; if wrong, excuses plead against it and are accusations of its wrongness. Those who

[132]

were invited to the wedding made excuses, which were indeed proofs of their denials, and that they would not come (Matthew 22. 3). Their seeming civilities and apologies were arguments that they were criminal. All our fig-leaf aprons and coverings are proof that we are ashamed of what we have done. Many times sin is laid at the wrong door. Nature is blamed as if the fault were in man's constitution. The Devil is blamed because he tempted and beguiled. And indeed, God Himself is blamed for permission, or even for more: 'the woman thou gavest me' (Genesis 3). What does all this prove but that in the eyes of sinners sin is a very ugly and abominable thing?

(c) *They deny that they have sinned.* They commit a sin to cover sin. It is a hard and difficult thing to bring sinners to confession, for sin is such a shameful thing. It is said of the adulterous woman: 'She eateth and wipeth her mouth and says, I have done no wickedness' (Proverbs 30. 20); she will sin to avoid the scandal of her sin. When Gehazi, by lying in his master's name, had taken a reward from Naaman the Syrian and returned, his master asked him where he had been; he said 'thy servant went no whither' (2 Kings 5. 25–26). He was so ashamed of what he had done that he dared not own it. This is a clear evidence that sin is an ugly thing, that sinners will not, dare not admit and justify it.

(ii) *Sinners dare not look into their actions nor call themselves to account.* Thus it is further apparent that sin is an unpleasing thing which sinners are ashamed of. It is as troublesome for sinners to look into themselves to examine their lives as it is for men whose business is declining to look into their books and cast up their accounts. 'Why is this people of Jerusalem slidden back by a perpetual backsliding? No man repented him of his wickedness saying, what have I done?' (Jeremiah 8. 5, 6). Such men would never look behind them or within themselves. They do not care to be alone lest the thoughts of their sins should stare them in the face. They study diversions and pastimes and run into company lest their sins, like ghosts and devils, should haunt and lay hold of them. And when these are over they sleep away the rest of their time. They cannot endure to be at home lest an upbraiding conscience, which is a worse thing than a scolding woman, should fall upon them. They can afford no leisure to think how they have idled and sinned away, and thereby have worse than lost, so much of their time. We read of people on whose hands time lay heavy, like a burden, who therefore studied arts and methods of laying it aside, that they might put the thoughts of the evil day far from them. Sometimes they lay on their beds, and being weary of that they would stretch themselves upon their couches, and then fall to eating and drinking, and so rise up to play and dance (Amos 6. 3–6). What does all this speak of but an unwillingness to have any sense of sin or even to look on its picture, so hellish a thing is it!

(iii) *They will decry and punish in others sin which they themselves are guilty of, the better to conceal their own, or to compensate for it by being severe to others.* When a thief has stolen and robbed he is the first that makes a hue and cry; they are loath to be found guilty themselves. Though Judah was guilty of incest himself, how forward he was to punish fornication in Tamar his daughter-in-law (Genesis 38). When our Saviour put the case to the Pharisees, what the lord of the vineyard would do with husbandmen who had abused and beaten his servants and, which was worse, slain his son, they could readily answer: 'He will miserably (that is, with a punishment as great as their sin) destroy those wicked men' (Matthew 21. 41). Thus when they did not know whom they condemned they condemned themselves and their own sin – out of thine own mouth art thou condemned, O sinner! It is true the case was altered when he said that they were the men; but by this we see that when men are not concerned or seem not to be so, how severe they are against sin! And indeed, they do so to hide their own wickedness (John 8. 7–9).

(iv) *They usually fly to the horns of the altar, to some fits of devotion and forms of godliness.* They act as if they would compound with God to save them. What is the meaning of all the purifications, sacrifices and atonements which the heathens used, but that their sense of guilt was too heavy to be borne; and what is more common among men of a better profession than to say as soon as they have sinned, Lord have mercy upon me, God forgive me! They kiss their crucifix, tell over their beads, and go to confession, and what does all this denote but that they have, they themselves being witnesses and judges, been injurious to God and to their own souls. Without reconciliation and pardon or at least an imagined pardon, they cannot be quiet.

(v) *They desire to die the death of the righteous.* Balaam and others who did not live the life of the righteous but accounted it madness, even so reckoned their end to be happy, and therefore desired that their own might be as that of the righteous. By this we see that no wicked man cares for sin's wages. Surely that work cannot be good for which the wages are so bad that no man cares to receive them, but says, O that my after-state may be with the righteous (Numbers 23. 10). The wages of sin is death and the end of sin is death; but Balaam wants no such death and no such wages. Though they go hellward while they live, yet they wish that they could go to heaven when they die. What are we to deduce from this but that sin is a damnable thing. Though sinners seek their happiness in their misery yet it is happiness that they seek and whenever they find their disappointment they grow angry with themselves, with sin, the devil and all.

One objection may be made against this witness of wicked men against sin: true, it will be said, there are some pitiful sneaking sinners, cowardly and timorous ones, who are daunted at and ashamed of sin, but there are others past shame, fear and sense, roaring boys, ranting and rampant sinners, rodomontade* blades who boast of their sin and glory in being wicked. They take pleasure in things worthy of damnation and yet scorn to be frightened by terrible preachers. They will sin in the face of the sun without a blush. We will hear what these have to say and be judged by these brave sparks and bold fellows.

* Boastful, bragging.

We must confess with sorrow for such as have none for themselves that there are some hardened sinners who are sunk into the image, the practice, and it may be the condemnation (as well as the snare) of the Devil himself. Indeed, they seem to outdo the devils, for they believe and tremble, which is more than some sinners do. Godly men rejoice with trembling, but some ungodly men sin without trembling and rejoice at it too.

There is a sad and dreadful judgment upon them, worse than any affliction that could befall them; it is of all judgments the most terrible, for it belongs to the suburbs of hell itself. To be punished for sin by sin is the worst of punishments. When God says of a person or people, that he will let them go, that they shall take their course and not be punished, that is by bodily and felt plagues, then he punishes them most and worst of all. To denote the greatness of it, it is three times said in Scripture that God gave them up, and gave them over (Romans 1. 24, 26, 28). It is no wonder that men act the Devil's part when they are under the Devil's doom.

This therefore is no more a commendation of sin than a madman's going naked and enduring the pricks of a pin in his flesh without feeling anything, commends his condition. Is it any part of handsomeness to have a whore's forehead? Shall we make blind men judges of colours, or dead men judges of the affairs of the living and their concerns? Who would accept the judgment of those who are void of judgment and are given up to a reprobate mind? If men have lost their senses and will say that snow is black or that honey is bitter, shall we believe them?

But even so, there is none of these hardened sinners who will not at one time or another bear witness against sin, and blush at their own impudence. We hear Pharaoh saying, who is the Lord? And yet, hardened as he was, the same Pharaoh says, I have sinned against the Lord. God has ways enough to bring them to confession. They who once were so wild as to call the saints' lives madness were at last tame enough to call themselves fools for it. There is a time coming when all such impudent and daring sinners will sneak and be ashamed. Either the grace or the judgment of God will awaken them out of their dead sleep; and then, though they dreamt of a feast, they will be hungry; and the mouth will confess, the eyes weep, the cheeks blush, the hands smite on the thigh, and the heart bleed and break. Cain felt little till he heard God calling from heaven and telling him he was cursed, and then sin became heavy in its punishment, even intolerable (Genesis 4. 9–13). Judas makes merry a while and chinks his thirty pieces, but soon cannot endure the money nor himself but went to his own place. The prodigal lived wantonly for a long time but yet at the last cries, I have sinned. And I find three occasions when hundreds of sinners have confessed their sins.

(a) *In a day of affliction.* When the plagues of God have taken hold of them and the judgments of God have been heavy upon them, then they confess. The story of Pharaoh is too long to rehearse; likewise that of Nebuchadnezzar (Daniel 4). But how God made their stout hearts stoop and brought them to their knees! Sinners who are shameless, and seem to dare heaven and challenge God himself and scoff at his threatenings, will then be made to change their tune, and to weep instead of singing. Joseph's brethren who were shameless in Canaan were ashamed in Egypt, and cried out, 'Verily we are guilty concerning our brother'. The cruel Adonibezek acknowledged the justice of God's retribution. Tell me what your desperadoes will say in distress and on a deathbed!

(b) *In the day of judgment.* Even if sinners do not awake and repent before, yet in the great and terrible day of the Lord they will be ashamed. They who now run to all excess of riot will not be able to stand then. The wicked shall not stand in judgment; they will then quake and tremble, for horror will take hold of and arrest them. They will not stand to justify themselves nor to be justified by anyone else. They will be found speechless, without a word to say for themselves or their sins, like the man who came to the wedding feast without a wedding garment. If the righteous be scarcely saved, or with difficulty, where shall the sinners and ungodly appear

(1 Peter 4. 18)? See how they run away and would fain hide themselves (Revelation 6. 15).

(c) *In the day of eternity.* In that long, everlasting day when they are in hell they will confess the sinfulness of sin. The place of torment will extort the confession of sin as it did from Dives (Luke 16). Where is the rustling of silk and satin now? Where are the dainty bits, the generous wines, and all the deceitful pleasures of sin now? Alas, although they have no pity shown them they will pity others, and wish that none might come into that place of torment. Then they will cry out, O sinful sin! O devilish and hellish sin!

This must suffice to show the sinfulness of sin from the confession of wicked men and I now proceed to call other witnesses.

### 4. THE WHOLE CREATION WITNESSES AGAINST SIN

There is not one creature in heaven or earth or under the earth, whether animate or inanimate, but proclaims the sinfulness of sin. And not only the sensible, but insensible creatures also can find a tongue and language to speak against sin. They do this with respect to themselves, and with respect to God and man.

### (1) *The whole creation witnesses against sin as having done it a great deal of wrong and injury*

It witnesses that sin has deprived it of its privilege, so that it is not now as when it came out of God's hand and was made by him. When God looked on all that he had made, behold it was very good (Genesis 1. 31). But how are things altered since sin came into the world! The angels he has charged with folly (Job 4. 18). The heavens are not clean in his sight (Job 15. 15). Man in his best estate is altogether vanity (Psalm 39. 5). The earth is under a curse (Genesis 3. 17, 18). Indeed the whole creation groans (Romans 8. 21, 22). By the whole creation the learned Grotius understands the whole universe, as do many others. The apostle had three times spoken of the creature (verses 19, 20, 21) and yet now speaks more fully in verse 22:

[138]

the whole creation, or every creature, is subject to vanity and under the bondage of corruption, which makes it groan and puts it to pain as a woman in travail. It is as if it cried out, O sinful sin! I was freeborn and though under dominion, yet not under bondage. Once I served man freely but now from fear (Genesis 9. 2). Every creature which is under the power of man may say to him, I did nothing of myself to make me liable to bondage, but being your goods and chattels, I suffer a part of the penalty of your treason. If you had not sinned, I would not have suffered. But now I groan and wait to be delivered from the bondage of your corruption. O sinful sin!

(2) *The creation witnesses against sin with respect to God and man*

It teaches man many duties and it convinces him of many a sin.

a. *The creatures teach man his duty.* They do so in general as well as showing him many special duties. In their courses and places they all praise God and fulfil his word, as you may read in Scripture (Psalm 148. 8; Revelation 5. 13). And no creatures, except the fallen angels and man, ever transgressed the law or disobeyed the word of their Creator. They are such good servants that when God bids them go they go, when he bids them come they come, when he bids them do this they do it. By this they teach man to do what God bids him, and what a sinful thing it is to break his law and to disobey his word. The creatures cry shame on us when we sin; they do this in several particular ways:

(i) *They teach man dependence upon God.* They depend on God and teach man to do so too. It is as our Saviour says, Take no anxious and soul-disturbing thought for your livelihood, but learn of the fowls of the air and lilies of the field, to trust God (Matthew 6. 25–34).

(ii) *They teach man to pray.* They call upon man to call upon God. For they cry to God and observe their morning prayer before they break their fast. The ravens do not forget it: 'He giveth to the beast his food and to the young ravens which cry' (Psalm 147. 9). This cry is made to God, 'who provideth for the raven his food; when his young ones cry unto God they wander for lack of meat' (Job 38. 41). They are no sooner hatched but they cry unto God. All the creatures do the same. 'These wait all upon thee, that thou mayest give them their meat in due season' (Psalm 104. 27). Indeed, beside their waiting they petition as well: 'Thou openest thine hand and satisfiest the desire of every living thing' (Psalm 145. 16). Now if you are a prayerless or distrustful person these creatures witness against your sin, for they teach you to pray and trust.

(iii) *They teach us to be weary of the bondage of corruption*. They are weary of it; they groan under it. And will ye not cry out, O wretch that I am, who shall deliver me from this bondage of corruption and this body of death! If not, the creature witnesses against you and teaches you to wait and long for a better state, and to long for the glorious liberty of the Sons of God.

(iv) *The creatures teach us to be fruitful*. They teach us to repay the trust and charges that God bestows on us. The earth w'·ich drinketh in the rain which cometh oft upon it, bringeth forth herbs, meet for them by whom it is dressed (Hebrews 6. 7 with Isaiah 55. 10). The ox knows his owner and the ass his master's crib (Isaiah 1. 3). The flock feeds the shepherd (1 Corinthians 9. 7). If you then are barren and unfruitful, your gardens and your fields will rebuke you. If you are disobedient, your ox and your ass will upbraid you. God himself appeals to heaven and earth against you (Deuteronomy 32. 1; Isaiah 1. 2).

b. *The creatures convince men of many sins*, as well as teaching them many duties. In both respects they are schoolmasters to man. The way in which we now use the creatures bears witness against sin. When we eat flesh we do so, for there was no such grant in the first blessing; since sin our appetite has been more carnivorous. Our clothes witness against sin, for in the Hebrew the same word signifies treachery or prevarication and a garment; the clothes that cover our nakedness tell us that sin despoiled us of better robes, that is, of our innocence. The dust tells us that, having sinned, we must return to dust. Also the vanity and disappointments, and hence the vexations we meet with from things created, witness against sin.

(i) *The creation witnesses against atheism* (Romans 1. 20). He that has said in his heart that there is no God is called a fool by every creature. The very idea of a creature supposes a God, and we may more reasonably argue that there is nothing than that there is no God. The fact that the creatures are made proves the First Cause, and who is that but God? It is so clear from the creation, says the apostle – that is, the eternal God-head – that men are left without excuse (Romans 1. 20). Rain from heaven is God's witness of his being and of his being good, as the apostle infallibly concludes (Acts 14. 15–18). Creation and providence, which is creation upheld and continued, are witnesses for God, so that we may say with Job: 'Ask now the beasts and they shall teach thee; and the fowls of the air and they shall tell thee; or speak to the earth, and it shall teach thee: and the fishes of the sea shall declare unto thee that the hand of the Lord hath wrought this' (Job 12. 7–9). If there is any being, there is a God, says the creation.

(ii) *The creatures witness against ingratitude.* They witness against man's failure to acknowledge how indebted he is to God. Even the dullest among the creatures witnesses against this (Isaiah 1. 3). God upbraids the ingratitude and rebellion of Israel with the gratitudes and services that the ox and the ass pay their owners. The rivers of waters return continually to pay their acknowledgments to the fountain-general, the sea (Ecclesiastes 1. 7). These waters upbraid those who make no returns but bad ones to God. They say in effect, what Moses did in words, 'O foolish people and unwise, do ye thus requite the Lord evil for good!'

(iii) *The creatures bear witness against the idleness of man,* and the sinfulness of that state. Man was not to be idle in paradise, and every man should have a calling to follow and should follow his calling. The apostle says, he that will not labour must not eat. From idleness comes no good, yet alas how many busy-bodies there are who do nothing but idle away their days! To these the creatures speak by their industry, and Solomon refers the sluggard to the ant to learn (Proverbs 6. 6–11). It is not only, Go to the infidel (for he that provides not for his family is worse than an infidel); but it is, Go to the ant. Perhaps your wife and children lack certain conveniences, even necessities, while you are idle. Go to the ant, thou sluggard!

(iv) *They bear witness against ignorance and its sinfulness*; against man's failure to observe divine appointments, and the judgments of God (Jeremiah 8. 7–8). The stork in the heaven knoweth her appointed times; the turtle, the crane and the swallow observe the time of their coming, but my people (however wise they think they are) do not know the judgment of the Lord? Though they pretend skill in discerning the face of the sky, yet they discern not the signs of the times; they scarcely know what time of day it is, nor that it is the day of their visitation (Luke 12. 56; 19. 44).

(v) *They witness against oppression and covetousness as very sinful.* The stone shall cry out of the wall, and the beam out of the timber shall answer it (Habakkuk 2. 11, 12). But what do these strange witnesses say? This: Woe to him . . .! And Woe to him . . .! Some men's lands and the furrows of their fields cry against them (Job 31. 38). Perhaps the poor labouring man who ploughed and reaped has not yet received his wages (James 5. 4). The gold and silver also, even the canker and rust thereof, the moth-eaten garments also, are a witness against these sins (James 5. 1–3). The ass rebuked the madness of the prophet when he was hastening after an evil covetousness (2 Peter 2. 15, 16).

(vi) *They witness against the sinfulness of refusing the offers of the Gospel and of grace.* There is a saying, Who but fools refuse gold when it is offered them? But there are such fools as refuse Christ and heaven and happiness when they are offered them, and will not be entreated to be reconciled that they may be saved. But they are set against the glory of God and their own salvation. Against these the stones of the street and the dust of the apostles' feet bear witness (Luke 19. 40; 9. 5; 10. 10, 11). Indeed there is not a sin which the creation as a whole and in its various parts does not bear witness against. The very dullest and worst-natured creatures, the ox and ass have excelled man. Even Dives's dogs had more humanity than Dives himself, and were witnesses against his cruelty. In short, whatever duties the creatures teach they thus convince of and bear witness against the sins which are contrary to those duties, and whatever sins they convince of, they teach the duties contrary to them.

(3) *The creatures are instruments in the hand of God to punish sinners*

This is another proof by them of the sinfulness of sin. And they do this with great readiness, as if they were avenging themselves as well as vindicating God. Witness the plagues of Egypt. The four elements have often borne their testimony: fire burnt Sodom; water drowned the old world; the earth swallowed up Korah; and the air has conveyed infection in the time of plague. And the sun, moon and stars have been warriors and fought in their courses against sin. The beasts of the field and fowls of the air have done likewise. But I will only hint at these things. There are two ways in which they show their displeasure and his, whose creatures they are, against sin in punishing sinners:

a. *By withdrawing their influences.* The heavens shall be brass and the earth iron; the one shall neither rain nor drop dew, the other shall not bring forth fruit (Deuteronomy 28. 23; Hosea 2. 18, 22).

b. *By acting contrary to their ordinary course and nature.* For waters to stand as a heap (Exodus 15. 8) and for fire not to burn (Daniel 3) are unusual and unnatural things. They do this to witness against the unnaturalness of sin, and both these were witnesses against the sin of persecuting God's Israel. On occasions the creatures continue to bear witness of this kind to this day. They are always bearing witness, though men do not observe it, which only infers their greater sinfulness.

[143]

This must suffice for the witness of the whole creation. But notwithstanding all these witnesses it may be said that we cannot put sin to death without a law, and if there is no law to condemn sin, we cannot condemn it. Therefore I shall proceed to show that there is a law against sin which condemns sin as worthy of death; for it is guilty of the death of many and of attempting the death of all. So legally and by the requirements of law, we ought to condemn sin and put it to death.

## 5. THE LAW WITNESSES AGAINST AND CONDEMNS SIN

The law of God is without sin in itself and is against sin in others. Since the law is holy, just and good, that which breaks the law must be unholy, unjust and evil. In its primary intention and promulgation the law reveals the authority, wisdom, will and goodness of God, for it was unto life. Sin must therefore be exceedingly sinful, for it is against all this. The law revealed man's duty and man's happiness. How evil then is sin, which is a contradiction of and opposition to the duty and happiness of man! Since sin is a transgression of God's good law, the sinfulness of sin appears by the commandment. The law is against sin both before it is committed and after it has been committed.

1. *The law is against sin before it is committed.* The committing of sin is against the being of the law. It is holy and wholly against sin, for it forbids sin. That is, all sin, whether of omission or commission, whether in thought, word or deed, whether against God or against man – the voice and cry of the law is this: Thou shalt not sin. So that in this sense, by the law is the knowledge of sin; it shows what is sin, as well as what sin is. 'Is the law sin?, God forbid – nay I had not known sin but by the law, for I had not known lust or concupiscence to be a sin except the law had said, Thou shalt not covet. Thou shalt not lust' (Romans 7. 7). The law shows that lust is sin by forbidding it. Indeed, the law not only forbids sin but forbids it upon great and severe penalties, upon no less than the pain of death, on the peril of a curse. It says, cursed be everyone that doeth not, and continueth not to do all things that are

written in the law (Galatians 3. 10). So the law is utterly against the commission of sin.

2. *The law is against sin after it is committed.* By the commandment sin appears to be exceedingly sinful after commission.

a. *The law reveals what sin is,* just as before it revealed what is sin. It shows how displeasing to God and how destructive to man it is, as a transgression of the law of God which was made for the good of man. The law is so far from indulging or justifying sin or the sinner or from concealing it, that no sooner is it committed than the law reveals it, and God's displeasure against it (Romans 3. 20).

b. *It condemns the sinner.* The law is not against the righteous, for against such there is no law or condemnation. But this law, like a good magistrate, is an encouragement to them that do well, but a terror to evil-doers. The apostle Paul says, When the commandment came and showed me sin as in a magnifying glass, sin revived; it got the victory over me and was too strong for me, for the law strengthened it against me (1 Corinthians 15. 56) and I died (Romans 7. 9). I was dead in law. I have this sentence of death within me; as he says in another place. The law, when transgressed, works wrath (Romans 4. 15); it sends out terrors, thunderings and flashes of wrath. It reveals wrath to them who by sin have made work for wrath.

Thus we see that the law is against sin before and after it has been committed. Yet we may show further how the sinfulness and the malignity of sin appears by the commandment.

1. *Sin takes occasion from its being prohibited and forbidden by the law, to sin against and transgress it the more.* There is in it such a malignity and an enmity that it will not be subject to the law of God (Romans 8. 7); It tries to break this bond asunder and to cast this cord far from it (Psalm 2. 3). The law stands in its way, and therefore it rushes to break it with the more violence. Sin grows angry and swells like a river which has been pent up and stopped in its course. The Apostle speaks of it in this way: 'Sin, taking occasion by the commandment,

wrought in me all manner of concupiscence' (Romans 7. 8). The law said, Thou shalt not lust; at this, lust grows mad and provokes to sin the more. Sin is proud and impetuous, so that it scorns to be checked or to have any chains put upon it. Such is the sinfulness of sin, we are apt to be the more proud, the more covetous, and the more wanton, because it is forbidden us.

2. *The law takes occasion by the commandment to deceive us*. The Apostle says that it did so to him (Romans 7. 11). It deceives us just as the Devil took occasion from the commandment to deceive our first parents; as if God were envious of us, or at least we mistake his meaning. Sin first corrupts our understanding, and by that our affections, and by that our conduct. The Devil and sin put their interpretations on God's text; they gloss and comment upon it and put queries: Hath God said? (Genesis 3. 1 and 2 Corinthians 11. 3). You need not fear, they say, there is no such danger, this command has another meaning. Such are the sly and cunning tricks that Satan and sin use with us to harden us by deceit (Hebrews 3. 13).

3. *Sin makes use of the commandment to kill us*. It works our death and ruin by it (Romans 7. 11–13). Sin at first makes us believe, as the serpent did Eve, that if we sin we shall not die but live better and be like gods. But we are tempted, enticed and drawn the way of our own lust, and when lust hath conceived it bringeth forth sin, and sin when it is finished bringeth forth death (James 1. 14–15). It brings forth every kind of death—natural, spiritual and eternal; for this is the wages and the outcome of sin (Romans 6. 21, 23).

Man no sooner sinned but he became mortal, dead in law; and by living in sin man becomes spiritually dead in sin (Ephesians 2. 1, 2). If grace does not prevent, man will die in sin and be damned for sin, which is eternal death. Thus the Apostle says; While sin flattered me and deceived me, as if I should go unpunished, it has brought me under condemnation and death. Even now upon some men God lets sentence of death pass, that he might raise them from the dead, yet these people find themselves dead first, before they pass from death to life, as was the case of the Apostle in this passage.

Conversion is a resurrection from the dead. Sin kills men, grace revives men; so, like the prodigal, they that were dead are alive. But by this we see the sinfulness of sin, that it makes use of the law which was ordained to life, to condemn and pass sentence of death upon sinful men. That which was made to be our strength against sin is become the strength of sin (1 Corinthians 15. 56). Death would be weak without its sting, which is sin, and sin would be weak without its strength, which is the law. So sinful is sin, exceedingly and beyond measure sinful, it works death by that which is good and which was ordained to life.

Even from the mouth of the law several things proclaim the sinfulness of sin. Do we not hear the law? (Galatians 4. 21); what dreadful things it speaks against the trangressors of it:

1. *The law will not pardon the least sin.* It allows us no favour. If we break it in one thing though we observe it in many things, if we do not keep it all, it is as if we did not keep it at all. There is no compounding with the law nor compensating for a sin by doing a duty. 'Circumcision verily profiteth if thou keep the law: but if thou be a breaker of the law thy circumcision is made uncircumcision' (Romans 2. 25); it does not profit at all. Just as one sinner destroys much good, so does one sin; it is like a dead fly in a box of ointment. 'Whosoever shall keep the whole law and yet offend in one point, he is guilty of all' (James 2. 10); for the nature of all sin is in every and any sin. If a man sins once, though only once, the law overthrows him, for the law is only the one will of God in various particulars. If any one of these is transgressed, it is against the will of God which runs through them all like a silken string through many pearls, for if that is cut or broken in only one place, the whole is broken. Wherever there is only one transgression the law pronounces the curse (Galatians 3. 10). Had not God provided a city of refuge, a new and living way, we should never have found any favour from or by the law (Romans 8. 2, 3).

2. *The law cannot justify any man*. Since sin entered it has lost its power and grown weak (Romans 8. 3). Even if it were pitiful, compassionate and friendly, yet it lacks the power to justify us. The law cannot give life, though it was made to that end. If there had been a law given which could have given life, verily righteousness should have been by the law. But the Scripture has concluded all under sin that the promise (of life) by faith of Jesus Christ might be given to them that believe (Galatians 3. 21, 22). 'If the law *could* have given life' – implying that it was not in the power of the law. But why not? It could at first! True, but it is weak through the flesh, for all are concluded under sin, the law is transgressed and therefore it cannot give life. Sinful sin has weakened the law as to the justification of sinners, but it has strengthened it as to their condemnation.

3. *The law makes sin abound and aggravates it greatly*. Of what use is the law? 'Wherefore then serveth the law – it was added because of transgressions' (Galatians 3. 19); to make sin appear in its own colours. The law written in man's heart was so obliterated that men could not discern sin by it as they had been wont to do. The Apostle says: 'I had not known sin but by the law' (Romans 7. 7), that is, as it was newly promulgated and written. I did not know it by the law in my heart for that let me alone. So the law was added to revive the sight and sense of sin, that men might see what an ugly thing sin is, infinitely worse than men are generally aware of until the commandment comes. 'The law entered that the offence might abound' (Romans 5. 20); not that men might sin more, but that they might see their sin more. It is that men might take a full measure of sin in all its dimensions, in its height, depth, breadth and length. The holiness, goodness, justice and severity of the law all show sin in its ugly shape and colours.

4. *The law has become as a schoolmaster to us* (Galatians 3. 24). We would scarcely ever have looked at Christ had not the law whipped and lashed us like a severe school-master. For this, not to exclude other meanings, is as I conceive it, chiefly the meaning of this text. The law kept us in awe and bondage by

its severity until Christ came. Compare this text with Galatians 4. 1-3): 'The heir, as long as he is a child, differs nothing from a servant but is under tutors and governors . . . so we were in bondage.' To be under tutors is the same as to be under a school-master and that is to be in a condition of bondage. Many go to school with an ill will, for they go to the rod, the whip, to bondage, to fear and torment. The law does nothing but frown upon us, gives us hard tasks and lashes us for not doing them, till Christ comes or until we come to Christ, just as the Egyptians did to the Israelites (Exodus 5. 14). The law is the state of bondage and fear; the very children are all subject to bondage through fear of death (Hebrews 2. 14-15).

This shows the sinfulness of sin, that it made the law such a dread and terror to us. For so it is to all till Christ come, who is the end of the law for righteousness (Romans 10. 4). He takes away the terrors of the school-master by taking us into the University of a higher and better state, that of believing on him for righteousness. By this we come to have a spirit, not of fear, but of power, of love, and of a sound mind, as St. Paul says (2 Timothy 1. 7).

5. *The law silences man from making any complaint*, however great the judgment of God upon him. Mark what and to whom and to what end and purpose the law speaks: that every mouth be stopped (Romans 3. 19). All the world must be silent when God speaks judgment, for all are guilty. If living man complains he has his answer soon and in short: it is for his sin (Lamentations 3. 39). There is no room for one who has sinned to complain when he is judged – a sinner and yet complain! O, I am punished, he says; yes, it is for sin – now this stops his mouth. Man has no reason to enter into judgment with God when God enters into judgment with man. What a wicked thing is sin, which has brought man into such a condition that he cannot speak one word for himself! If he were to open his mouth the law would stop it by saying to him, Thou hast sinned. The law tells man that he is without excuse and therefore it is in vain to plead. Everything on this side of hell is mercy, for it is the Lord's mercy we are not consumed; and

hell itself is just judgment. Under this or that, any or all judgment, man under the law has no cause to complain. He must be silent for he has sinned.

6. *The law leaves a man without hope.* When once it has passed sentence on a man, there is no reversing it by the law. Hope is one of the last succours, and when it fails the heart breaks and sinners are broken-hearted. Christ came to save sinners and to heal the broken-hearted, that is, men without hope (Isaiah 61. 1), men who are in a desperate and despairing state. The law condemns without mercy (Hebrews 10. 28); it leaves no place for hope from it. No matter how many petitions you present it with, and seek a pardon with tears, yet the law is inexorable. The sinner is cursed and shall be cursed, says the law. Now if there is to be any reprieve or hope of pardon, that comes from the grace of heaven's prerogative, which is above the law. This can revoke and disannul its sentence, indeed bestow blessing where the law pronounced a curse. But the law itself admits of no altering; it is like that of the Medes and Persians, peremptory and unalterable. What I have written, I have written, says the law.

Thus in all these ways, sin by the commandment and the law becomes and appears exceedingly sinful. But it may be said by someone that, though the law is severe to sinners, yet the Gospel is propitious and merciful to them. Therefore sin does not seem to be so vile a thing as before. To this I must answer, and make it evident that the Gospel also bears witness against sin.

## 6. THE GOSPEL ALSO BEARS WITNESS AGAINST SIN

Truly it is the greatest and purest testimony against sin. Though sinners find favour from the Gospel, sin finds none. The Gospel is not in the least indulgent to the least sin. The whole voice of the Gospel is, 'These things are written that ye sin not'. The Gospel is the declaration of the life and death, the design and doctrine of our Lord Jesus Christ, which was and is wholly against sin. The design of Christ was indeed to save sinners (1 Timothy 1. 15) but to destroy sin (Romans 8. 3;

1 John 3. 5, 8). He came to save his people from their sins; not from the petty and contemptible evils of reproaches and afflictions, but from the great and formidable evil of sin; from the guilt for time past, and from the power for time to come. He came to redeem us from all iniquity (Titus 2. 14). And this is the blessing with which he blesses us: to turn us every one away from every one of our iniquities (Acts 3. 26). Thus whoever names and calls upon the name of the Lord, that is, makes a profession of being a Christian, is thereby obliged to depart from iniquity (2 Timothy 2. 19). How the life and death of our holy and blessed Saviour witnessed against sin I showed before. I shall now deal with the doctrine of the Gospel which so fully comports with and is adequately fitted to his aim and design, which is the taking away of sin.

The sum of Gospel doctrine preached by Christ himself, and confirmed to us by them that heard him, was and is repentance and faith (Mark 1. 15); under these, the Apostle comprises the whole counsel of God (Acts 20. 21, 27). Now both these doctrines speak loudly against sin as being exceedingly sinful. Repent, says the Apostle, for the remission of sins. What an evil then is the thing which man must repent of, and which none but the God of all grace who is rich in mercy can remit and forgive! This forgiveness proves him to be a God of great love and rich mercy, or else sin could not be forgiven. For as our Saviour tells us, it is easier to heal diseases than to forgive sins (Matthew 9. 5, 6). To forgive sins is a manifestation of power, as Moses said in his prayer: 'Let the power of my Lord be great to pardon' (Numbers 14. 17–20). Repentance takes in many things. It is made up of sorrow and shame, confession and reformation, all of which speak of sin's sinfulness. 'Repent, that your sins may be blotted out' (Acts 3. 19); if sin is not blotted out then man is undone, and his name will be blotted out of the book of life.

Faith also, like repentance, speaks against sin. Faith says men are void of righteousness and life, for these are both only by faith. If men do not repent, they will not be forgiven. Likewise, if they do not believe, they will be damned; for not only those who do not know God, but those who do not obey the Gospel of our Lord Jesus Christ will have vengeance taken on them, and be punished with everlasting destruction from the presence of the Lord (2 Thessalonians 1. 8, 9). And how can they escape (that is, there is no possibility of escaping) this great damnation who neglect the great salvation (Hebrews 2. 3)?

If we take the doctrine of the Gospel apart, it is in every part against sin. There is not one Gospel doctrine that in its application does not strike against sin. 'The grace of God bringing salvation (the saving grace of God) hath appeared to all men (and so it is against the sin of all men and against all sin), teaching us that denying ungodliness and worldly lusts (without exception) we should live soberly (as to ourselves) righteously (as to others) and godly (to God) in this present world (that is, all the days of our life, as in Luke 1. 74, 75)' (Titus 2. 11). The Gospel is a witness against the old man with all his corrupt affections, passions, lusts, and deeds, and is all for new light and knowledge, new love and affection, new life and conduct. Its design is that man should be no longer an old, but a new creature (Ephesians 4. 17–25; 2 Corinthians 5. 17). It is against all sin and for all righteousness and holiness; against hypocrisy and for truth; against formality and for spirit and power.

The several parts of the Gospel are against sin, as we shall show.

1. *The doctrinal part of the Gospel.* This is the part which flesh and blood is inclined to interpret as an encouragement to sin, and from which it takes occasion to abuse the Gospel:

i. *The doctrine of God's free and abounding grace* (Romans 5. 20, 21). St. Paul had taught that where sin abounded grace did much more abound, and that grace did reign to eternal life. From this some are apt to take occasion to sin, as if they were encouraged to do so by grace (Romans 6. 1). But with what detestation and abhorrence the Apostle speaks against it! Shall we sin either because grace abounds or that grace may abound? God forbid! And when men would do evil that good might come of it, he speaks like a son of thunder, and tells them that their damnation is just (Romans 3. 8). St. Jude writes an epistle expressly against such people as turn the grace of God into wantonness, thus perverting the end of grace. He calls them ungodly men, and men ordained to this condemnation (Jude 4).

ii. *The doctrine of redemption by the blood and death of Jesus Christ.* Christ Jesus died for our sins, and some wicked wretches are apt to conclude that they may live in sin because Christ has died for sin. But he died for sin that we might die to sin (Romans 6). He gave himself for us to redeem us from all iniquity and to purify us to himself (Titus 2. 14). The death of Christ calls for us to die to sin and to live to him that died for us (2 Corinthians 5. 15).

iii. *The doctrine of privileges is against sin.* God has dignified his people and given them titles of honour compared with which the names of Caesar and Emperor are but trifles. Behold, as a matter of wonder, what manner of love the Father has bestowed upon us, that we should be called the sons of God! (1 John 3. 1). And you, says St. Peter of believers, are a chosen generation, a royal priesthood and, which is more glorious, a holy nation (1 Peter 2. 9). Therefore, he says, abstain from fleshly lusts, and show forth the virtues and thus the praises of him who has called you out of your marvellous darkness into his marvellous light.

iv. *The doctrine of judgment to come* is against sin. Wicked men scoff at this (2 Peter 3), and think that if they are let alone until that day, then they will do well enough. But remember that for all things we must come to judgment, and therefore learn to fear God and keep his commandments, as the wise man teaches us (Ecclesiastes 12. 13, 14). Speaking of the day of judgment, the Apostle says: 'Knowing the terror of the Lord, we persuade men' (2 Corinthians 5. 11); we persuade them, not to sin, but to live in righteousness and holiness. Seeing this must be, what manner of persons should we be in all holy conversations and godlinesses! (for the Greek is plural). We must take heed not to fall into the errors of the wicked but to grow in grace, as St. Peter concludes (2 Peter 3. 11, 17, 18). Thus all the doctrines of the Bible from the beginning of Genesis to the end of Revelation are a continual preaching and witnessing against sin.

2. *The mandatory part of the Gospel witnesses against sin.* By this we mean the commanding and exhorting part of the Gospel. What are men commanded and exhorted to do but to serve God in righteousness and true holiness all the days of their lives? To depart from iniquity, as from the way to Hell, and to walk holily in Christ Jesus, as in the way to Heaven? Indeed God condescends so far as to implore men to be reconciled that they may be happy (2 Corinthians 5. 20). What does this show but that sin is both displeasing to God and destructive to man? That is, it is sinful sin.

3. *The promising part of the Gospel is against sin.* God has given to us exceeding great (in the Greek, the greatest) and precious promises, that by these we might escape the pollutions of the world through lust, and be made partakers of a divine nature (2 Peter 1. 4); and that, having these promises, we should cleanse ourselves from all filthiness of flesh and spirit, to perfect holiness in the fear of God (2 Corinthians 7. 1). Promises of good are against the evil of sin.

4. *The menacing and threatening part of the Gospel is against sin.* God threatens before men sin that they may not sin, and he threatens after men have sinned that they may repent of sin. Not only the law, but the Gospel also threatens sinners, and with no less than damnation (Mark 16. 16). When any have sinned, God threatens the execution of threatenings if they do not repent (Revelation 2. 5, 16, 22; 3. 3, 19). This also witnesses against sin.

5. *The exemplary part of the Gospel witnesses against sin.* The examples recorded in the Gospel, as are those in the Old Testament, are registered as witnesses against sin. The examples of good men and good things are set up as signposts to show us what to avoid. The good examples are given that we may not sin by omission of good (Hebrews 12. 1); the bad that we may not sin by commission of evil (1 Corinthians 10. 6–11).

[154]

Abraham's faith, Moses' meekness, and Job's patience are examples for us to follow. We should tread in their steps. On the other hand, Ananias and Sapphira's lying, Judas's covetousness and apostasy, and similar cases, are written for our example, that we might hear and fear and not do so wickedly.

6. *The experimental part of the Gospel witnesses against sin*. Any experiences that men have had of God's goodness, and of their own deceitful and evil hearts, and what they have suffered by sin, all bear witness against sin. Has God been good in this and that way, and are you so foolish as to requite the Lord evil for his goodness, which should have led you unto repentance (Deuteronomy 32. 6)? God was angry with Solomon because he departed from the Lord God of Israel who had appeared to him twice (1 Kings 11. 9). We should draw inferences as Ezra did: 'After all that is come upon us for our evil deeds, seeing thou hast punished us less than our iniquities deserve, and hast given us such deliverance as this . . .' (Ezra 9. 13, 14). What then? What use is to be made of this? 'Should we again break thy commandments? Wouldest Thou not be angry with us till our lusts consumed us?' Yes, we could expect nothing else. What, have you had so many experiences of your deceitful heart, and yet are so foolish as still to trust it (Proverbs 28. 26)?

It is sad and dangerous to sin after experiences. It is impossible, that is, very difficult and at least morally impossible, for those who have been enlightened and have tasted of the heavenly gift, to renew them again to repentance if they fall away (Hebrews 6. 4–6). You have had many an aching heart for sinning already. So sin no more, lest a worse thing come unto thee. Having such a cloud of experimental witnesses, let us lay aside the sin that so easily besets us. If you sin against these witnesses, these witnesses will witness against you, and aggravate your condemnation. Let us therefore say to our sins, as Ephraim did to his idols, with great indignation – 'Get ye hence, what have we any more to do with you!'

That I may conclude, I have only one more witness to produce against sin:

## 7. THE WITNESS OF SIN ITSELF

I shall show that sin proclaims its own sinfulness both by its names which it cannot disown, and by the arts which it uses to disguise itself.

(1) *Sin's names*. These it cannot deny, but confesses that they belong to it. I shall give only two examples:

1. *It is called the work of the Devil* (1 John 3. 5, 8). This is not to say that man's sin is not from himself, or that it is only of the Devil; but sin is what the Devil does and what he tempts others to do. Thus to sin is to act and work like the Devil; he who sins is of the Devil. Man indeed is of God, but the sinner or sinful man is of the Devil. The Devil was the first sinner, and he that sins is of him as if he were his child (John 8. 44). He who does the Devil's work is of the Devil; sinning is the Devil's trade and he who follows this trade is of the Devil; he lives a devil's life. The Devil does nothing but sin; this is his business, and those who tread in his steps are of him and like him: they are devils incarnate.

a. *To sin and to live in sin is to do as the Devil does*. It is to be like him and conformable to him. Sin is his work. He is so evil and wicked that he is called emphatically and by way of eminence *the* Evil and *the* Wicked One (1 John 2. 13; 3. 12); as if no-one were evil or at least as evil as he. Truly the devils are not only wicked, but they are called wickednesses in the abstract (Ephesians 6. 12) and abstracts denote essences. He sinned from the beginning and continues sinning to this day; and they who imitate him in his work are his children as much as if they were begotten of him: 'Ye are of your father the Devil, and his works (or his lusts) ye will do'; he was and is a murderer: he attempted it upon God, but effected it on himself and man (John 8. 44). He is the Abaddon and Apollyon, the murderer to this day (Revelation 9. 11). It is true that he is a liar, a deceiver and a tempter, but he does all these in subservience to his reigning sin (for he is called a king in Revelation 9. 11), which is that he is a destroyer or murderer (1 Peter 5. 8). Now exactly the same is said of those who sin: they destroy their own souls (Proverbs 8. 36); they are *felones de se*, self-murderers. Sin is devil's work.

b. *He who sins works for the Devil.* Not only does he do such work as the Devil does; he is the servant and slave of the Devil. The Devil works in the children of disobedience and they work for him. He is their prince and their god, whose servants they are, and whose works they do. 'His servants ye are whom ye obey', the Apostle says (Romans 6. 16). So that they who serve and obey the Devil are his servants, and sin is the work sinners do for him. What wages then are they who serve such a master likely to have!

Though sinners defy the Devil in words, yet they deify him in works, and at last he will devil-ize them and bring them into the same nature and misery as himself. Sinners are led by him at his will: they are like his dogs on the end of a string. When men are converted they are delivered from his power (Acts 26. 18) and they who apostatize or who are excommunicated are delivered again to Satan. Thus in whatever state a sinner is a sinner, whether an infidel, a formalist or an apostate, he is under the power of the Devil, doing the Devil's work for the Devil's wages.

c. *He who sins is a devil.* So much does he belong to the Devil and do his work that he has the name of a devil. He is a devil to God, to himself and to others. For one sin St. Peter had the name of Satan (Matthew 16. 23), but wicked men are called devils: Judas was a devil (John 6. 70). Sin made angels devils, and it makes men devils, traitors, as Judas was, to their Lord and Master. It is said, 'The Devil shall cast some of you into prison' (Revelation 2. 10); surely the Devil did not appear in person to do this, but by his instruments and agents, devils incarnate. O sinful sin, the work of the Devil!

Let me here take the opportunity to show you some sins which are especially said to be the Devil's sin. They who do them are of the Devil, work for him, are like him, and are called devils:

a. *Murder*, especially soul-murder. Anti-Christ, the Devil's son, is most guilty of this making merchandise of souls (Revelation 18. 13). So also are lying prophets that hunt souls (Ezekiel 13. 18–20) and devour and destroy souls (Ezekiel 22. 25, 27). The Devil was a murderer from the beginning (John 8. 44), and they who murder are (as Cain was) of the Devil (1 John 3. 12). Murder originates in anger and hatred: 'Whoever hates his brother is a murderer' (1 John 3. 15). Therefore the Apostle says, 'Do not be angry so as to sin; let not the sun go down upon your wrath, for that is to give place to the Devil' (Ephesians 4. 26, 27). Pride is all for contention, and contention for murder. Pride produces discontent, and discontent envy, and envy hatred and malice. Hence comes murder. If you have bitter envying and strife in your hearts, this is not only earthly and sensual but devilish (James 3. 14, 15). Originally the Devil's sin and his condemnation was from pride (1 Timothy 3. 6). Pride made him discontented, envious, angry, and a murderer; and so it did Cain, his eldest son. The proud spirit lusteth to envy (James 4. 5–7). Thus when St. Peter teaches us how to resist the Devil he tells us it must be by submission and humility (1 Peter 5. 5–8).

b. *Lying* is the second sin that calls the Devil father, and marks out those who do it as his children. The Devil is a liar and the father of lies (John 8. 44). When Ananias told a lie, the Apostle said that Satan had filled his heart (Acts 5. 3). They who lie are of the synagogue of Satan, members and sons of the synagogue of Satan (Revelation 2. 9 with 3. 9). God says of his children that they will not lie (Isaiah 63. 8). They who love and make lies are without among the dogs and devils (Revelation 22. 15); they are without the gates of the City of God, and they have their portion with the Devil in the lake of fire (Revelation 21. 8).

c. *Deceivers and seducers* are of the Devil. He is the deceiver (Revelation 12. 9; 20. 2–3), the old serpent who deceived Eve and who deceives the whole world. They who deceive the souls of men are like the Devil, whether it be done by calling the truth into question as the Devil did at first, and against which the Apostle speaks (2 Corinthians 11. 2–3); or by the abusing and wresting of falsely-quoted Scripture (2 Peter 3.

[158]

16) as the Devil did (Matthew 4. 6); or by transforming themselves into angels of light as the Devil does (2 Corinthians 11. 14). There are deceivers who sin in the name of the Lord, and attribute that to the Spirit which is only their own fancy, if not a falsehood. They may even deceive by false and pretended miracles after the manner of Satan (2 Thessalonians 2. 9,10).

d. *Tempting man to sin.* They who do this come under the Devil's name and do his work. He is the tempter (Matthew 4. 1; 1 Thessalonians 3. 5); he tempts all men to one sin or another. The Devil had a hand in Cain murdering his brother (1 John 3. 12); in Judas's treason (Luke 22. 3); in Ananias's lie (Acts 5. 3); in David's numbering the people (1 Chronicles 21. 1); in Peter's denying his Master (Luke 22. 31, 32). He tempted to the first sin, and ever since he has tempted all men to sin and to commit every sin. It is the Devil's work and sin to tempt others to sin, and they who do this do the Devil's work.

e. *False accusing.* Slandering, evil speaking and back-biting others is of the Devil and like him. He is the accuser of the brethren (Revelation 12. 10). He accused Job and Joshua, and he accuses others very often without cause. The tongues of those who do this are set on fire of hell (James 3. 6). Breeders of strife, slanderers, and calumniators are called by the Devil's name, *Diaboloi* – so we read in three places in St. Paul's Epistles (1 Timothy 3. 11; 2 Timothy 3. 3; Titus 2. 3). To carry slanders is the work of the Devil.

f. *Hindering others from believing and closing with the truth of the Gospel.* This is another sin which is the work of the Devil and which makes them who do it like the Devil. This may be done in several ways:

(i) By keeping them in ignorance, and blinding them (2 Corinthians 4. 4). This may be done either by stealing and taking away the Word (Matthew 13. 4, 19), or by hindering and keeping away the means of grace from them (1 Thessalonians 2. 18).

(ii) By sowing tares among the wheat (Matthew 13. 25, 27, 38, 39).

(iii) By perverting the ways of the Lord (Acts 13. 10) which are represented as tedious and dangerous. Whoever keeps means from men, or men from means, or makes false representations of the ways of God is of the Devil.

g. *Apostasy* (John 8. 44). The Devil did not abide in the truth but left his first love, life and state (2 Peter 2. 4; Jude 6). Hence Judas is called devil (John 6. 70) and apostates are said to turn aside after Satan (1 Timothy 5. 15). As converts are turned from Satan to God, so apostates return from God to Satan. He who does not abide in the truth is like the Devil. I will mention only one more sin in this list:

h. *Persecuting the righteous for righteousness' sake* is the Devil's work (1 John 3. 12; Matthew 23. 35). They who do it are of the Devil and are called devils. Some he oppresses, some he possesses; and where he is dispossessed there he turns persecutor: 'The devil shall cast some of you into prison' (Revelation 2. 10); this was a persecuting devil incarnate.

Thus sin is the work of the Devil, which is a great witness against it. I may add at this point that in some ways the sin of man is more horrible and heinous than that of devils. I do not mean the first sins of either, but the sins since the time when God revealed his pleasure concerning the disposal of devils and men. The devil has some sort of gratification in tempting man, for it is a kind of victory or revenge; but men only wrong and torment themselves. Moreover the devils are past hope and have grown desperate, being rejected of God (2 Peter 2. 4); for Christ Jesus did not take them on him (Hebrews 2. 16). They are hardened against God who punishes them, and have grown so envious that they will be avenged on man seeing they cannot be on God. If only they had a door of hope opened, it is probable they would not be so wicked as they are. When there is no hope, persons are more resolute (Jeremiah 2. 25). But for men to sin whom God has spared, for whom indeed he spared not his own Son, whom he calls and woos and even begs to be reconciled and happy – for these men to sin, what horrible ingratitude is this! What an aggravating and inexcusable sin it is! It is worse than the Devil's sin, for devils do not sin against second mercy and offers of grace as men do. But I must hasten to sin's second name:

2. *Sin is all filthiness of flesh and spirit* (2 Corinthians 7. 1). This denotes its loathsomeness and its infectiousness.

a. *Sin is a loathsome thing.* This is clear when we begin to consider that which sin resembles, unto which it is likened, as the most offensive and most loathsome diseases: a canker or gangrene (2 Timothy 2. 17). Now men are loath to eat and drink with those who have these diseases. Sin is likened to the rot, to the filth and corruption of the foulest disease, which is so foul and rotten that one would not touch it with a pair of tongs, as the proverb goes. The Apostle tells us that some, like Jannes and Jambres, resist the truth; he calls them men of corrupt or rotten minds. And Solomon would have us know that just as a sound heart is the life of the flesh, so envy (anything opposed to the sound heart) is the rottenness of the bones (Proverbs 14. 30). Indeed, sin is likened to the plague from which everyone flies. It is so offensive and loathsome that it separates the nearest relations. Now sin is called the plague of the heart (1 Kings 8. 38, 39) which is much worse than any sore of the body.

And this is not all. Sin is not only likened to the most loathsome diseases, but also to the other most loathsome things there are. It is likened to the blood in which infants are born, which is loathsome (Ezekiel 16. 5, 6). It is likened to mire and dung, to the very excrements that lie in ditches and sewers in which sows and swine wallow, and even to the vomit of dogs (2 Peter 2. 22). It is compared to the putrefaction of graves and sepulchres (Matthew 23. 27, 28), which stink, as Martha said of Lazarus when he had been some days dead (John 11. 39). It is also likened to poison (Romans 3. 13). All these things, and others which I shall not name, are loathsome things at which men stop their noses and from which they hide their eyes. Yet sin is more loathsome than all of them if we consider that nothing but the fountain open for Judah and Jerusalem to wash in, nothing but the blood of Jesus can cleanse from this filthiness. All the nitre and soap in the world cannot get it out.

Besides, it is not only filthy but filthiness, not only corrupt but corruption, in the very abstract. All the things to which sin is likened fall far short of sin; they are only shadows which are very imperfect representations of the reality.

Now all the former examples reach only to the body and do not defile the man. But sin reaches to and seizes on soul and spirit, and defiles the man (Matthew 15. 19, 20). This is the canker, the rottenness, the plague, the poison of the soul, and sin is not only worse than any, but than all of these. What is more, if our righteousness is but as a menstruous rag (Isaiah 64. 6) how filthy must our sin be! The Apostle Paul counted his righteousness which was of the law to be but dung (Philippians 3. 8); what then did he reckon his injuriousness, persecution and blasphemy to be—surely as bad as death and hell. If not only our righteousness, but our righteousnesses, indeed all our righteousnesses, are as filthy rags (Isaiah 64. 6), what is our sin, our sins, and all our sins? Truly filthy beyond expression or imagination.

b. *Sin is a polluting and infectious thing.* Since sin is of a pestilential and poisonous nature, it has caused not only corruption, but pollution and defilement (2 Peter 2. 20). Many things may make a man foul and loathsome, such as leprosy and ulcerous tumours, and yet the soul of a man may be still pure and fair, as Job's was when his body was all over a scab or sore, and he sat on the dunghill. But as we suggested before, sin defiles the man, and soaks into his very spirit and infects that. We will attempt to take a clearer and fuller view of sin's pestilential and infectious nature and operation, and so consider it in various ways:

(i) *In its universality.* See how it has extended and spread itself over all the world; there is no land or nation, tribe, language, kindred or people where it has not been known from the rising of the sun to the going down thereof. All climates, hot and cold, all quarters of the world, American, African, Asian and European, have all been infected. Not only Sodom and Samaria, but Jerusalem and Sion were infected and ruined by it. It is here, there and everywhere, except Heaven!

Besides this, it has infected all ages; it is almost as old as the world. It has run in the blood from Adam to Moses, and so on to this day. It is the plague which has lasted almost six thousand years. Indeed, what is more, not one man has escaped it; all kinds of men, all ranks, high and low, rich and poor, kings and beggars have been infected by it (Romans 3. 9, 10); the wise and learned as well as the foolish and illiterate. Who is there that has lived and sinned not, our Saviour excepted? If any man says he has not sinned, he sins in saying so. By one man sin came into the world, but since, not one man but every man has sinned. All have sinned and come short of the glory of God (Romans 3. 23), and death came upon all, inasmuch as all had sinned (Romans 5. 12). If all men are mortal, then all are sinners, for death came in by sin; where there is no sin there is no death, as in Heaven (Revelation 21. 4). All men have died of this plague; indeed our Lord and Saviour would not have died if he had not been made sin for us. Moreover, this leprosy has not only spread itself on mankind as a whole, but on the whole of man; every part of man is infected. It has made flesh and spirit filthy (2 Corinthians 7. 1). From the crown of the head to the sole of the foot, there is not one sound part in him, for all his members are servants to sin. It is no better within, for his heart is evil; the thoughts of his heart are evil; the imaginations of the thoughts of his heart are evil; the very thoughts of his thoughts are evil. Indeed every creature of the heart is evil (Genesis 6. 5). I showed above how the understanding is darkened and depraved. That the heart is desperately wicked and deceitful beyond any knowledge but God's the prophet assures us from God himself (Jeremiah 17. 9). The mind and conscience is defiled (Titus 1. 15, 16). The world has become perverse and stubborn; and worse, it is wilful and mad, set upon sin and Hell (Ecclesiastes 8. 11). The affections which are lustful are inordinate, and the passions which are irascible, are unruly. Man is more headstrong than the horse which rushes into the battle. Sin has made some men so restless that they cannot sleep unless or until they have done mischief (Proverbs 4. 16).

[163]

Sin spreads its infection by defiling man's duties and holy things. It defiles his natural and civil actions so that the plough-ing of the wicked is sin (Proverbs 21. 4). Man should do everything from the highest to the lowest duty to the glory of God, but which of his deeds is not ill-done and to the dis-honour of God? Sin infects men's prayers. The prayers of the wicked are an abomination to the Lord (Proverbs 28. 9), even though offered up with incense to perfume them (Isaiah 1. 13). Under the law, Aaron was to bear the iniquity of the holy things (Exodus 28. 38). Israel brought God many a present, but sin, like a dead fly in a box of ointment, spoilt everything (Isaiah 1. 11, 16).

Sin also infects all that belongs to man. When man was created, God furnished his house for him, gave him the world and the fulness thereof. It was good then, but alas, how it has changed, for sin has made everything that belongs to man vanity, that is, empty and unprofitable (Ecclesiastes 1). The fulness of the creature cannot fill a man: the eye is not satis-fied with seeing, nor the ear with hearing, for all is vanity. The gloss and beauty, the pleasure and profit of creature-enjoyments have become vanity; indeed, what is more, sin has made them vexation too. Sin has embittered man's enjoy-ments. Man, among his comforts, lives but a vexatious life. In the fulness of his sufficiency he is in straits, and likewise, in the fulness of his comforts he is in sorrow, and in the midst of laughter his heart is sad. Man's enjoyments are disappoint-ments; they fail his expectations and so are not to his con-tentment, but to his vexation. Neither the length nor the comfort of his life is in the abundance of these things (Luke 12. 15). What is even worse, his sin has not only made things very vexatious, but a snare and temptation to man; they are sin's baits by which it catches men. What are honours, pleasures and riches but snares to the children of men (Pro-verbs 30. 8, 9).

(ii) *How suddenly sin infects*, increases and multiplies! Sin is not barren, but all too fruitful to beget and bring forth more; it is not lazy but gains ground continually. How great a fire

[164]

hath a spark kindled! Adam's posterity has not been so numerous as his sins. A little cloud, no bigger than a man's hand – so it seems at first – grows and spreads to cover the whole hemisphere. The water that at first seemed little and shallow, swells more and more from the ankles to the knees, from the knees to the loins, from there to the head until it grows into such a great river that it cannot be passed over. In this way grows sin; and it is a very monster for its growth. Let us notice how it increases in our own selves and then how in others:

(a) *How it increases in ourselves.* Sometimes the same sin increases from little to great, growing from an infant to a man. It is as a snowball that grows bigger by rolling it in the snow. The little grain of mustard grows to a great tree. A little seed of sin becomes a big tree. Adam's sin was only one but it was a breeding and pregnant sin, and the mother of all abominations. One sin transgresses the whole law (James 2. 10). When lust has conceived it hastens to bring forth, and when it has brought forth, it brings it up until it comes to its full stature (James 1. 14, 15). It is at first only a lust, an appetite, inclination, or motion; from there it proceeds to enticement; by that to draw us aside; and then to tempt and impregnate us. By this temptation it conceives, and there is an embryo; this grows in the womb and when it is brought forth it is a sin; and this being finished or perfected proves deadly. The tongue is a little member, but as a little spark of fire, but when kindled it becomes a world of iniquity and defiles the whole body and sets on fire the whole course of nature (James 3. 5, 6).

Just as a little leaven leavens the whole lump, so sometimes one sin begets many more sins, not only of the same kind, but others also. God had forbidden his people to take the accursed thing (Joshua 7. 11), but when they had taken, they dissembled also and put it among their own stuff. You may see how one sin led to another when Achan confesses his sin (verses 19–21): he says 'When I saw, I coveted, and when I coveted, I took, and when I had taken, I hid them'; thus one sin begat another.

This thing grows into a greatness and multiplies itself. If we do not abhor the garment we may be spotted with the flesh. If we do not withdraw from occasions of evil we may by the occasions be drawn to evil; and not abstaining from appearances of evil, be brought to apparent evil. There is one chapter in Scripture that gives us two sad examples of this, Genesis 34. Dinah, out of curiosity, must make a visit to the daughters of the land and while going to see the daughters the son saw her; and having seen her, he took her; having taken her, he lay with her; and by lying with her defiled her. When the report of this came to Jacob's sons they were grieved, and being grieved, were wroth, and being wroth they meditated revenge; meditating revenge they spoke deceitfully; having deceived, they slew, and having slain they fell upon the spoil. How hard it is then to sin once, and only once. Sin grows upon us.

(b) *How sin increases in others and infects them*. It went from one man to every man. How soon the world got the name of un-godly world or the world of the un-godly (2 Peter 2. 5)! And after the Flood, how soon the world became overspread with sin from seven or eight persons! One root cf bitterness defiles many (Hebrews 12. 15). Man's bad examples are very pestilential and pernicious; a little leaven leaveneth the whole lump. Or, as our country proverb has it, one scabbed sheep infects a whole flock. The world grows worse and worse; the latter days are most perilous because most sinful. And as if there had not been sin enough already, some set up projects and trades of new sins, being inventors of evil things (Romans 1. 30). How spreading and catching is this infection, for others will very soon follow these newly-found fashions of sin and sinning.

(iii) *The infection of sin is almost incurable*. The cure is impossible to us and only possible with God, and that, at a costly rate, by the blood of Christ himself. The reason why it is very hard to be cured is that sin is within us and dwelleth in us (Romans 7. 17, 20). An ulcer in the flesh is more easily cured than one in the lungs. A disease that is within cannot

[166]

be so well reached. Indeed, sin is not only in us but is riveted in us; it has got into the flesh and spirit as if it were one with us, like the leopard's spots and the Ethiopian's blackness. Under the law there was a leprosy so inveterate that though they scraped a house outside and inside and threw out the dust, though they took other stones and mortar, yet it returned again (Leviticus 14. 42–44). When diseases become, as it were, natural, and are in the constitution, they are hard to be cured. It is not easy to obliterate that which is written with a pen of iron and the point of a diamond. It is difficult to soften a heart of stone.

Besides, this filthiness has long been in possession, even time out of mind. It pleads prescription: a custom of such long standing has become a law and, as it were, the course of nature (Jeremiah 13. 23). To show how hard it is for sin to be cured and rooted out, we now observe that very forcible means have been used for cleansing it, and even so, it has not been removed. God poured out a whole flood of water which washed away most sinners; yet sin, as I may say, kept above water, and was found alive and strong after the flood. When God sent fire and brimstone or Hell, as one old writer put it, from Heaven, on Sodom, that centre of sin, still sin escaped with Lot and his daughters. Now fire and water are very cleansing and purifying things, and yet you see that even they cannot do it. When some others sinned, the earth swallowed them up, yet sin remained, it did not die. After all these judgments the same sins are still in the world. Even in the saints themselves, with all the forces that faith can muster, sin is scarcely kept under, but the flesh will be lusting against the spirit. And when their affections do not cleave to sin, yet sin will cleave to their affections and make them cry out with St. Paul, O wretch that I am, who shall deliver me from this body of death? The victory is by Christ Jesus; it is death which kills sin.

(iv) *Sin lives in its effects when we are dead and gone*. It follows us to the grave and there rots our bodies. When it can no longer reach our souls to make them vile, still it does not

[167]

refrain from making our bodies putrid and vile. He who did no sin saw no corruption, but we who have sinned see corruption, and stink within a few days as Lazarus did, so sinful and infectious is sin!

Thus we have seen the names of sin and how they witness against it. There remains only a second aspect—the witness of sin against itself, namely,

(2) *The arts that sin uses to disguise itself*. If sin were not an ugly thing, would it wear a mask? If it did not have evil designs, would it walk in disguise and change its name? Truth is not ashamed of its name or nakedness; it can walk openly and boldly. Sin, on the contrary, is a cheat, a lie, and therefore lurks privily and puts on false names and colours; for if it were to appear like itself—as it sooner or later will do to all, either for conversion or confusion—it would frighten men into dying fits, as it did the Apostle, and when they come to themselves they would abhor and hate it, as Paul and the Prodigal did. Men would never be so hardy in sinning but that sin hardens them by deceiving them; so the Apostle says, 'Take heed lest any be hardened through the deceitfulness of sin' (Hebrews 3. 13). Sin uses all manner of arts, methods and devices to attract us and inveigle us. It uses many tricks on us and has all the knacks of deceiving and cheating us. So I may with truth say that sin has not learnt but taught all the deceits, dissimulations, flatteries and false diplomacies that are found in courts; the stratagems of war; the sophisms and fallacies of the schools; the frauds of tradesmen, whether in city or country; the tricks of cheaters and jugglers, the ambushes of thieves, the pretensions of false friends, the various methods of false teachers—these and every other kind of cheat and deception in the world, sin teaches and practises upon us all to make us sin.

It is impossible to count up all the ways in which the deceitful hearts and sins of men abuse them. I will, however, give a few examples as a warning to sinners and a witness against sin, and so conclude this section of our book.

(1) *Sometimes sin persuades us that such and such a thing*

*is not a sin, though it looks like a sin.* Thus the Devil dealt with Eve in the beginning and so deceived her. She was a little suspicious and shy, that what the Devil urged her to do was evil, but he cunningly insinuated that however it seemed to her, yet it was not so. In this way the pride and wantonness of people is maintained – that though these things appear to be evil, they are not evil. But, alas, it is the next thing to being a sinner to look like a sinner; appearance in good is too little and in evil it is too much. It is a very hard thing to look like a sinner and talk and dress like a sinner and not to be one. It is more than likely that what the Devil grants to be like a sin, is a sin. Those who are persuaded otherwise are deceived by him, as Eve was. If we like the picture, the odds are great against us not liking the thing. Though an idol is no God, nor even like him, yet God has utterly forbidden graven images, for they are of the Devil's carving.

(2) *Sin would persuade that what may be sin in another cannot be sin in you, all things considered, because you are necessitated.* For example, a poor man is forced to steal. But no man is necessitated to sin, even though under necessity; sin is sin in any or in all. Though temptations may mitigate and excuse somewhat, yet they cannot excuse totally from its being a sin, and they cannot un-sin sin.

(3) *It is one sin only, and this only once*, says Sin. But if sin is good, why only once, and if evil, why once? One sin though committed but once is one and once too much. Besides when the Serpent's head is in, it is hard to keep out the whole body; one makes way for the other. It is almost impossible to sin once and only once.

(4) *It is only a little one*, says Sin. But that which is against a great God and deserves so great a punishment as death cannot be a little sin; for the wages of sin and of every single sin is death (Romans 6. 23).

(5) *It is in secret and no-one will see it*, says Sin. But this is a cheat, for it is impossible to sin so secretly but there will be at least two witnesses. God and conscience know all the sins that man can commit.

(6) *Yes, but you will hate it and dread it ever after*, says Sin. Thus some go to Mass to show their distaste of it, and to plays to see the folly of them. But who would be a burnt child to learn to dread the fire? Such costly experiments may indeed cost us the loss of our souls. It is dangerous to meddle with that which is an appearance and may be an occasion of evil, and much more to parley and tamper with sin itself.

(7) *But I promise you that you shall gain by it*, says Sin. You will have so much profit, so much pleasure and so much honour. Sin's gain is loss, however; for he who gains even the world by sin pays too dearly for it. It means the loss or at least the hazard of his soul. The pleasures of sin are grievous, and its honours are disgraces and shame. Did not our first parents find it so, and do not we (Romans 6. 21)? The precious substance promised by sin ends in a pernicious shadow, and the spoils we get by sin only spoil us. Sin promises like a God but pays like a Devil. Sin tells us that we shall not die but live like gods, but we find nothing but death and such a life as they have in Hell. Sin's performance is altogether contrary to its promises; it promises gold and pays dross. If any man, then, has a mind to have true miseries, let him pay heed to sin's false promises.

(8) *But others do it*, says Sin, *and why may not you?* It is not what others do, however, but what they ought to do that we are to follow. We must not follow any man or a multitude of men to do evil. If others will risk their damnation, what is that to us? It will be no comfort to have had companions in sin and to meet them again in Hell.

(9) *But you have only to repent*, says Sin, *and God will forgive you*. To this we must say that he who promised forgiveness to them that repent has not promised repentance to them that sin. Besides, even if sin were to cost no more than repentance, anyone in his right mind would be loth to buy repentance at so dear a rate; for repentance, though it may free them from greater, puts men to more grief and pain than ever sin could afford them pleasure.

(10) *Yes, but you have escaped well enough hitherto*, says

Sin. No evil has befallen you. If this is so, however, it may be so much the worse for us. Not to be punished may be the worst punishment (Isaiah 1. 15; Hosea 4. 14, 17). What will it cost if God does awaken me, and if not, what will it cost when God shall damn me?

(11) *It is only your infirmity*, says Sin. You cannot help it. Tell sin that this is a thing that none but fools and children can accept. Besides, to plead for infirmities is more than an infirmity. That which is only an infirmity today may become a disease tomorrow, if not prevented. Once the will is engaged, it is past an infirmity and has become a sin.

Now if these and other arguments do not succeed, then Sin speaks more openly. It says, there is no such thing as sin. There is no difference between good and evil. As all things come alike to all, so all things are alike. And also, says Sin, evil is good in God's sight, or he would judge it (Malachi 2. 17); his silence makes you think that he is such an one as yourself (Psalm 50. 21). But tell Sin that this defeats and refutes itself and proves nothing so clearly as that sin is exceedingly sinful. If there is no sin, and no difference between good and evil, to what purpose are these different words used by Sin to prove that there is no difference? To say that it is only in imagination and not real is to deny that there is any such thing as sense and conscience, which every man admits, and no-one can deny without denying himself and God. Between good and evil there is more difference than between light and darkness, life and death, ease and pain, food and poison, and these are real, and not differences made by our fancy only. That all things come alike to all is not always true; there are contrary examples. To say that all things are alike is never true but is a manifest contradiction. To say that evil is good in God's sight and that he is such an one as a sinner is to deny God to be, for if he is not good and just, he is not God. But this bespeaks man to be woefully ignorant, for the flood which drowned the old world, the fire which fell from Heaven on Sodom, the judgments which God executes in the earth continually, witness that God is displeased with and the avenger of sin, just as his giving us rain from heaven and fruitful seasons is witness that he is good and does good. The fact that his sun shines and his rain falls on the unjust as well as on the just is to persuade men of his goodness which calls for repentance and which also witnesses that sin is evil.

But if sin were not exceedingly sinful, what need would it have to use all these tricks and subterfuges? If it and its deeds were not evil, why does it seek to avoid the light? Why, like a maker of counterfeit money, does it put the King of Heaven's stamp on its base metal? Why does Jacob call himself Esau and counterfeit his brother if sin were not abominable? Why did the Gibeonites pretend to have come from afar if they did not wish to be unknown? If sin were not false and a robber, why does it creep in unseen, climb up a narrow way and avoid the door? Why does it flatter and deceive? Why does it never keep its promises, but break all it ever made? It is because it is sinful sin.

I have now shown what sin is and in what its sinfulness consists, and proved it by many witnesses including sin itself. But before I come to the next thing, that is, to the application of this doctrine, I shall briefly sum up the charge against sin. That which sin is accused of and proved to be guilty of is high treason against God. It attempts nothing less than the dethroning and un-god-ing of God himself. It has unmanned man, made him a fool, a beast, a devil, and subjected him to the wrath of God, and made him liable to eternal damnation. It has made men deny that God is, or affirm that he is like themselves. It has put the Lord of Life to death and shamefully crucified the Lord of Glory. It is always resisting the Holy Ghost. It is continually practising the defiling, the dishonour, the deceiving and the destruction of all men. What a prodigious, monstrous, devilish thing is sin!

It is impossible to speak worse of sin than it really is, or even as badly of it as it really deserves, for it is hyperbolically sinful. There are not enough words; we need more, and stronger ones to speak of its vileness. And if we were to say that it is worse than death and the Devil, the very Hell of

Hell, this would not be to rail at it, but tell it only the truth about itself. Sin is the quintessence of evil; it has made all the evils that there are and is itself worse than all the evils it has made. It is so evil that it is impossible to make it good or lovely by all the arts than can be used. A poison may be corrected and made medicinal, even if it is not nourishing. But sin is sin, and can be nothing else; its nature cannot be changed, not even by a pardon. It is not only ugly but ugliness, not only filthy but filthiness, not only abominable but abomination. There is not a worse thing in Hell itself; it has not its fellow there. All this and much more may be said of and against sin. Having laid this groundwork, then, I shall now build upon it, and proceed to the application and usefulness of the doctrine of sin's sinfulness.

# SECTION FOUR

# THE APPLICATION AND USEFULNESS OF
# THE DOCTRINE OF SIN'S SINFULNESS

―――――

## I. IN GENERAL, SIN IS THE WORST OF EVILS; THE EVIL OF EVIL, AND INDEED THE ONLY EVIL

Nothing is so evil as sin; nothing is evil but sin. As the sufferings of this present time are not worthy to be compared with the glory that shall be revealed in us, so neither the sufferings of this life nor of that to come are worthy to be compared as evil with the evil of sin. No evil is displeasing to God or destructive to man but the evil of sin. Sin is worse than affliction, than death, than Devil, than Hell. Affliction is not so afflictive, death is not so deadly, the Devil not so devilish, Hell not so hellish as sin is. This will help to fill up the charge against its sinfulness, especially as it is contrary to and against the good of man.

The four evils I have just named are truly terrible, and from all of them everyone is ready to say, Good Lord, deliver us! Yet none of these, nor all of them together, are as bad as sin. Therefore our prayers should be more to be delivered from sin, and if God hear no prayer else, yet as to this we should say, We beseech Thee to hear us, good Lord!

## (1) *It is worse than any evil affliction*

There are afflictions of several kinds, and they are all called evils. 'Is there any evil (of any kind whatever) in the city and I have not done it?' (Amos 3. 6), says the Lord. You see that God will own himself the author of that evil, but not of

[177]

sin, for that is a bastard begotten and bred by another. The evils of plagues and afflictions are brought by God, though deserved by sin. And now indeed no affliction seems to be joyous for the present (Hebrews 12. 11); although they are not to be desired yet they may be endured. Sin on the contrary is neither to be desired nor endured. Any sin is worse than any suffering, one sin than all suffering, and the least sin than the greatest suffering.

What then? Is sin worse than to be whipped, to be burnt or to be sawn asunder? Yes, by a great deal! It is clear from what our Saviour says: 'Fear not them that can kill but fear him that can damn' (Matthew 10. 28). That is, it is better to be killed than to be damned. You may more easily suffer from man than sin against God. One may suffer and not sin, but it is impossible to sin and not to suffer. They who avoid suffering by sinning, sin themselves into worse suffering.

This seems to be clear enough. Yet the truth is so seldom properly applied until it is believed, and seldom believed until it is fully proved. I shall therefore demonstrate more fully that sin is worse than suffering. In general, this is so because sin is all evil, only evil, and always evil, which no affliction is or can be. In my flesh, says the Apostle, no good dwells, not even the least, and this is ever present with me. Now it cannot be said of afflictions that there is no good in them, or that they are always present with us. There are some *lucida intervalla* (bright intervals), some spells of sunshine in winter. We may say, 'It was good that I was afflicted' (Psalm 119. 71), 'It is good to bear the yoke in one's youth' (Lamentations 3. 27). But one can never say, 'It was good that I sinned, no, though it were but in my youth' (Ecclesiastes 11. 9; 12. 1). All things may be corrected and made to work for our good, so that we can say not only that God who afflicted me was good, but that the affliction worked for good (2 Corinthians 4. 17); but we can never justly say that sin did us good. Many can say, 'Periissem nisi periissem' (I would have perished had I not suffered); but no-one can say, 'Periissem nisi peccassem' (I would have perished had I not sinned). No! It is by sin that we perish and are undone. Many people have thanked God for affliction, but no-one ever thanked him for sin. Some indeed misunderstand the meaning of Romans 6. 17, as if the Apostle were thanking God that men were sinners. But this is not the case by any means! He thanks God that they who once were sinners had become obedient to the Gospel; the proper sense and reading of this text is, 'Thanks be to God, *though* ye were the servants of sin (in time past), yet (now) ye have obeyed the form of doctrine which was delivered to you', or as it is in the margin and the Greek, 'whereunto ye were delivered'. Sin, in itself, is good neither before nor after its commission; it is not good to be committed, nor good after it is committed. It does us no good, but hurt, all our days. Other evils, however, though we cannot call them good before, so that we might desire them, yet afterwards we can call them good and so we can thank God for them. I will illustrate this in detail.

1. *Suffering may be the object of our choice, which sin cannot be.* That which is evil and only evil cannot be the object of our volition and choice; it is against nature. If men did not call evil good and good evil, they could never love the evil nor hate the good. Nor may sin be chosen as a means to a good end; for as well as being evil and nothing else, it does evil and nothing else. Affliction on the contrary, though not chosen for itself, may yet be chosen for a good end, and chosen rather than sin. It may be chosen although the only good result were the avoidance of evil. We have examples of this, such as the three young men whose gallantry of spirit was such that though they should not be delivered by their God, yet they would not sin against their God (they were holily wilful), nor even as much as demur, deliberate or take time to consider whether they should suffer or sin; it was past dispute with them, brave and noble souls that they were (Daniel 3. 17). We find the same of Daniel himself (Daniel 6) and of St. Paul (Acts 20. 24). Notice that when the Apostle speaks of his afflictions, he calls them light (2 Corinthians 4. 17), but when he speaks of sin, he speaks of it as a burden that pressed him down and made him cry out, 'Wretch that I

am!'; it made him groan, being burdened (2 Corinthians 5. 4). Moses' choice is famous the world over, for it was not made when he was a child but when he came to forty years of age; he preferred suffering, not only before sinning but before honours, riches, and pleasures. He accounted the worst of Christ – namely, reproaches – better than the best the world could give.

There is a further example which is more than all the rest, and it is that of our blessed Saviour. To him was the greatest offer made that ever was made, but though he was tempted, and suffered by being tempted, he scorned and abhorred to sin (Matthew 4). He endured the cross and despised the shame (Hebrews 12. 1–4); he met the cross, shame and pain, and in addition the contradiction of sinners. Yes, all this he endured rather than sin. It is described as a striving against sin (Hebrews 12. 4). And when St. Peter wished him to decline suffering, he called him Satan and said to him, 'Get behind me, Satan'. Thus he teaches us that it is better to suffer than to sin.

2. *We ought to rejoice in suffering.* Not only should we choose suffering rather than sin, but we must do it with all joy, we must, in the highest degree, glory in tribulation. Sin on the contrary is the cause of shame and grief, not of joy. 'Count it all joy when ye fall into divers temptations' (James 1. 2); not simply joy, or a little joy, but all joy; it is a reason for glorying. By temptations we are here to understand tribulations, for St. Paul says that temptations were for the trial of faith (Romans 5. 3). The trial of faith is the furnace of affliction (Isaiah 48. 10 with 1 Peter 1. 6, 7). Now if any were to glory in their sin, and pride themselves on that, they glory in their shame (Philippians 3. 19). Indeed if we fall into sin it is a matter for grief and shame. Suffering is as far to be preferred before sin, as joy is before grief, and glory before shame.

We may add that God himself takes pleasure, joy and delight in the trials of good men. Though he does not delight to grieve the children of men, yet he laughs at the trial of the innocent (Job 9. 23); for in this sense this text is understood by many. God does not laugh at them as at the wicked, by way of derision and scorn, but by way of pleasure. It is as when a general in a war sends on a dangerous mission a company of men of whose courage and skill he is confident. Though he knows that some of them must bleed and perhaps die for it, yet it pleases him to see them engaged in it. Thus God laughs at the trial of the innocent, for he sees that they are men who can abide a trial, as the excellent expositor on the Book of Job puts it, with much more to this effect.

God takes pleasure in the sufferings of his people just as he did in the sufferings of Christ and as Christ himself did. He boasted to the Devil's face that Job still held fast his integrity even though he were afflicted by the Devil who had moved God against him, to destroy him without a cause (Job 2. 3). One ingenious and eloquent commentator says on this text: 'Surely one may call Job more than happy since if, as David tells us, the man whose sins God is pleased to cover is happy, what may that man be accounted whose graces God vouchsafes to proclaim?'

We see then that God takes pleasure in and laughs at the trial of these his champions and heroes. The heathen moralist, Seneca, ventured to say that if there were any spectacle here below noble enough and worthy to entertain the eyes of God, it was that of a good man generously contending with ill-fortune (as they call it), afflictions and sufferings. But when men sin God laughs them to scorn. If his sons and daughters sin it provokes him to grief and anger; but the sins of others provoke him to laugh at and to hate them (Psalm 2. 4, 5; Psalm 37. 13). Which is better? To suffer and please God or to sin and grieve him? To undergo that which by patient suffering of it will rejoice God and give him occasion to magnify us, or to do that which will provoke him to be angry with us, until we are consumed, and then to laugh at our calamity? (Proverbs 1. 26, 27).

3. *Many encouragements are given us to suffer but none to sin*. On the contrary there are all kinds of discouragements

against sinning. It is all encouragement and no discouragement to suffering, but all discouragement and no encouragement to sin. For example, when we suffer for God, God suffers with us; but when we sin, God suffers by us. We read that in all their (his people's) affliction he was afflicted, he sympathised with them (Isaiah 63. 9; Hebrews 4. 15). But when he speaks of sin, it is, 'Saul, Saul, why persecutest thou me?' (Acts 9. 4); Saul's sin persecuted Christ Jesus. God complains of his people's iniquity as of a burden, as if they made a cart of God and loaded him with sins as with sheaves (Amos 2. 13).

When we suffer for God he has promised to help and assist us with counsel and comfort, with succour and support; but when we sin, God leaves us and withdraws his presence and consolations. If Jacob is in the fire or the water, God will be with him (Isaiah 43. 1, 2). On the other hand God says, 'If ye do forsake me I will forsake you' (2 Chronicles 15. 2). Sin is a forsaking of God and it makes God forsake us. Now which is best, to have God with us or against us? If God is for us it does not matter who is against us (Romans 8. 31); but if God is against us and departs from us, then all is Ichabod (1 Samuel 4. 21, 22; Job 34. 29). Furthermore, sufferings for God are evidences and tokens of his love, that we are his children and darlings (Hebrews 12. 6–8); but sin is a proof that we are not born of God (1 John 5. 18, 19), but are children of wrath and heirs of the Devil and Hell. Thus the encouragements to suffering, and discouragements to sinning, pronounce sin to be the worst of all evils.

4. *Suffering, even for sin, is designed to cure us and kill sin.* Surely the remedy is better than the disease. But sin kills us and strengthens sin. They who add sin to sin feed it, give it nourishment and new life and strength. They add fuel to the fire which sufferings are to quench and put out.

Affliction is better than going astray: 'It is good for me that I was afflicted because before I was afflicted I went astray' (Psalm 119. 67, 71). The fruit of affliction is the taking away of sin (Isaiah 27. 9); it is to make us partakers of his holiness (Hebrews 12. 10), which is the end of the greatest promises

(2 Peter 1. 4; 2 Corinthians 7. 1). We see then that God has the same aim in bringing threatened evils on us as in making good promises and fulfilling them to us. Is this not better than sin? For did sin ever do such kindnesses for us? Alas, its mercies are cruelties, its courtesies are injuries and its kindnesses are killing. It never did nor meant us any good, unless men are so mad as to think that it is good to be defiled, dishonoured, and damned!

5. *Sufferings tend to make us perfect, but sin makes us more and more imperfect.* The second Adam was perfected by suffering (Hebrews 2. 10), but the first Adam was made imperfect by sinning. And thus it fares with both their seeds and children as it did with them. A sinner is without strength (Romans 5. 6), without God, without Christ, without hope (Ephesians 2. 12). But a sufferer, after a while, shall be perfected by the same God of all grace as has called him unto eternal glory by Christ Jesus (1 Peter 5. 10). But the more a sinner, the more imperfect and the fitter for hell.

6. *Suffering for God glorifies God, but sin dishonours God.* Suffering calls on us to thank and glorify God for it (1 Peter 4. 14, 16). By it the saints are happy as God's martyrs (1 Peter 4. 14); but by sinning, sinners are made miserable as the Devil's martyrs (1 Peter 4. 15). Which, I pray you, is better? to suffer for God or for the Devil? To be suffering saints, or sinners?

7. *Sufferings for God, Christ and righteousness add to our glory, but sinning only adds to our torment* (Matthew 5. 10, 11, 12, and 2 Corinthians 4. 17). Light afflictions work an exceeding weight of glory; but sin works an exceeding weight of wrath and torment (Romans 2. 5). It accumulates heap upon heap, load upon load, to make up a treasury of wrath.

Which then is the greater evil—I speak as to wise men, judge ye what I say—light affliction or heavy sin? Which is better, treasures of glory or treasures of wrath? Or, which is all the same, to suffer or to sin?

Hitherto I have proved that sin is worse than affliction. It may be said, however, that if we do not suffer unto death, it is no great suffering; skin for skin, all that a man hath will he give for his life. But if to die is dreadful, it is worse to sin, as I shall now prove.

## (2) Sin is worse than death

We have a saying, Choose the lesser of two evils. Now to die is cheaper and more easy than to sin. God's loving kindness is better than life, that is, we would do better to part with the latter than the former. In the same way sin is worse than death: it would be better for us to undergo the latter than to commit the former; better submit to death than commit a sin, as I hinted before from Matthew 10. 28.

Let us compare them. Sin is more deadly than death. Now the separation of soul and body, that dissolution of the frame of nature and of the union between soul and body is regarded as a great evil, as is apparent from man's unwillingness to die. Man would rather live in sickness and pain, and would be in deaths often, rather than die once. And it is not only an evil in man's apprehension, but it is really so to human nature, for it is called an enemy (1 Corinthians 15. 26). It is true that death is a friend to grace, but it is equally true that death is an enemy to nature. There are four ways in which death is evil, and an enemy to man, and in all of them sin is more an enemy to man than is death.

1. *Death is separating.* It separates the nearest and dearest relations, even that which God has joined together, man and wife, soul and body. It separates us from possessions and ordinances, as I showed before. Thus death is a great evil and enemy. True! But sin is worse, for it brought death and all the evils that come by death. Sin separates man, while alive, from God, who is the light and life of our lives. Death does not separate from the love of God, which sin does (Romans 8. 38, 39; Isaiah 59. 2).

2. *Death is terrifying.* It is the king of terrors (Job 18. 14). It is very grim, a very sour and harsh thing. It is ghastly and frightful, for men are not only unwilling, but afraid to die. Yet all the terror that is in death is put there by sin. Sin is the

sting of death (1 Corinthians 15. 56), without which, though it kills, it cannot curse or hurt any man. Thus sin is more terrible than death, for without sin either there would have been no death, or for certain no terror in death. When the sting is taken away by the death of Christ, there is no danger or cause of fear (Hebrews 2. 14, 15). When the Apostle Paul looked at the Prince of Peace, he was not afraid of the King of Terrors, but to challenge and upbraid it (1 Corinthians 15. 55).

3. *Death is killing, but sin much more so.* Death deprives of natural and temporal life, but sin deprives us of spiritual and eternal life. Death kills only the body, but sin kills the soul and brings upon it a worse death than the first death, that is, the second death. Men may kill us but only God can destroy us, that is damn us, and he never does that except for sin. Thus sin is more killing than death is killing.

4. *Death is corrupting.* It brings the body to corruption, and makes it so loathsome that we say of our dearest relations, as Abraham did of Sarah when she was dead, 'Bury her out of my sight'. Death makes every man say to the worm, 'Thou art my mother', and to corruption and putrefaction, 'Thou art my father' (Job 17. 14). But sin corrupts us more than death, for he who died without sin saw no corruption. It defiles us and makes us stink in the nostrils of God and man (Genesis 34. 30). The old man and his lusts are corrupt and do corrupt us (Ephesians 4. 22). They corrupt our souls, and that which corrupts the soul, the principal man of the man, is much worse than that which corrupts the body only. Sin, however, corrupts the body too, while it is alive; intemperance and uncleanness corrupt soul and body. So sin is even in this worse than death.

Our Saviour tells the Jews that their great misery was not that they should die, but that they should die in their sins (John 8. 21). By this he intimated that sin was worse than death, and was that which made death a misery. Better die in a hospital or a ditch than in sin. It is better to die anyhow than to sin and die in sin. Therefore the Church Father told

Eudoxia the Empress, when she threatened him, *nil nisi peccatum timeo* (I fear nothing but sinning). And that Queen spoke royally who said that she would rather hear of her children's death than that they had sinned. They of whom the world was not worthy, being too good to live long, chose rather to die than sin (Hebrews 11). Thus many a good man, like St. Paul, desires to die, because his dying will prove the death of sin. Yet sin is worse not only than death.

### (3) *Sin is worse than the Devil.*

The Devil is indeed a terrible enemy, the evil and envious one, the hater of mankind. Yet he knows that he can neither damn nor hurt men without sin. Sin can do, without the Devil, that which the Devil cannot do without sin, and that is, undo men. God and the Devil are not so contrary as God and sin; for the Devil has something left which was of God, that is, his being. Sin, however, never was nor can be of God; he is neither the author of it nor the tempter to it (James 1. 13). Sin made the Devil what he is. For the Devil was not made as a devil by God. It is true that the Devil now seeks to devour man, that he cannot do it apart from sin, and that he cannot compel any man to sin.

1. *Though the Devil tempts, it is man who sins.* Satan's temptations to sin are not sins, nor are they the way to hell; but the very temptations of sin are sins, and the way to more sins and so to hell. A man's own lusts are more and worse tempters than the Devil. The Scripture speaks as if a man were not tempted, nor indeed is he effectually, until his lusts do it (James 1. 14). If a man were tempted by the Devil forty days and yet remained without sin as did Christ, if he were tempted all his days and yielded not because the grace of God was sufficient for him, he might, as St. Paul did, glory in his infirmities and triumph over the messenger of Satan (2 Corinthians 12). The Devil gives up for a season; but sinful lusts scarcely ever do so, for they haunt men more than the Devil does. There is a scum of filthiness boiling or bubbling up even when the Devil does not meddle with us. 'Free me from the

[186]

evil man that is myself' was St. Augustine's prayer and it should be ours; for indeed no man or devil is as bad to us as our evil self is to us. The serpent beguiled me and I did eat, was no excuse. The Devil had a spite against me and paid it, will not do for an apology. It is man who sins, and sin that damns, neither of which can the Devil force upon man.

2. *Sin is worse than the devil as a tempter and it is a worse tormentor.* The Devil is cruel enough, a roaring lion. Many times he takes possession of men and handles them most unmercifully. And he will torment them much more in Hell. But during all this the Devil is outside a man's spirit; but sin is there, taking possession of and tormenting that. It is a sorrowful thing to be tempted to sin, but it is a torment to be a sinner. God does more for us, for our ease and refreshment, when he pardons us than if he cast out of us as many devils as he cast out of Mary Magdalene or out of the man called Legion (Mark 5. 9). Yea, in Hell the gnawing worm of a guilty and upbraiding conscience torments man more than devils do. It would be a relief to a man in Hell if he could only have peace in his conscience, or if he could say that he was there without his fault, and that his perdition were not of himself.

(4) *Sin is worse than Hell.*

Hell is only a punishment, but sin is a crime. It is more evil than the punishment, and it is that of which Hell is the punishment. The very greatness of this punishment argues the greatness of the crime and the sinfulness of sin. That God is glorified on men in such a way is a clear and full proof what an evil thing it is to sin against and dishonour God. Consequently Hell itself does not inflict so much hurt as sin does. Hell, indeed, is a dismal place of horror and torment, the extremity of suffering, but it never had any existence till sin had. Nor could Hell have such names and such torments as it does now if sin were not there. It is reported as a saying of Anselm that if sin and Hell were set before him and he must go through one of them, he would choose to go through Hell rather than sin. Sin is the worst of Hell and worse than Hell. It is what makes sinners cry out for the uninhabitableness of devouring fire and ever-lasting burnings, which are no terror to righteous and upright souls (Isaiah 33. 14, 15). It is sin that makes Hell to be Hell. God was never angry until sin made him so; his wrath was never kindled except by sin. Now just as sin made Hell, so the more sin the more Hell, as Tyre and Sidon suffer more than Sodom and Gomorrah. Even if there were no Hell but such as Cain and Judas felt within them, it would still be a great one. They would tell you that it is damnation enough to be a sinner and to feel the horrors of a guilty and accusing conscience.

(5) In every way *sin is the worst of evils*. I will show this yet a little more:

1. *There is more evil in it than there is good in the whole creation*. That is, it does us more hurt than all the creation can do us good. When we are sick or wounded, many of God's creatures of a medicinal nature can help to recover and cure us. There is no cure, however, for this evil of sin by any or all of the creatures. Sin was too much for that good in which we were created, and all created good ever since has not been able to recover us from it. No! It is only by God that we can be either pardoned or purged of it. All the angels in Heaven could neither pay our debt for us nor cleanse our hearts for us. God himself new-makes us, for mere mending would not serve our turn. Therefore man's recovery is called a new creation and the new man is said to be created in righteousness and true holiness (Ephesians 4. 24). It was David's prayer, 'Create in me a clean heart, O God' (Psalm 51). Sin is an evil beyond the skill and power of all the creation to cure and cleanse.

2. *There is no evil but sin to be repented of*. God allows us to sigh and groan, to mourn and lament for other evils; but for this he calls for and requires repentance. This is a severe thing, full of rebuke and disgrace to man, although it is a grace. How great is that evil for which a man must cry, I have sinned, and to bring him to the confession of which, and to repentance for and from it, other evils are inflicted!

3. *The greatest punishments are those which are made up of sins.* It is worse to be let alone and given up, than if man were sent immediately to Hell. As it is, they live only as reserved to fill up their measure to the brim, and to undergo the more of Hell, to grow rich in wrath having treasured it up against that day. As the best of comforts is to have assurance of the love of God, and to be sealed to the day of redemption, so the saddest of judgments is to be given up (as is said three times in Romans 1) to one's lusts, to a hardened heart, a seared conscience, a reprobate mind. Then God will say, 'Let him that is filthy be filthy still' (Revelation 22. 11); and 'They shall not see nor understand, lest they be converted' (Isaiah 6. 9, 10). This last is a fearful Scripture, for it is six times quoted in the New Testament, as you may see in the margin.

4. *God hates man for sin.* It is not only sin (Proverbs 6. 16, 19) but sinners that God hates, and that for sin. It is said of God that he hates the workers of iniquity (Psalm 5. 5); not only the works of iniquity, but the workers of it.

Hatred is known not by judgments, nor by the evil of suffering, but by the evil of sin which is before us (Ecclesiastes 9. 1, 2). It is because of sin that the merciful God says, 'He that made them will not have mercy on them, nor shew them any favour' (Isaiah 27. 11). As a certain scholar expresses it, This is the highest that can be spoken of the venom of sin, that in a sense, and to speak after the manner of men, it has put hatred into God himself; it has made the Lord hate and destroy his own workmanship. God is love, and judgment is his strange work; yet sin makes him out of love with men and in love with their destruction at last. Though he does not delight in the death of a sinner who repents, yet he does in the death of one who is impenitent.

5. *Christ is the best and the greatest of Saviours,* and his salvation the best and greatest salvation. This proves sin to be the worst and greatest of evils. He came to save sinners not from the petty evils of sickness, affliction and persecution, but from sin, the greatest of all evils (Matthew 1. 21; 1 Timothy 1. 15). To be saved from Egypt was of old reckoned great; but being

[189]

delivered out of the North was a greater salvation (Jeremiah 23. 8). Salvation from sin, however, is the greatest salvation of all, and therefore sin is the worst and greatest of evils.

Thus we have proved sin to be the worst of evils, the evil of evil, with which nothing is to be compared for evil. I will now apply this in detail, and show what we should infer from the sinfulness of sin as against God and as against man.

## 2. Inferences from the Sinfulness of Sin against God

### (1) *The patience and long-suffering of God with sinners is wonderful*

If sin is so exceedingly sinful, that is, contrary to and displeasing to God, then surely his patience is exceedingly great, his goodness exceedingly rich, and his long-suffering exceedingly marvellous, even such as to cause wonder! That God should entreat sinners, his enemies, to be reconciled (2 Corinthians 5. 20), that God should stand at a sinner's door and knock (Revelation 3. 20), that God should wait on sinners to be gracious to them (Isaiah 30. 18) is not after the manner of man, but of God. Truly, it is a characteristic of the God of grace and patience, and to be admired for ever! It was a wonder that in the beginning God should think thoughts of good and not of evil, of peace and not of wrath, but visit man in the cool of the day. Yet when he had imparted and commended his heart's love to us through his Son (Romans 5. 8) and both were rejected, that he should still continue to offer and call and wait is a miracle of miracles. What shall we say? It is God who is the God of grace and patience (Romans 15. 5) and rich in both (Romans 2. 4; 2 Peter 3. 9; 1 Timothy 1. 13–16). He is as his Name is (Exodus 34. 6; Numbers 14. 18; Psalm 86. 15), and as he was yesterday so he is today. We are all living monuments and examples of his goodness and patience. It is of the Lord's mercies that all of us are not altogether and utterly consumed, and that in Hell (Lamentations 3. 22).

[190]

Sin is so sinful, contrary and displeasing to God, and has made man so much God's enemy, that it is a miracle that he should find his enemies and let them go away safely. God who is of purer eyes than to behold iniquity looks on the sin of men. His eyes so affect his heart as to grieve him. It tempts and provokes him to anger, wrath and hatred. And yet God keeps his anger, which is like burning coals in the bosom; he does not let out all his wrath and ease himself of his burden by avenging himself on his adversaries, but he woos and waits on sinners. Such is the power of his patience, the infiniteness of his mercy and compassion, and the riches of his unsearchable grace! God sees sin. He is not ignorant. God is sensible of it and concerned; for it grieves and vexes him. God is able to avenge himself when he pleases; yet he forbears and is patient. Wonder at it! And consider further:

1. *The multitude of sinners* in the world. If it were only one or two, they might be winked at and passed by. But all the world lies in wickedness (1 John 5. 19). There is none righteous, no, not one—if there had been only ten, God would have spared Sodom although ten thousand sinners might be there. Yet there is not a man to be found who does not sin. All have sinned, Jew and Gentile, high and low. What grace, then, what patience is this!

2. *The multitude of sins* committed by every sinner. The sins are more numerous than the sinners. If all men had sinned only once it would have mitigated the matter. Sin, however, has grown up with men; they are not only conceived and born in sin, but go astray before they can walk, even from the womb. Not a good thought is to be found in their hearts (Genesis 6. 5). Sin grows up faster than men do; they are old in sin when still young in years. They are adding iniquity to iniquity and drawing it on with cords and ropes, committing it with both hands greedily, as if they could not sin enough. They dare God himself to judge them. They drink down iniquity like water, as if it was their element and nourishment and pleasure also. Moreover, among the rest, God's sons and daughters provoke him with their sins, which

[191]

go very near his heart (Deuteronomy 32. 19). Yet, behold, how miraculously patient and long-suffering is God!

3. *The length of time.* This multitude of sinners has committed these multitudes of sins from the beginning even until now, generation after generation. If all the world had sinned, and committed all kinds of sins, yet only for an hour or a day, it would not have been so provoking. But as length of times aggravates misery, so it does sin. God reckons up 120 years of patience – and there were many before that – as to the old world (Genesis 6. 3); and to Israel, forty years (Hebrews 3. 17). He came to the fig tree of the Jewish nation three years in person, seeking fruit before he cut it down, or so much as gave the order for it (Luke 13. 6, 7). He had waited much longer with all of these, but these years were, as it were, borrowed time, such as landlords allow their tenants after Quarter Day, space given before sending in the bailiffs. We were quite old enough to be damned when we were young; but God has given us an over-plus of time, space for repentance, and has not yet cut us down as those who cumber the ground. Such is his patience!

4. *Sins cry to God against us.* Moreover, the Devil for sure is constantly pleading against us. The cry of Cain's sin went up (Genesis 4. 10). The cry of Sodom's sin was great (Genesis 18. 20, 21; 19. 13). The keeping back of labourers' wages cries (James 5. 4); indeed, all oppression cries (Habakkuk 1. 2, 12–17). Yet God, as if he were loth to judge us or to believe reports against us, comes down to see if these things are so and, as it were, sets Abraham and his friends interceding, by telling them what he is about to do (Amos 3. 7). Such is the goodness of God!

5. *Many aggravating circumstances attend the sins of men.* In addition to the greatness of sin's own nature, these greatly provoke God. Men's sins are not only many and great; they are both multiplied and magnified, aggravated by many circumstances. Men increase and heighten their sin by not repenting of it, and aggravate their impenitence by despising the goodness of God which should lead them to repentance

(Romans 2. 4). This makes them inexcusable, and incapable of escaping the judgment of God. Men sin against deliverances, as if they were delivered to do all manner of abominations, and to sin more than before (Jeremiah 7. 8–10). Men sin against their resolutions and promises, vows and protestations, made on sea or land, on sickbeds or at any times of danger, and return like dogs to their vomit. They bargain with God in time of fear and danger, but put him off with nothing when the danger is, as they think, over. Men sin against means, and the means of grace. They have precept on precept, line on line, and yet sin still and more. Whatever way God takes with them, nothing will suit them. God says, This and this have I done, yet you have not returned (Amos 4. 6–11). Mourn or pipe to them, it is all the same, they will not hearken. And, what is more, men sin against knowledge and conscience. Though they know God, they glorify him not as God (Romans 1. 21). They know their Master's will, but fail to do it (Luke 12. 47; James 4. 17). It would be useless, because impossible, to count all the aggravating circumstances of men's sins, which make them more sins, the degree, multitude, and magnitude. Yet notwithstanding all this, God waits to be gracious! Oh, grace, grace unto it! Is it not a wonder that men are spared, especially if we consider how quickly God cast away the angels that sinned! Wonder of grace!

## (2) *The judgments of God are just*

Though God is so patient, beyond what we could ask or think, yet sometimes he does, and will for ever, punish sinners who do not repent. Thus this is a second inference from the sinfulness of sin. God often punishes less than iniquity deserves, but never more. The greatest sufferings are neither more nor less than sin deserves. The worst on this side of Hell is mercy, and the worst of and in Hell is but justice.

1. *Consider the nature of God*. He is and cannot but be just. Shall not the God and Judge of all the earth do right? Can he or will he do wrong? No! 'For he will not lay upon man more than right; that he should enter into judgment with

God' (Job 34. 23). Cain could say that his punishment was intolerable, but he could not say that it was unjust; though greater than he could bear, yet it was not greater than he deserved. God will not argue the case with men merely as a Sovereign, but as a Judge, who proceeds not by will only, but by rule. Repeatedly, when the judgments of God are spoken of in Revelation, they are said always to be just and true and righteous (Rev. 15. 3; 16. 7). Though his ways are unsearchable, yet they are true and just and righteous. He makes war in righteousness. Death is only the due wages of sin (Romans 6. 23). Therefore it is said, Their damnation is just (Romans 3. 8); and every sin has a just recompense of reward (Hebrews 2. 2). Guilt stops men's mouths when they suffer the judgment of God (Lamentations 3. 39; Romans 3. 19; Psalm 51. 4; Romans 3. 4). If God judges man, God is found true; but if man judges God, man is found a liar.

Would we complain of the Devil, as Eve did? It is true that he is to blame, but he is not so much the cause of man's sin as man himself is. The Devil, certainly, could tempt, but he could not compel. So it is man who sins although he is tempted to sin; though man could not prevent himself being tempted, he could have refrained from sinning.

Would we complain of God? What would we charge him with? Did not God make man in the best state in which a creature could be? Did not God tell him what was evil and the danger of sinning? God might say as he did of Israel, What could I have done more that I have not done? So man must say that he has rewarded evil to himself by doing evil and that his perdition is of himself (Hosea 13. 9). Sinners have their option and choice; why then do they complain?

2. *Consider the nature of sin*. It is Deicide, God-murder. Thus it is just for God to do with sinners what they would unjustly do with him, that is, take away from them all good and glory, displease and destroy them, because they would do so to him. If we consider the person who is sinned against, and that the aim of sin is to ungod God, what punishment can be thought bad enough? The Schools rightly tell us that

objectively sin is infinite. What punishment then can be too great for so great an evil? If its deed had answered its intention and will – horror of horrors! – God would have been no more. As none but infinite power can pardon it, so none but infinite power can punish it sufficiently. Just as its aim is infinite, so is its desert. Therefore, though its punishment is also infinite, it is but just. Seeing sin contains all evil, it is not strange that its punishment should be answerable and proportionate. That all sin should undergo all misery is not unjust; God renders sufferings to man only according to his doings (Jeremiah 17. 10).

3. *Consider the impenitent state in which sinners die.* Thereby they treasure up this wrath against the day of wrath and revelation of the righteous judgment of God (Romans 2. 5). They who die impenitent continue as they die; consequently they sin and are impenitent for ever. Is it unreasonable that everlasting sinning should be everlastingly punished? It is no severity in God to damn such men for ever. Let man repair the injury he has done and pay the debt he owes God to the utmost farthing and he shall go free. If he says he cannot, that is his crime as well as his misery, for he chose whether or not to do the injury and to run into this debt. Besides, he cannot plead the satisfaction made by Christ, for he made no satisfaction for final unbelief and impenitence; a man who never accepts Christ on the terms of the Gospel cannot plead Christ's name or righteousness before God, and there is no salvation in any other. Thus on all accounts sin's sinfulness vindicates the justice and judgments of God. But though God's judgment is just, yet he is pleased to pardon and forgive some sinners, which brings me to my third inference.

## (3) *How precious a mercy is the forgiveness of sin!*

It is a wonder that anyone is pardoned. The preciousness of this mercy, in the forgiveness of sins, may be seen in various ways:

1. *It is a New Covenant mercy.* The New Covenant is called a better covenant, and its promises better promises (Hebrews

8. 6). The old Covenant, that of works, granted no pardon; but this is the mercy of the new Covenant, that it is a Covenant of grace (Hebrews 8. 12).

2. *Forgiveness of sins is the fruit of the precious blood of Christ*. His blood was shed for this end. Now that which costs so great a price must needs be precious. We were redeemed with no less than blood, and no worse blood than that of the Lamb and Son of God (1 Peter 1. 18). This redemption is called forgiveness of sins (Ephesians 1. 7; Colossians 1. 14).

3. *By forgiveness of sins we have the knowledge of salvation* (Luke 1. 77). They who have their sins remitted are blest, and they shall be blest (Romans 4. 8).

4. *By the forgiveness of sins we have ease and rest for our souls, and cause to be of good cheer*. The sense of pardon will take away the sense of pain. What! are you sick when pardoned? No! I am no more sick (Isaiah 33. 24). When sin is taken away, the sickness which remains is as nothing. The sense of sin makes us sick, but the sense of pardon makes us well. We can say, like the psalmist, 'Return unto thy rest, O my soul; for the Lord hath dealt bountifully with thee' (Psalm 116. 7). A man who is sensible of sin and not of pardon can hardly sleep or take any rest; but when the joyful sound of a pardon is proclaimed and received, the soul which is justified by faith has peace with God and within itself and is at rest. Though the man sick of the palsy was not cured, he had good cause to be of good cheer, because his sins were forgiven him (Matthew 9. 2). This is called speaking comfortably, or to the heart: 'Comfort ye, comfort ye my people. Speak ye comfortably to Jerusalem, and cry unto her, that her warfare is accomplished.' Is that all? No! But, which is more, 'Tell her that her iniquity is pardoned' (Isaiah 40. 1, 2). It is a greater comfort to hear that our sins are pardoned than that our afflictions are at an end. It makes us able as well as willing to undergo afflictions, sufferings and persecutions.

Now if we consider what a sinful thing sin is against God, how displeasing to him, it is a wonderful thing that God should pardon any man's sin. God does more than man can do for himself or expect that God should do for him. Indeed, it costs God more – witness the blood of Christ – and requires more of his power than to heal all our diseases and bestow all the good of this world upon us. Our Saviour tells us that it is easier to say to an impotent man, Arise, take up thy bed and walk, than to say, Thy sins are forgiven thee. The latter is a declaration of his power (Matthew 9. 5). When Moses prays that Israel might be pardoned their sin, he says, Let the power of the Lord be great (Numbers 14. 17–19). It is called riches of mercy and great love (Ephesians 2. 4). It is such power as that by which Christ was and we are raised from the dead (Colossians 2. 13; Ephesians 1. 19–20). 'Who is a God like unto thee, that pardoneth iniquity?' (Micah 7. 18). This is the mystery into which angels pry and at which they wonder (1 Peter 1. 12).

God, as it were, acts against His own word (Genesis 2. 17); he revokes his threatening. It is more than we could ask or think; it is beyond our reach, as it is expressed in Scripture (Isaiah 55. 7, 8, 9). When men are sensible of sin they can hardly believe that God will or can forgive it; they are apt to say as Cain did, Our iniquity is greater than can be forgiven. Man's mercy is large when it reaches to seven times; what is God's then that reaches to more than seventy times seven in a day! (Matthew 18. 21). When good men have prayed concerning the ungodly, Lord, forgive them not (Isaiah 2. 9; Jeremiah 18. 23), yet God has pardoned: even when he himself was so put to it as to say, 'How shall I pardon thee for this?' (Jeremiah 5. 7). Yet God offers pardon and teaches men what to say to him in such cases that they may be forgiven (Hosea 14. 1–4).

## (4) *Sin is not to be committed on any account whatsoever*

It is not to be committed for any reason because it is contrary to God, against his will and glory. This reason overbalances and outweighs any reason that can be given for sinning. It was once said of a Roman ambassador, '*Romanus tamen*' (he is a Roman nonetheless). Similarly, no matter how plausibly sin and sinners plead, no matter how gainful or pleasurable sin is, yet still it is a sin, that is, it is against God, which is a greater reason why it should not be committed than any that can be adduced why it should. It should not be so much as debated, whether a sin should or should not be committed, for no reason can equal this, that it is against God. There is a common saying by which people excuse their own and other men's sins, namely, that they are no man's enemies but their own, and that they wrong no-one but themselves. Now even if that were as true as it is in fact false, yet still sin should not be committed. But sinners *are* God's foes and they are injurious to God, which is more than being so to anyone else or to themselves. We should do good not only because it is good for us, but because it will glorify God, which is a higher end, and so much higher as God is above us. In the same way we should forbear to do evil not only because it is against us, but because it is against God, who should be more beloved by us than ourselves.

There are many aggravations of sinning against God. It is against God who made us, indeed, fighting against God who made us. We are all the offspring of God, the children of God by the first nature, though children of wrath by corrupt nature. It is noticeable how the genealogy runs: '. . . which was the son of Adam, which was the son of God' (Luke 3. 38). Adam was, and so were we, the children of God by creation. God was our Father who made us, and woe to him that striveth with his Maker (Isaiah 45. 9). It is a calamitous thing to sin against God as a Maker. How unnatural it is to sin against our parents! So heinous was it, that 'he that smiteth his father or mother shall die' (Exodus 21. 15). What is it then to smite the Father of our spirits, the Father of our father and mother! If the ravens of the valley shall pick out the eyes of them that curse father and mother (Proverbs 30. 17), what is likely to happen to them that make nothing of cursing God himself!

Sin is against God in whose hand our breath is, and whose are all our ways (Daniel 5. 23), which is a reason we should glorify him. He has our being and well-being at his disposal; he can crush us as the moth and turn us not only to the dust but to the Hell of death. What he does for us and what he can do against us put us under an immense and powerful obligation not to sin against him. We are beholden to him for all the good we have. That nakedness to which the creatures once paid reverence would now cause them to scorn us if God did not clothe it. The creatures would not serve us nor be serviceable to us if God did not command and bless them. We should have no bread nor any good by it if he did not provide and bless it. What could weak things do to strengthen or dead things to keep us alive, did not his Word do more than they? We live not by bread but by his Word. If God should deny us bread by day or sleep by night, what would become of us? How then can we find it in our hearts to sin against God? There are two great wonders: the one, that God should be so good to man, who is and does evil against him; the other, that man should do evil against so good a God. O foolish people and unwise, thus to requite the Lord!

It is God who preserves our going out and coming in. He keeps us from an infinite number of invisible, as well as many visible dangers abroad and at home. If we only knew our dangers we should go in fear of our lives every moment. The earth would swallow us up, the fire would burn us, the water would drown us, if God were not with us to preserve us. He could have sent us down to Hell long ago, and yet he gives space for repentance and waits to be gracious. It is true, he will at last judge us, and what shall we do then? How shall we stand if found to be sinners, when he rises up to judge terribly the earth? What sanctuary or city of refuge shall we fly to that we may be secure? Alas! there will be no escaping; his vengeance in that day will overtake and ruin us.

Think of this, and think whether you can find it in your heart to sin, or to think it a little or light thing to sin against God, and such a God, whatever may be the pretext for it. Let me say this further, that even if God had not laid so many obligations upon us, yet we were bound not to sin against his sovereignty and the authority he has over us. But when he

[199]

humbles himself and grants so many kindnesses to us, it would be monstrous ingratitude and rebellion to sin against him, no matter what profitable pleasure might come to us thereby, and no matter what reason may be alleged or pretended for doing so.

### (5) *How transcendently and incomparably beautiful a thing is holiness!*

How lovely a thing it is in the eyes of God and ought to be in the eyes of men! This is the thing that is so agreeable and pleasing to God, so adorning and beneficial to man. The black spot of sin sets off the beauty of holiness. But I have already spoken of this in a separate discourse which is being published. I will therefore, refer you to that and shall say no more on this subject here.

### 3. INFERENCES FROM THE CONTRARIETY OF SIN TO THE GOOD OF MAN

### (1) *That they who seek for any good in sin are miserably mistaken*

As sin is, so are its effects, wholly evil to man. There are some who call evil good (Isaiah 5. 20), or as it is in the margin, who say concerning evil, IT IS GOOD. They think, and do not hesitate to say as they think, that evil is good. They place their chief happiness in the chiefest evil, that is, in sin, and they love evil more than good, as is said of Doeg and such as he (Psalm 52. 3). How many there are who not only undo themselves but take pains and pleasure to do so! They think it strange indeed, that others are not so mad as they, and run not with them to the same excess of riot (1 Peter 4. 4). All this proceeds from the same mistake, that evil is good, that is, good to them, bringing profit, honour or pleasure to them. This is called the lust of the eye, flesh and pride of life (1 John 2. 16); from it came the first sin (Genesis 3. 6). But the event proved then, as it will always do, that they gather no grapes from thorns nor figs from thistles. They seek the living among the

[200]

dead, and may as well find ease in and from Hell as good in and from sin.

The morsels of sin are deceitful, though called dainties. Sin is a mere cheat; with false shows it deceives the heart of the simple. However sweet the stolen waters of sin seem to be in the mouth and to the taste, they will be gall and wormwood in the belly, bitterness in the latter end. All the corruption that is in the world came in by lust (2 Peter 1. 4), and all lust is deceitful (Ephesians 4. 22). Thus the woman was first deceived and by her the man (1 Timothy 2. 14). Instead of being as God which they thought was promised, they became as the Devil, which was the thing intended and designed by him. Sin first deceived and then slew St. Paul, as he says (Romans 7. 11). It pretends to bring milk and butter in a lordly dish, as Jael did to Sisera, but the hammer and nail is in its heart and hand. They who serve diverse lusts are deceived, as the Apostle says (Titus 3. 3). All the servants of sin are deceived, not of sin's wages, but by sin's promises. Though they sport themselves, while they play and nibble at the bait like silly fishes, it is only to their own deceiving, for an evil heart has deceived them (2 Peter 2. 13). Therefore the Apostle exhorts us to take heed lest we be hardened through the deceitfulness of sin (Hebrews 3. 13). Sin's first work is to deceive us, and when it has thereby drawn us in, it hardens and so destroys us. I shall seek to prove in various ways the deceitfulness of sin.

1. *There is not, nor can there be any profit to man by sin.* Can that which wrongs his soul be profitable? What doth it profit a man to gain the world and lose his soul? Sin costs dear, but profits nothing; they make a bad purchase who buy their damnation. What did Cain get by killing Christ in Abel, his type, or Judas by selling Christ? Surely he bought damnation dearly though he sold his Saviour cheaply. Take your money, he said, I have sinned. The knowledge that he had committed that sin made him weary of his gain and of his life. He got Hell, or, as it is said, Devil and All. What profit does anyone have by that of which they are ashamed (Romans 6.

21). All the works of darkness are unfruitful as to any good (Ephesians 5. 11), but good works are profitable (Titus 3. 8). Sin is a very expensive thing; it cannot be maintained without great cost. Men might build hospitals at a cheaper rate than they can maintain their lusts. Some men's sins cost them more in a day than their families do in a week, perhaps in a year. Some starve their families to feed their lusts, which have turned many out of house and home, and reduced great estates to a crust of bread, quite apart from what will happen hereafter. Lusts consume health and wealth (Proverbs 5). Gluttony, drunkenness and uncleanness are costly and expensive sins.

*Objection.* It may be said, It is true that these are costly sins indeed, but what have you to say about covetousness, that frugal and thrifty, saving and getting sin?

*Answer.* Covetousness and all it gets or saves is unprofitable. For consider:

(i) *All that is gotten is not gain.* I will tell you what a wise man saw and said: 'There is a sore evil which I have seen under the sun, namely, riches kept for the owners thereof to their hurt' (Ecclesiastes 5. 13). Here are riches, and riches kept, but it is to the hurt and detriment of the owner. Better for him not to have had them or not to have kept them. Did they profit him? Yes! if hurt can be profit! but not otherwise. 'Those riches perish by evil travail: and he begetteth a son, and there is nothing in his hand' (verse 14). He can leave his son nothing, for it is not in his hand. While he had his riches, he could not sleep for them (verse 12), and his abundance made him poor. Perhaps it was his crime that he was rich, and someone more powerful than he, like Vespasian, finding him like a sponge swollen and full, must needs squeeze him and leave him hollow and empty. The histories tell us of times when the acquiring of estates has been the greatest crime people have been guilty of, even though they have been charged with sedition or treason.

(ii) *Covetousness itself may be a thief, and rob men of the use and comfort of their own possessions.* The covetous man always needs more and is in truth the poorest man in the world; 'There is one alone, and there is not a second; (he is a single man, unmarried, without a second-self) yet is there no end of all his labour . . . neither saith he, For whom do I labour, and bereave my soul of good?' (Ecclesiastes 4. 8). Is this profitable? No! It is a sore travail, for he has not the power to eat thereof (Ecclesiastes 6. 2). To fill his purse he starves his belly and begrudges himself food.

(iii) *No matter how much you have, and how much you use it, it will never satisfy, and therefore must vex you.* No satisfaction, no profit! A man's aim is satisfaction (Luke 12. 19), but the eye is not satisfied with seeing nor the ear with hearing (Ecclesiastes 1. 8). Now if these things cannot satisfy the senses (Ecclesiastes 6. 7), much less can they satisfy the souls of men. What adds to the vexation is that the love of money increases faster than the money, so that 'he that loveth silver shall not be satisfied with silver; nor he that loveth abundance with increase' (Ecclesiastes 5. 10, 11).

(iv) *You will not carry away with you one penny, and where then is the profit?* It may be that you will say that none of the above arguments fit your case. But this must be your case. What you leave behind you is none of yours, but you die the poorer for leaving your riches behind you and not having laid up your treasures in heaven (1 Timothy 6. 7, 19). The rich man said to his soul, Thou hast goods; but our Saviour said to him, Thou fool, thou must die tonight, and whose shall these things be? Not thine! What do you get by all your getting, to leave everything behind you? Indeed, perhaps you will leave everything to the very persons whom you would least wish to enjoy it (Psalm 39. 6; Ecclesiastes 2. 18–21). To go naked out of the world is a sore evil and of no profit (Ecclesiastes 5. 15, 16). If you enjoy everything to your dying day yet then you lose all; and perhaps you not only lose it, but lose by it. Riches do not profit in the day of wrath, and surely that cannot be worth much while we live that will be worth nothing when we die.

Besides, there is no man in more danger to lose by getting

than the covetous man, who is in the ready way to lose his soul; for the love of money is the root of all evil, which while some have coveted after, they have got nothing by it but the loss of their souls, being drowned in perdition (1 Timothy 6. 9, 10). Moreover, take riches here for the present, while they are at their best; the pains of getting, the cares of keeping, and the fear of losing, eat out the comfort of having. So all must subscribe to what our Saviour said, that a man's life – neither the length, health or comfort, much less the happiness of a man's life – does not consist in the things he enjoys in this world; life needs more and better things. What silly foolish things are sinners! To place the good of profit in that which is not only unprofitable, but expensive! To pay so dear a price for so vile a commodity! To pay according to the rate of Heaven and to be put off with Hell! We laugh at the simplicity and childishness of little ones who will part with gold for a toy or a novelty; but how much more ridiculous and worse than childish are they who risk their precious souls for that which does not profit! They are like the king who is said to have sold his kingdom for a draught of water; or like Israel whom God upbraided that they changed their glory for that which did not profit, and left and parted with a fountain of living waters for an empty cistern that had none, indeed, for a broken cistern that could hold no water, not even a drop (Jeremiah 2. 13).

Sinners often ask this question, What profit is there if we serve God? (Job 21. 15). In answer I say that godliness is profitable at all times, for here and hereafter; it has the promise of both lives, this and that to come (1 Timothy 4. 8). But let me ask them what I wish they would often ask themselves, What profit is there if we sin? as Judah asked his brothers, What profit is there if we slay our brother? (Genesis 37. 26). Surely there is none but shame and sorrow. You may put your gains in your eyes and weep it out; if not, a greater loss will come to you.

Thus we have seen that no good by way of profit comes by sin, no, even by that which is called the most profitable sin, covetousness. So our inference holds good, that though you seek good in evil, you are mistaken.

2. *There is no honour to be gained by sin*. Sin is not a creditable thing. Granted, there are some who glory in and boast of their sin, but they glory in their shame (Philippians 3. 19), and surely sooner or later they will be ashamed of their glory! Sin is not a thing of good report; it hears badly of itself and has a bad name throughout the whole world. Can that be honourable which is unreasonable? Can that be an honour to man which debases and degrades him? The unreasonableness of sin is apparent from the reasonableness of the law; sin has no reason for it, for the law is against it. That sin degrades men I have showed already. Take the finest things of this world, in which men pride themselves; they cannot cover the nakedness of sinners, much less be an ornament or honour to them; for that which is a disgrace to the soul can never be an honour or grace to the body. That which men, generally, are ashamed to own, at least under its own name, cannot be an honour to them. Yet even if all the world were to admire and celebrate the grandeur of sinners, God counts them vile, though they are exalted in the world, and God is doubtless the best judge of honour. That which is abominable to God cannot be honourable to man. Even an appearance of righteousness, which is highly esteemed among men, is an abomination in the sight of God, much more then is sin itself (Luke 16. 15).

3. *There is no pleasure to be had from sin*. It is true, indeed, that the pleasures of sin are much talked about. We read of some who take pleasure in unrighteousness (2 Thessalonians 2. 12) and of some so impudent and brazen-faced that, though they knew the judgment of God, yet they took pleasure in doing, and in them that did, such things as were worthy of death (Romans 1. 32). There have been those, too, who have lived in pleasure on the earth, and seemed to grow fat by it, nourishing themselves, but it was only for the day of slaughter (James 5. 5). Notwithstanding all this, we do not doubt that we shall make it evident that there is no such thing as men

talk and dream of, that is, pleasure in, from or by sin. Pleasure is the contentment and satisfaction of a man's mind in what he does or has; but sinners have none of this from sin.

a. *There is no peace to the wicked.* This is told us by the God who searches their hearts and knows what is there (Isaiah 57. 21). The Septuagint reads this verse: There is no joy, no peace, nor pleasure, no serenity, nor one halcyon-day, for they are like the raging sea, casting up mire and dirt by reason of its rolling and disquiet. To appearance, men seem to laugh and be merry, but God sees that they have no peace within. And I would rather believe the God of truth than lying men, for lie they do when they say that they have peace or pleasure in sin. Solomon 'said of laughter, It is mad, and of mirth, What doeth it?' And in the midst or heart of laughter, the heart is sad.

b. *Sin in its very nature cannot afford pleasure, since it is contra-natural to Man.* Therefore the heathen philosophers could say that punishment follows on the heels of guilt, as the Scripture says, If thou doest not well, sin lieth (like a dog) at the door (Genesis 4. 7). Another writer says more expressly that punishment not only succeeds sin but that they are born together and are twins. For they who deserve punishment expect it, and whoever expects punishment suffers it in a degree. Thus the sinner is his own tormentor and sin his torment. Our knowledge of having erred keeps returning and complaining of the faults, and the impression of the fault will bring fear, which fear has torment, even if there were no more torment to come. The upbraidings of conscience mar mirth and make pleasure very displeasing. What pleasure can it be to feel the reproaches of meat even though it tastes pleasant? Poison itself may be sweet to the taste but not therefore pleasant; for regrets and ominous belchings do not speak of pleasure. Whatever crosses and thwarts nature is a punishment, not a pleasure, and such is sin to primitive and created nature. And if habit and a seared conscience seem to deny the sense of such regrets, yet that only argues the case the worse. For what pleasure can that be which benumbs a man and makes him not only stupid but dead? They who live in such pleasures are by the infallible truth declared to be dead while they live (1 Timothy 5. 6). When stupidity may pass for pleasure, and death for life, or dreams for enjoyments, sin may then be pleasant.

c. *Sin cannot fill up the boundless and infinite desire which is in the heart of man, but disappoints it.* There can therefore be no satisfaction by it, but of necessity, much vexation. Lusts are like the horse-leech and the grave which never have enough, but cry, Give, Give. To desire shows that something is lacking, and again to desire shows the continuance of this lack. Hence, sin has changed so often, or, as the Apostle says, serves diverse lusts. These changes and varieties clearly show the poverty of their entertainments and the emptiness of their pleasure. While men seek to quench the thirst of sin by giving it salt water to drink they only increase it. Indeed, every man may find it much more easy, pleasant and satisfactory to mortify than to gratify sin, to deny rather than fulfil the desires of the flesh. For men to be constantly contradicting and swimming against the stream of their conscience, which tells them they ought not to sin, and if they do, chides them for it, must needs be uneasy and unpleasant. Men's sins make them sick, as Amnon's did; so far are they from being pleasures. To desire the presence of what is absent, or the absence of what is present; or the continuance of what cannot be kept or would, if kept, surfeit a person, as constant drunkenness and intemperance does, must inevitably be very tedious. Such men, even in the fulness of their sufficiency (Job 20. 22), cannot help but be in straits. If they gratify one of their lusts, they displease another: if they gratify pride and prodigality, they displease covetousness and so are still far from pleasure. They are distracted and slain by one or other of their lusts all the day long. They have fightings without and within; indeed, good men are not persecuted more by the Devil and the wicked world than these men are tormented by their irregular and inordinate fleshly appetites and carnal inclinations.

Yet for all this men are loth to believe that there is no pleasure from sin. They say that this is contrary to the expressions of Scripture and to their experience. The Scripture mentions the pleasures of sin (Hebrews 11. 25), and we find pleasure in it. Thus men are apt to plead for sin and to be its advocate. They will cling to any scripture that only speaks of such a thing as sinful pleasures, even though it disowns and disallows them. As for that misunderstood text in Hebrews, let me say that Moses cannot be charged with any sin from which he drew pleasure; and therefore by the pleasures of sin are not meant such pleasures as flow from, but such as lead to sin. That is, he declined the pleasures which would have inclined him to sin. Pleasures are allurements and baits to draw men to sin, as in the case of Eve; the tree was pleasant to the eyes and inviting, but her taste and digestion found no pleasure but bitterness from the fruit. Thus Moses lived where there were pleasures which tended to or were abused to sin. Indeed, there were such pleasures as he could not have enjoyed without committing the great sin of afflicting the people of God, which the Egyptians did, and of being cruel to them, instead of delivering them. So this scripture says nothing in favour of sin, or that there are any pleasures to be had by or from it.

Yet even if we were to take this text as they interpret it, all that can be said of it is this, that it speaks as they think; not that there are, but that there are thought to be, pleasures of sin. It is a common thing for a scripture to speak of a certain thing as if it were, and to say that it is, when it is only supposed to be so by others. For example, 'There be gods many, and lords many' (1 Corinthians 8. 5); not that there really were any such gods, but that by others they were reckoned so to be. Similarly in this text, he speaks according to the manner of men concerning the pleasures of sin, as they are reputed. This is confirmed by a passage of the Apostle Peter, 'They count it pleasure to riot in the daytime' (2 Peter 2. 13). It is no pleasure, but they accounted it a pleasure. Certainly, it was no pleasure, for they only enjoyed a mock-sport or pleasure, while they sported themselves in their own deceivings. So in counting it pleasure to riot, they deceived themselves; they supposed it sport and pleasure, but it is not so.

Yet again, if there is any pleasure, it can only be to the physical and sensual part of the man, which is a pleasure to the beast, not to the man. The body is only the case of man, a mud-walled cottage thatched over with hair. It is the soul that is the excellency and glory of the man, the man of the man. Whoever, then, would take a right measure of what is good or evil to man must take it especially with respect and relation to the soul. That man who bade his soul take its ease in eating and drinking greatly mistook its nature. Alas! The soul cannot feed on flesh, for it is a spirit and must have a diet peculiar and proper to a spirit, that is spiritual. Quite often the pleasure of the body proves to be the soul's pain. To eat and drink is the body's pleasure, but gluttony and drunkenness, which are the sins of eating and drinking, are the soul's pain, and many times the body's too. To rest when one is weary is the body's pleasure, but to be idle, which is the sin of rest and ease, is an affliction and trouble to the soul.

Furthermore, that which men call the pleasure of sin is both their dying and punishment. Many laugh and are merry because of the sickness and disorder from which they are suffering; they say of those who are bitten by the tarantula that they will laugh themselves to death. Some people are so ticklish that they will laugh at the waving of a feather, but this is a proof of their weakness and folly, two ill diseases. Many people take pleasure in eating lime, mortar, coals and such-like trash, but it is from a sickness which vitiates and corrupts their palate. Would they otherwise feed on ashes if they did not suffer from the disease of green sickness? So whoever pretends to find pleasure in sin proves himself to be distempered and diseased, and suffering from the old and deeply-rooted disease of being in sin, indeed dead in sin.

Sin is a punishment as well as a disease. It is false pleasure, and what truer misery is there than false joy? It is like the pleasure of the man who receives much money, but it is all counterfeit, or the pleasure of the man who dreams of a feast and awakes so hungry and vexed that he could eat his dream. For this reason sin should be doubly hated, because it is ugly and false, because it defiles and mocks us.

Yet even if there is any pleasure, it is only for a season, a very little while. It is soon over and gone, like the crackling of thorns under a pot; 'The triumphing of the wicked is short, and the joy of the hypocrite but for a moment' (Job 20. 5). The miseries of sin, on the contrary, may be and indeed, without repentance, will be eternal. Just as the sufferings of this present life are to the godly not worthy to be compared with the future glory, so the pleasures of the wicked are, even the best of them, as nothing, compared with the future misery which awaits them. Certainly, then, those pleasures which men must repent of, or be damned for to all eternity, are woeful and rueful pleasures.

All in all, then, the inference is undeniable that there is no profit, honour, or pleasure to be had by sin, and that they who seek for all or any of these things in sin act as those who would seek ease in Hell, the very place and element of torment. If good is not good when better is expected, how miserably vexatious must their disappointment be? When men look for good and peace, but evil and trouble, and nothing else, comes upon them; when they bless themselves and say, We shall have peace though we walk in the imaginations of our heart, to add drunkenness to thirst, the Lord will not spare them, but then the anger of the Lord and his jealousy shall smoke against them (Deuteronomy 29. 19). When they shall say, Peace and safety, then sudden destruction will come upon them, as travail upon a woman with child, and there will be no escaping (1 Thessalonians 5. 3).

There are still other inferences to be drawn from the sinfulness of sin. I shall make only a few brief comments upon them.

## (2) *Time spent in sin is worse than lost*

Most of the pastime in the world is lost time, but sinning time or time spent in sin is worse than lost, for it must be accounted for, and who can give a good account of evil doing? While men live in sin, they do nothing but undo themselves. Man was not sent into this world only to eat, drink, sleep and play, much less to sin, but as into a great workhouse, to work for the glory of God (John 17. 4), and so to work out his own salvation, and that with fear and trembling (Philippians 2. 12). They who live in sin, however, work out their damnation, and that many times without fear or trembling; but they will have a great store of these when they come to receive their just doom and damnation.

Time is a most precious commodity, for eternity depends upon this moment. As men sow in this seed-time, they will reap in that harvest. Time is a prophet for eternity: as men live here so must they live for ever. They who sow sin must reap death (Galatians 6. 8). Time is to be redeemed (Ephesians 5. 16), and every day is to be numbered, greatly valued and improved, that we may apply our hearts to wisdom (Psalm 90. 12). And this is wisdom, the fear of the Lord; and this is understanding, to depart from evil (Job 28. 28). This is wisdom, to know and do what is the acceptable will of God (Matthew 7. 24; Ephesians 5. 15–17). We may be said to be, but not to live, if we do not live to God, and all time that is not so spent is but mis-spent and worse than lost. Poor people who are demented and have lost their understanding wear out their days to less loss and disadvantage than do sinners.

## (3) *They who mock at sin are worse than fools and madmen*

'Fools make a mock at sin' (Proverbs 14. 9). Tell them, as Lot did his sons-in-law, the danger therein, the judgments that hang over their head and, as with Lot, ye seem to them as one that mocketh (Genesis 19. 14). They laugh at it, as if God were not in earnest when he threatens sinners, and as if they who preach against sin were only ridiculous persons. 'It is as sport to a fool to do mischief' (Proverbs 10. 23), and there are some who sport themselves on their way to Hell, as if it were but a recreation! What fools they are who laugh at their own folly and destruction! It is a devilish nature in us to mock at the calamity of others, but to laugh at our own calamity seems to be worse than devilish. There are many, too many, who mourn under affliction, yet laugh over their sins; they sigh and weep when they feel any burden on their body but make merry at that which destroys their soul! Can anything be more mad than this, to laugh, mock and make sport at that which is a burden and weariness to God (Isaiah 1. 14; Amos 2. 13); which is the wounding, piercing and crucifying of Christ Jesus (Zechariah 12. 10; Hebrews 6. 6); which is a grief to the Spirit of consolation (Ephesians 4. 30); which is a trouble to the holy angels (Luke 15. 7, 10); which wrongs and undoes their own souls (Proverbs 8. 36)! Such is sin.

## (4) *Sin being so sinful, infectious, and pernicious, it can never be well with a man while he is in his sins*

Was it well with Dives, though he fared deliciously every day? No, it was better with Lazarus who lay at his gate full of sores. For that is well which ends well, which is never the case with sinners. Even if judgment is not executed speedily, it will surely come, for they are condemned already, being sons of death and perdition. No man, then, has any cause to envy the prosperity of sinners; it is not good enough to be envied, but it is bad enough to be pitied. They are only fattened for, and thereby fitted to destruction. 'The prosperity of fools shall destroy them' (Proverbs 1. 32). It is their folly alone which actually destroys them, but their prosperity doubles it, and does it with a vengeance. The prosperous sinner is in the worst plight of all sinners; they are set in slippery places and shall be cast down from their height to the depths of destruction (Psalm 73. 18).

### (5) Sin's utter sinfulness argues that men should become religious without delay

This may prevent a great deal of sin which, unless a man is religious, and strictly so, early in life, is certain to come about. How precious and dear should that thing be to us which prevents so pernicious and destructive a thing as sin! How industriously careful we should be to keep ourselves from that which will keep us from happiness! How ambitious we should be to enjoy that which capacitates us for enjoying God for ever and which gives us the first-fruits of it here! Indeed, we cannot be too soon nor too much religious, but the sooner and more the better. If ever you mean to be religious, there is no time like the present, no day better than today. 'Remember *now* thy Creator' (Ecclesiastes 12. 1), for so the word runs, that is, God in Christ, for he created all things by Christ Jesus (Ephesians 3. 9; Colossians 1. 16). Remember now, in the days of thy youth, before the evil days come, when thou shalt say, I have no pleasure in them (Ecclesiastes 12. 1); not only will you have no pleasure in the evil days of sickness, death and judgment, that evil day which you put far from you, but none in the remembrance of your youthful days. Youth is the most proper season of all our days, and *now* is the most proper season of all our youth to remember God in. If you say, we will do that when we are old, for it is now springtime with us (our May-time), and we will think of religion in a winter's night; do not boast of tomorrow, young as you are, for you are old enough to die. This night your soul may be taken from you, and you may be in Hell tomorrow!

Therefore take the wise man's advice, 'Rejoice, O young man, in thy youth, and let thy heart cheer thee in the days of thy youth, and walk in the ways of thine heart, and in the sight of thine eyes' (Ecclesiastes 11. 9). Yes, you say, with all our hearts we will take this advice; we like it well, for it is pleasing doctrine. We would rather mind this than to be holy; we will be debonair and jovial, for we do not care for severe preachers of strictness and devotion. We will laugh and sing, drink and dance away our time while we have it. But do not mistake, Solomon speaks ironically and has something else to say; take all, and then, if you rejoice, it will be with trembling; rejoice, *but*; let your heart cheer you, *but*; walk in the ways of thine heart and eyes, *but*; but what? 'But know thou, that for all these things God will bring thee into judgment' (Ecclesiastes 11. 9). How will you answer for your vanity and follies, your pride and wantonness, your drunkenness and debauchery then? Oh, remember your Creator before that evil day comes, and prevent a life of sin which is the most miserable life in the world! For God has promised that if you seek him early you will find him, and in finding him you find everything (Proverbs 8. 17–21).

Remember him in your youth, for memory is then in its prime and most flourishing. Shall he, who gave you your being and memory, be forgotten by you? If God did not remember you, what would become of you? See what is likely to become of you if you forget God (Psalm 50. 22). However good and however excellent your memory is, I am sure that you have a very bad one if you forget and do not remember your Creator in the days of your youth. A young man's glory is his strength, and will you give your strength to sin, which is due to God (Mark 12. 30)? God's sacrifices were to be young; the first-ripe fruits and the first-born (which is the strength, Genesis 49. 3) were to be dedicated to God; he will not be put off with less now. God's chiefest worthies have been and are his young men (1 John 2. 13, 14); God's men of valour are young men. The princes of this world, like the Romans of old, make up their armies of young men, the flower of their army is of young and strong men; and shall the King of kings be put off with what is decrepit and worn out? No, he will not! Go, offer it to your governor, will he be pleased with or accept such persons (Malachi 1. 8, 13, 14)? He will not, neither will God, who is a great King, the Lord of Hosts, whose Name is dreadful.

They who have been religious early are greatly famed and

honoured in the Scripture records. God is taken with and remembers the kindness of their youth (Jeremiah 2. 2). Abel, though dead, is spoken of with an honourable testimony, even that of God himself, for serving God so young and so well (Hebrews 11. 4). Joseph was very early religious; so was Samuel. Jeroboam's little son is not to be forgotten, for God has honoured him. King Josiah, Daniel, and the three children or young man of Israel are all enrolled in the court of honour and heaven. In the New Testament, St. John is called the disciple whom Jesus loved, his bosom-favourite and darling, and the reason usually given is because he came to Christ and became his disciple while still very young. It is said in commendation of Timothy that he knew the Scriptures from a child (2 Timothy 3. 15).

Many parents are afraid to have serious and divine things taught their children lest it make them melancholy and depress them. But is anything better able to fit them for service to God or man than religion? Or is any spirit comparable to that true greatness and gallantry of spirit which consists in being afraid to sin? We should teach children moral and religious courage and bravery, which fears to sin more than to die, and to make the choice of Moses, preferring the reproaches of Christ before the treasures and pleasures of this world. In this way they are likely to attain better names and greater wealth, to enjoy more pleasure and preferment than any that this world can confer upon them. They who are taught to love and serve God best are best bred; and they attain most honour who honour God, for them will God himself honour.

I do not speak in derogation of anything that passes for virtue among men, and that is attractive and genteel. I would, however, press you to more, to what is commendable to God and in his sight of great price, that is, to remember him in the days of your youth. For evil days are coming; sickness, old age, death is approaching; the Judge is at the door. Certainly that is best while we are young that will be best when we are old and die; and that can be worth very little at the beginning which will be worth nothing at the end of our days.

The sins of youth will lie heavy upon old age. Even if God give repentance to you when you are old, it will cost you the more because you did not repent sooner, and you will regret that you have been so long in sin and that you have only a little while to live in which to testify your conversion. Job thought it sad to possess the sins of his youth (Job 13. 23, 26). Things that are sweet in youth often prove the bitterness of old age, and what are pleasures while young bring pains when old. This made King David pray to God that he would not remember against him the sins of his youth (Psalm 25. 7). Though I might add much more, I suppose this will suffice to show how important it is for us to be religious early, since sin is so dangerous and destructive a thing.

### (6) Sin being so pernicious, how welcome should the Gospel be!

It brings the good and joyful news of the Saviour, telling us how to be saved from sin, the cause of wrath, and from wrath as the effect of sin. How beautiful, then, should be the feet of those who bring this blessed remedy to us (Romans 10. 15)! If we had gout or a gallstone what would we not give for a remedy, an infallible medicine to cure us? We always welcome surgeons though they cause us pain, and apothecaries though they bring us loathsome drugs; indeed, so dear is health to us, that we not only thank but reward them too. What a welcome, then, should Christ and his gospel have! They come with saving health to cure us of the worst of diseases and plagues, that of sin. Surely we should press with violence, and be so violent as to besiege heaven and take it by force; and we should no less hasten to receive the gospel, and take into us the wine and milk thereof and the waters of life, seeing that we may have them so freely for the asking! It is true that our salvation cost Christ Jesus dearly, but he offers it to us at a cheap rate and we should not let Heaven be so thinly, and Hell so populously inhabited, when salvation may be had at an easier rate than going beyond the sea for it (Romans 10. 6–10 with Deuteronomy 30. 12–14). Since

[216]

it is so faithful a saying and worthy to be received, do not be so unworthy as to refuse it, and with that to refuse your own salvation!

## 4. EXHORTATION AND COUNSEL

It may be that some poor soul or other may be pricked in heart and cry out like the Jews, What shall we do? (Acts 2. 37), or as the jailor, Sirs, what must I do to be saved? (Acts 16. 30). Is there any hope for poor sinners? Is there any balm in Gilead, or any physician there (Jeremiah 8. 22)? Yes, surely there is! As one scholar puts it, God would never have suffered so potent and malicious an enemy to have set foot in his dominions unless he had known how to conquer it, and that not only by punishing it in Hell but by destroying it. He will not only pardon, but subdue your sins. If you will hear him, hear then, that your soul may live. Hear the call of Christ Jesus, behold he calleth thee, Come to me, ye that are weary and heavy laden, and I will give you rest (Matthew 11. 28). All who were in debt and distress came to David; you are such an one, come to this David, for so Christ is called, take his counsel and you will do well. You shall live, and sin shall die. What is this counsel of his?

*Answer: Repent and believe the Gospel* (Mark 1. 15).

(1) *Repent.* Jesus Christ came to call sinners to repentance (Matthew 9. 12, 13). This was one of the errands upon which he came into the world. Repent then not only for, but from dead works (Hebrews 6. 1). Abhor both your sin and yourself, repenting as in dust and ashes (Job 42. 6). Be full of indignation against, and take a full revenge upon your sin and yourself, as true repentance does (2 Corinthians 7. 11). To be merciful to sin is to be cruel to yourself; to save the one alive is to put the other to death. Therefore do not spare it, but repent unfeignedly from the bottom of your heart. Let it grieve you that God is displeased with you for your sin, but much more that he has been displeased by you and by your sin. Bring forth fruit worthy of repentance, amendment of life, that your repentance may appear to be a change of heart and

life, of your mind and manners, not only a reformation but a renovation, showing that you are a new man.

The goodness of God leads you to repentance; he might have driven you into it by terrors, but he gently leads you. It is indeed an evidence of his goodness that he will admit us to repent, but that he will call and lead to repentance is goodness much more. And what goodness is it that he puts us to no greater penance than repentance (Jeremiah 3. 13)! God might have said, You must lie in hell so many thousand years to feel the smart of your sin. If he had bid you do some great thing, would you not have done it? How much more when he says, Wash and be clean – to allude to the words of Naaman's servants to him (2 Kings 5. 13). Indeed, what is even more, God waits to be gracious, and is patient even to long-suffering. He might have called and knocked at your door once and then no more, but he has stood and knocked and begged, and given you space and means (Revelation 2. 21; Luke 16. 31). And why has he done all this, but that you might come to repentance (2 Peter 3. 9)? If, then, you do not repent, it is a greater affront to God than was your former sin. *Humanum est errare,* it is human frailty to sin, but to continue in it without repentance is devilish. It is to despise God's goodness (Romans 2. 4); it is to justify your sin and to upbraid God with a scoff as did those who said, 'Where is the promise of his coming? (2 Peter 3. 4). In order that God's goodness may still prevail, I beseech you to consider further :

### 1. *If you repent you will be forgiven.*

'Repent and be converted, that your sins may be blotted out' (Acts 3. 19); they shall be as if they had not been. Where God gives repentance for sin, he also gives remission of it (Acts 5. 31). He who hardens his heart in impenitence shall not prosper; but he who confesses and forsakes his sins shall have mercy (Proverbs 28. 13, 14). God looks upon men, and if anyone says, I have sinned and perverted that which was right, that is, if anyone repents, he will deliver his soul from going into the pit, and his life shall see the light (Job 33. 27, 28).

[218]

Indeed, God is not only merciful, but if we confess our sins he is faithful and just to forgive us our sins, and to cleanse us from all unrighteousness (1 John 1. 9). How this obliges us to repent!

2. *Repentance is, according to God's interpretation, the undoing of all the evil you have committed and the doing of the good you have omitted.*

Indeed, he who repents of his sin tells all the world that if it could be done again he would not do it. And he who repents for not having done the will of God, does it in repenting (Matthew 21. 29). What goodness is this, to put such a construction on repentance! Shall we not, then, repent?

3. *By repenting, you cause rejoicing to all whom you have grieved by your sin.*

You have grieved your own soul; repentance will cheer it. For though repentance springs from sorrow, it ends in joy and will never be repented of (2 Corinthians 7. 10). You will rejoice the generation of the righteous. Yea, there will be joy in heaven; God and angels will be glad and rejoice at your return (Luke 15). It is the sin of men, and greatly aggravated, that they repented not to give him glory (Revelation 16. 9); sin dishonours but repentance gives glory to God. Therefore Joshua said to Achan, confess thy sin and give glory to God (Joshua 7. 19). At the same time we rejoice the heart, and glorify the name of God by repentance! Shall we not repent? O repent! repent! But if there is no repentance.

4. *Know that God has appointed a day in which he will judge you.*

This truth calls upon you, at your peril, to repent (Acts 17. 30, 31). If you do not do so, you only enrich yourself for hell, and by your hardness and impenitent heart treasure up wrath against the day of wrath and the revelation of the righteous judgment of God (Romans 2. 5). But God who is long-suffering will not be all-suffering; he who is the God of patience now, will, if that patience is abused, be a God of vengeance hereafter to the abusers of his patience. God's patience will be at an end one day; he will wait for you no more, no longer. He waited forty years but then swore in his wrath (Hebrews 3. 11). He waited on the Jewish fig tree three years, but at last cut it down.

God has set you a day and that is today. While it is called today, hear his voice, and harden not your hearts. When this day of patience is over, if you are still found unprovided, woe to you, for you are undone for ever! I pray you, think of it, have you not grieved God enough yet? Nor wronged your own soul enough yet? Are you afraid of being happy too soon? Or of going to Hell too easily and cheaply, that you will not repent or that you delay it? If in this your day you do not consider the things of your peace, you may have them hidden from your eyes, and go blindfold to Hell and be damned for ever; and then God will require payment to the utmost farthing (Matthew 18. 23–34). He will be paid all that is due; for time, for talents, for means, for mercies, for patience and forbearance, he will be paid for all. If he is not glorified by you now, he will be glorified upon you then. I hope, however, that you realise this, and that I shall not need to urge or press this any further upon you. Therefore I shall pass to the second counsel:

## (2) *Believe the Gospel*

It is not only repentance toward God but faith in our Lord Jesus Christ that is required for the pardoning and purging of sin, for destroying sin and saving you. Repentance is not enough, for righteousness is not by repentance but by faith (Philippians 3. 9). Prayers and tears, sighs and sorrows are not our saviour; it is Jesus only who saves from sin (Matthew 1. 21). None can put our sins to death but he who died for our sins. Do not think you can strike a bargain with God; if all the riches of the world were yours to give, and if you were to give them all, it must cost more than that to have your soul justified and saved (Psalm 49. 6–9). If all the men in the world were to lend you their blood, and you were to offer it up, and with that, your own and that of your firstborn too, it would all be too little (Micah 6. 7). Bring all your repentance and righteousness, and it cannot compensate or make amends for one sin. If all the angels in heaven lent you their whole stock of righteousness – and it is a great one – yet it would not do.

No satisfaction could be made nor anything merited for you but by the Son of God; he and he alone is the Saviour from sin, neither is there any name given under heaven except his whereby we must be saved, nor is there salvation in any other (Acts 4. 12). Look to him, then, and be saved, for whatever your sins are he can save to the very utmost all who come to God by him, for he ever lives to make intercession for them (Hebrews 7. 25).

But if you do not believe in Christ Jesus, though you repent of sin and live, as touching the law, a blameless life, as Saul of Tarsus did (Philippians 3), though you enjoy the reputation of a saint and may seem too good to go to Hell, yet without Christ and faith in him you will not be good enough to go to Heaven. Though there is a Christ to be believed in who has died for sinners, yet if you do not believe in him you may die and be damned notwithstanding that. Come then, come to and close with Christ, not with an idle and dead, but with an effectual and lively faith. Receive a whole Christ; not only Jesus, but Lord; not only Saviour but Prince (Colossians 2. 6). Be as willing to die to sin as he was to die for sin, and as willing to live to him as he was to die for you. Be as willing to be his, to serve him, as that he should be yours to save you. Take him on his own terms, give up yourself wholly to him. Forget your father's house, depart from all iniquity, and become wholly and entirely his. Let your works declare and justify your faith, by purifying your heart (Acts 15. 9), by sanctifying you (Acts 26. 18), by overcoming the world, both the good and evil, the best and worst, the frowns and flatteries of it (1 John 5. 4, 5). This Moses and the rest did by faith (Hebrews 11). Thus come, and thus make good your coming to and believing in Christ.

Then you shall be saved; as the apostle told the jailor, Believe on the Lord Jesus Christ, and thou shalt be saved (Acts 16. 30, 31). They who unfeignedly and with their heart believe in Jesus shall not be destroyed by this destructive thing, sin, nor shall they be damned by this damning thing, sin. Just as there was need of a Jesus Christ, and as faith in Jesus Christ is required, so salvation is made certain and assured to them who believe in Jesus Christ. He who perseveres to the end shall find the end of his faith, the saving of his soul. Hasten, then, to take hold of him, close with him and cleave to him, if ever you would be saved from your sin and God's wrath. Do you like the end, and not the way? Is salvation desirable and is not faith? Without faith it is impossible to please God here, or to be saved hereafter. Have you not souls as well as bodies? Would you not be saved from sin as well as from sickness? Hasten to Jesus Christ, then, the physician, the Saviour of souls. Is there any other Christ? Is there salvation in any other? Has God any more Sons to send? Is there any other way to Heaven? Have we not been in peril long enough? Come now to Christ; if ever there were reason for it, there is now. Will you need him? You do now. Will he be lovely hereafter? He is now. These things being so, we should fly like doves to the windows and not stand a moment longer lest we die, and die in our sins, and then farewell to happiness and hope for ever. But I trust that this is not in vain. I am willing to hope that I have not preached from nor prayed to God in vain, that I have not expostulated with and besought you in vain, but that you will yet repent and believe the Gospel.

There is still another thing to which I would exhort you on this occasion:

### (3) *Sin no more, nor return again to folly*

Hear and fear, and do no more wickedly. It is sad to lick up vomit, and after being washed to wallow in the mire; the latter end of such is worse than their beginning and it had been better for them that they had not known the way of righteousness, than after they have known it to apostatize and depart from the holy commandment (2 Peter 2. 21–22). It will be difficult – next to impossible – to renew such again unto repentance (Hebrews 6. 6). What can they expect but judgment, fiery indignation and vengeance (Hebrews 10. 26–30). O how the sin and condemnation of apostates is and will be aggravated! What! after all his kindness will you kick with the heel against him! After sin has cost you so many sighs and tears and aching hearts, will you make work for more? You will have your belly-full, for the backslider in heart shall be filled with his own ways (Proverbs 14. 14); he will have enough of it one day, and will then cry out, O what an evil and bitter thing is apostasy! O this evil heart of unbelief that made me again depart from the living God, after returning to serve him!

(4) *Take heed of living in any one (and especially any known) sin*

Let us lay aside all the remains of naughtiness, and the sin that does most easily beset us. Let us not have any favourite sin, but out with our right eyes and off with our right hands, rather than offend. Yea, let us cleanse ourselves from all filthiness of flesh and spirit, without and within, that we may perfect holiness and grow up to a perfect man, the measure of the stature of Christ Jesus. Shall we continue in sin? No! Not in one, God forbid! The Apostle speaks (Romans 6) as if it were not only inconsistent but impossible for those to do so who have seen and tasted that the Lord is gracious. For now they see the sinfulness of sin much more than they did before, as being that which attempted to murder God, and did indeed put the Son of God to death. And they say, Shall we crucify him again? King David would not drink the water that hazarded man's blood; how then, they say, can we do any wickedness and sin against the blood of God, which was shed to cleanse us from our sin? Shall we take pleasure in that

[223]

which put Christ to pain, and live in that which put Christ to death? No! By no means! Shall his love and power have no better influence and effect than that? Have we put off the old man, and shall we put it on again? Are we dead, and shall we not cease from sin? Can we say we believe in him, and not obey him? No! No! Get you hence, all idols! In this way gracious souls and new creatures both reason and resolve this case.

I caution and beseech you then to take heed of living in any sin, whether in thought, word or deed:

### 1. *Take heed of sinning in thought.*

Seeing that sin is so sinful, it is evil even to be a thinking sinner, or a sinner though only in thought. It is too commonly said that thoughts are free. They are indeed free in respect of men, who cannot judge us for them, but God can and will. Many people who seem to be modest and sparing as to evil words and deeds will still make bold with thoughts and, as the saying is, pay it with thinking. Such are speculative, contemplative sinners.

There are some who are so wise as not to say with their tongues, yet such fools as to say in their hearts, that there is no God (Psalm 14. 1). There are some who do not actually murder, yet by anger and envy are murderers in heart or thought, as Joseph accused his brethren in saying, You thought evil against me (Genesis 50. 20). There are thought-adulterers, who perhaps never were or durst be adulterers in actual deed (Matthew 5. 28). There are blasphemers in heart, who do not speak it with their mouths but are like those who heard Christ forgiving sin and thought in their hearts that he blasphemed, and so they themselves blasphemed him (Matthew 9. 3–5). Some talk of the world and declaim against it as a vanity, but they think vainly in their heart that their houses shall endure for ever (Psalm 49. 11); like the rich man who said within himself, Thou hast much goods laid up for many years, as if he thought these things his happiness. But it is said of the former that this their way is their folly (Psalm 49. 13), and of the

[224]

latter, Thou fool (Luke 12. 20). For the thought of foolishness, or the foolish thought, is sin (Proverbs 24. 9). Therefore it is said, Take heed that there be not a thought in thy wicked heart (Deuteronomy 15. 9), that is, that there be not a wicked thought in thy heart.

It is true, that all thoughts of evil are not evil thoughts, just as all thoughts of good are not good thoughts. A man may think of evil and yet his thoughts may be good; and a man may think of good and yet his thoughts be evil. A man thinks of evil with good thoughts when he thinks of evil to grieve and repent for it, to abhor and forsake it. And a man thinks of good with evil thoughts when he thinks of good to neglect and scorn it, to call it evil and so to persecute it. But thoughts of sin may be sinful thoughts, with respect to sin past or sin to come.

When men please themselves in the thoughts of their past sins, when they chew the cud and lick their lips after it, or as is said in Job 20. 12, 13, they hide it under their tongue, as if it were a sugar-plum, then they do the sin over and over again by thinking of it, although they do not act it. In this sense, some interpreters understand the scripture, 'She multiplied her whoredoms in calling to remembrance the sins of her youth' (Ezekiel 23. 19). She acted it over again in her memory, in new speculations of her old sins. On the other hand, some men, perhaps the same persons, think sinfully of the sins they have not done, grieving at and regretting they had not taken such and such opportunities, and embraced such and such temptations as they had to sin.

Also, with respect to sins to come, men think sinfully in plotting, contriving and anticipating what sins they will do, although they do not do them. Against this we are charged to make no provision for the flesh (Romans 13. 14); the word is, do not plan and cater for the flesh. Do not lay in fuel for such fire; do not lie in bed and plan to fulfil the lusts hereafter which you cannot practise at present. I would make mention of certain considerations that you may see the sinfulness of evil thoughts:

### (i) *Sinful thoughts defile a man.*

This they do although they never come to words or deeds, and are never uttered or practised. Out of the heart proceed evil thoughts, murders, adulteries, etc., and these defile the man (Matthew 15. 19, 20). Not only murder and adultery, but the thought of murdering and committing adultery defiles the man, as this text says; and our Saviour says the same in another text (Matthew 5. 22, 28). Thus Job made a covenant with his eyes that he might not think (lustfully) of a maid (Job 31. 1). So should we take heed to our ways, that we may not offend, not only with our tongues, but in our thoughts. For thoughts are the words of our hearts and their deeds; and all the words of our mouths and the acts of our lives come from our hearts. Therefore, above all keepings, keep thine heart (Proverbs 4. 23).

### (ii) *Sinful thoughts are an abomination in the sight of God.*

God has a special eye to the thoughts of men's hearts, to those of good men (Malachi 3. 16), and to those of bad men (Genesis 6. 5). In good men God very often accepts the will for the deed. If the will is present with them, though to do they have not the power; if they are as willing to do as to will the deed, God accepts the will for the deed although they cannot do it (2 Corinthians 8. 12; Matthew 26. 41). Similarly when men will and think wickedly, God takes their will for their deed. Just as he takes the good man's will for the deed with acceptation, so he takes the wicked man's will for the deed with abomination; for the thoughts of the wicked are an abomination to the Lord (Proverbs 15. 26). Their wicked thoughts are like filthy vapours and smells in the nostrils of God. Sin is a filthiness, and sinful thoughts have their filthiness as well as sinful actions. Therefore it is said, 'O Jerusalem, wash thine heart from wickedness, that thou mayest be saved. How long shall thy vain thoughts lodge within thee?' (Jeremiah 4. 14). The very remedy tells of the disease; if they must be washed then surely they were filthy, for sweeping will not serve the turn. And what was the wickedness of their heart? It follows in the text, the vain thoughts which were there, and these must be washed or they could not be saved. So abominable in the sight of God is the villainy and vanity of thoughts.

(iii) *Thought-sins are root-sins and the roots of all other sins.*

They are the mother-sins, actions being their issue (Proverbs 4. 23). Evil deeds are the offspring and children of evil thoughts, the branches and fruit which grow out of this root. Thoughts are the first-born of the soul; words and actions are only younger brothers. They are the oil that feeds and maintains the wick, which would otherwise go out; life-sins receive their juice and nourishment from thought-sins. St. James speaks as if our thoughts were the belly and womb where sin is conceived (James 1. 15). Now when men would curse grievously, as Job did, they curse the day and place of their birth, the womb that bore them; so should you curse sin even in the very womb that bore it, laying the axe to the root of this tree.

The wickedness of men's lives is charged upon their thoughts, that it has its root and rise there: murders, adulteries, etc., all come out of the heart, as out of the belly of a Trojan horse (Genesis 6. 5; Matthew 12. 35; 15. 19). One would wonder (as we do at some birds, where they nest all winter) to see so many flocks and herds of wickedness. One would wonder from what corner of the world they come. Why, they all come out of the heart, the rendez-vous of wickedness, the inn where lodge all the thieves and travelling lusts that are in the world and that do so much mischief in it. All the unclean streams flow from this unclean fountain, this ocean and sea of sin. Holy David says, I hate vain thoughts (Psalm 119. 113); that is, any thoughts that are against thy law which I love. We all hate that which is against what we love. But why does David hate the thought of sin? Because evil thoughts beget evil words, and evil words corrupt good, and beget bad behaviour. Vain imaginations beget vain conversations. It is hard for those who think well to do ill, and harder still for those who think ill to do well, for as the root is, so is the fruit, and by that the tree is known (Matthew 7. 17).

(iv) *If we had no other sins to be pardoned, yet we must beg pardon for sinful thoughts.*

A man may think himself to Hell, if the sinfulness of his thoughts is not forgiven him. St. Peter said to Simon Magus, Repent of thy thought – wickedness, and pray if perhaps the thoughts of thine heart may be forgiven thee (Acts 8. 22). If God were to pardon all our word-sins and evil deeds, and leave only our thought-sins unpardoned, we would be undone for ever. Indeed, blessed David was so afraid of sin that he begs God to cleanse him from his secret sins which lay lurking in his heart and were undiscernible there (Psalm 19. 12). Even if such thoughts do not increase to more ungodliness, which they will attempt and too easily effect, yet there is impiety and ungodliness enough in them to ruin us everlastingly. I wish that those who make light of vain thoughts, and even of evil thoughts, as if they had no evil in them, would think of this.

(v) *It is the great design of the Gospel to bring thoughts to the obedience of Christ Jesus.*

It is far easier to reform men's manners than to renew their minds; the laws of men may do the former but it is the law of God which does the latter. Many men, even though they had no other company, could live along with the sins of their hearts and thoughts, pleasing themselves and blessing themselves, too, in their own vain imaginations, and acting sins in their fancy. Indeed, they will more easily surrender the sins of their tongues and hands than their heart-sins. Now the Gospel comes to throw down these strong towers, to cast down imaginations, to conquer whole armies of thoughts, to reduce these straggling and thievish highwaymen into good order and obedience. This is the glory of the Gospel, beyond all the philosophy in the world, that it has such a great influence on the hearts and thoughts of men (2 Corinthians 10. 4, 5).

(vi) *Conversion begins, is carried on and is completed in the hearts and thoughts of men.*

It begins there, for while men are dead in sins they do not consider or regard what is in their heart and thoughts. But when the grace of God comes in power, and they receive it in truth, they begin to think and consider, What shall we do to be saved? Men are in a great quandary in their thoughts, they begin to be disturbed, and their bowels are turned within them. For this reason, regeneration is called the renewing of the mind, and repentance is a change of mind; the heart becomes a new heart, and when the heart is gained, all the rest follows. If the wicked forsake his thoughts, he will quickly forsake his ways (Isaiah 55. 7). The first turn is in the thoughts. 'I thought on my ways, and turned my feet unto thy testimonies' (Psalm 119. 59); the thoughts go before and the feet follow after. The first movements of the Prodigal were in his thoughts; when he came to himself he said within himself, I will arise and go to my father. While he was thus thinking – it is said, while he was afar off, just taking the first step – his father saw him and had compassion on him.

Not only is conversion begun in, but it is carried on in the heart and thoughts especially, though not exclusively. When others, like the Pharisees, study only to make the outside look fair and beautiful, the godly man is employed about his inside, to keep his heart clean. The prayers of godly men are chiefly taken up about their hearts: 'Create in me a clean heart, and renew a right spirit within me' (Psalm 51. 10). And as one excellent writer puts it, In what lies the difference between sincere-hearted Christians and others, but in the keeping of the thoughts, without which all religion is but bodily exercise? Papists may mumble over their prayers, hypocrites may talk, but this is godliness. As conversion begins and is carried on in the thoughts, so it is completed, finished and perfected in them; it ends there. For when a godly man comes to die, his chief and last employment is about his thoughts, He is done with works, he has made his will and concluded all outside him; perhaps his speech fails him, and then his main work and the conclusion, the shutting up of the whole matter is in his thoughts. So that when he comes into the new world of the regenerate, while he continues there, and when he is going into the world to come, his main employment is about and in his thoughts: there he began and here he ends.

(vii) *God keeps an account of, and will call us to account for thoughts as well as for words and actions.*

He has a book of remembrance written for them that think on his name; yes, and for them who think on their sins too with sinful thoughts! There is no thought hid from him; all things are naked and opened before him with whom we have to do (Hebrews 4. 13), or as the words may be read, before him to whom we are to give account. God knows our thoughts afar off (Psalm 139. 2), long before they come out into words or actions (Deuteronomy 31. 21). So the father saw the prodigal, while he was still afar off and only thinking to return. Indeed, he searches and tries the heart to this very end, that he may give to every man according to his ways (Jeremiah 17. 9, 10). God will judge righteous judgment, not according to appearance, as men do; as the man thinketh, so is he, and so shall he be judged. Men judge our inside by our outside; our heart by our work; but God judges our outside by our inside, our works by our heart. It is for this reason that we should fear God and keep his commandments, because God will bring not only every work, but every secret thing to judgment, whether good or evil (Ecclesiastes 12. 13, 14). When the Lord comes, he will bring to light the hidden things of darkness, and make manifest the counsels of the heart, that is, all the secret designs and projects of it (1 Corinthians 4. 5). He will judge the secrets of men by Jesus Christ, as our Gospel teaches (Romans 2. 16). Think, then, that for thoughts you must be judged, and therefore make conscience of them, for not only God's knowledge (Scientia divina) but man's conscience (Conscientia humana) will be one of the books opened as witness in that day, according to which men shall be judged.

Well then, what do you say, or what shall I say to you? Have you thought evil? Lay your hand upon your mouth (Proverbs 30. 32), not only if you have done foolishly but if you have only thought evil; lay your hand on your mouth, that is, be humble and abased. The vanity and vileness, the folly and filthiness of our thoughts should make us ashamed. And lay your hand on your mouth for prevention also. As people lay their hand on their mouth when they cough, lest any unsavoury or unseemly thing should come from them, so do you. For what we say in our hearts we shall soon say with our lips, if we do not lay a hand on our mouth to stop the issue of vain thoughts from flowing out into and infecting our lips and lives, our words and actions. This hive of drones will swarm if you do not lay your hand on your mouth. This cage of unclean birds will be opened and they will take their flight. Your thoughts will run waste like water beside the mill if you do not keep a strong hand over them. O keep your heart with your hand with mighty power, and suppress sinful thoughts, thus preventing them from expressing themselves.

In relation to this, take the following directions for your help and assistance; for know this, that of yourself you are not sufficient to think one good thought, nor to subdue one evil thought:

(i) *Humbly make your address and supplication to God.*

Your heart is in his hands, and to him alone heart-work belongs. He only can search, cleanse, new-make and keep the heart. Pray to God, not only that past sins may be forgiven but that there may not be future ones needing forgiveness. Beg him to new-make your heart and to create a clean one in you. Would you be rid of sinful thoughts? Pray against them, lift up a prayer, and cry out as St. Paul did against the messenger of Satan. Pray without fainting, that even if they are not removed, his grace may be sufficient for you. Cry out as a virgin would do in a case of rape, and God will hear the cry of the oppressed and of them who groan. Be often in spiritual ejaculations, which will be as so many deadly darts to wound and kill sinful thoughts. Call God to your relief; tell him you cannot stand before these troops and armies that defy Israel and Israel's God, and beg him to vindicate his own Name by his own power, as he can easily do; for not only are the hearts of kings in his hand, but he is the King and Ruler of all hearts, and can by his Word command them into, and keep them in order and obedience.

(ii) *Hide the Word of God in your heart that you may not sin against him.*

Do as holy David did, that you might be more holy (Psalm 119. 11). Apply the plaster to the sore place; the heart is the seat and centre of sin; apply the Word there, lay it up, and it will rout and root out these Canaanites and daughters of the land who are a grief of heart to you. Sin is in the heart: hide the Word there, as if it were in ambush to cut off sin upon its first appearance. The Word of God is the sword of the Spirit, and there is nothing like it to wound and kill sin with. It is one of the weapons of our warfare, which is mighty through God to cast down and cast out wicked imaginations (2 Corinthians 10. 4, 5). Put on therefore this and the whole armour of God, that you may be strong in the Lord and in the power of his might (Ephesians 6. 10–17). He is a God who works wonders, even in this matter and of this kind, by his Word and Spirit. Hide this Word, then, which is the sword of the Spirit, and that by which he achieves such glorious conquests over hearts and thoughts.

(iii) *Begin the day with thoughts of God and good things.*

Do not let fancies and vain imaginations get the start of you in the morning. Fancy was our playfellow for many a year before we knew what reason and understanding was; our childhood and youth was vanity. You know that many times schoolfellows and playfellows get such an intimate acquaintance and familiarity with us that it is hard to break it off. But fancy and imagination, these childish things which still have a strong hold of and strong holds in us, must be cast off before our thoughts can become obedient to Christ, as the Apostle tells us (2 Corinthians 10. 5). Therefore mount up with the lark, begin with God, think much and often that he sees and observes you. It was said by the Romans, Watch yourself, for Cato sees you. God's watching should awe you as Cato's did them (Psalm 44. 20, 21), and so it did David (Psalm 139. 17, 18). If vanity gets possession in the morning it will strive to keep it all the day. What a dish is first seasoned with, it keeps the flavour of for long after. Take, as it were, a good draught of the Word in the morning to prevent the windy vapours of vain thoughts. As soon as you wake there are many fiddlers at your bedroom door to sing you wanton songs; but do not listen to them; tell them and all the suitors and clients who solicit you, that you are otherwise engaged and have business of consequence to mind. Do not listen to any sirens. Stop your ear against all such charmers, no matter how pleasingly they sing and charm, for it can never be wisely nor to advantage. Thus, if when you awake, you are with God in meditation, you are likely to walk with God in your whole behaviour, and to be in the fear of the Lord all the day long.

(iv) *If this will not suffice, chide and check vain thoughts.*

If they still haunt you and, like flies that are beaten off, return again, use severity and sharpness. Alas! we are all too indulgent, courteous and gentle to these bold, intruding travellers, for so they are called (2 Samuel 12. 4). There came a traveller to the rich man – a lust to David in the case of Bathsheba, for it refers to that – and he killed another man's lamb for this traveller, this lust. If he had only examined it, he would have found it to be a spy or a vagabond, which should not have been feasted but sent to the whipping-post. The reason why we have so many pedlars coming to our doors is because we buy and take their trifles, and the reason why so many of these beggars and wandering gipsies knock at our doors is because we give them alms and lodging. If we only frowned on them and executed the law upon them, we should probably have none or less of their company.

(v) *Turn away your eyes from beholding vanity.*

Avoid occasions and appearances of evil; for the world is cheated by appearances and shows. Men become thieves when opportunity is offered them, who without it perhaps would not have thought of being so. Just as the heart inflames the eye, so the eye affects and inflames the heart. Curiosity to see and hear the silliest pictures and wanton songs has often induced persons to think such thoughts and to do such things as otherwise they would scarcely have dreamed of. Vain objects and vain speeches engender vain fancies and imaginations, and so proceed and increase to more ungodliness (2 Timothy 2. 16). Therefore the apostle warned Christians not to tell stories of fornication, uncleanness or covetousness; they should not be so much as named or mentioned (Ephesians 5. 3). Such stories, even though only romances, leave bad impressions on men's fancies. We need to keep a strict watch over eyes and ears if ever we would preserve our hearts and thoughts pure and chaste, lest we tempt the tempter to tempt us and to make our hearts worse by opportunity and custom than they are by nature. This made King David beg of God to turn away his eyes from beholding vanity (Psalm 119. 37), and good Job was so much afraid of himself that he made a covenant with his eyes, lest he should think (unbecomingly) of a maid. Looking produces lusting as lusting puts on looking (Matthew 5. 28).

(vi) *Beware of idleness.*

Every man should have a calling to follow, and follow his calling, which is an excellent preservative from evil thoughts. Idle people have no business but to sin, and they who follow their calling have no leisure to sin; their thoughts are too intent to be diverted. Time lies heavy on some men's hands for want of employment, and therefore they become busybodies, gadding and wandering about as their fancy or the Devil, like the wind, drives them, or like a decoy draws and allures them (1 Timothy 5. 13–15). Indeed, these idlers or busybodies are joined with evildoers, thieves and murderers (1 Peter 4. 15). They know that their time is passing away and will pass away, but they do not know how to pass it away, so that whatever temptation comes, they seem to be ready. The wink of an eye or the holding up of a finger prevails with them. They follow the Devil's whistle, and dance to his tune. They spend their days like vagrants, and their life is a mere diversion from that which is the business of it. They cannot endure to be with themselves, and therefore trifle away their precious time, and adventure the loss of their precious souls, by becoming sinners for company.

Our thoughts are so active and restless that they will be doing something or other, and like unruly soldiers, if others do not employ them well, they will employ themselves ill. God has therefore in mercy appointed us callings to take up our thoughts, that they may be not only innocent but profitable to ourselves and others. Paradise had employment, and Heaven also will not be without it. Idleness is an hour of temptation; and we can have no excuse to stand idle in the market place when God himself offers to employ us. The best way to rid our ground of weeds is to till it, and the best way to free our hearts from evil thoughts is by good employment. Only remember this, that your particular calling must not jostle out nor infringe upon your heavenly calling, nor should your being a tradesman make you forget that your conversation, your trading, must be for Heaven. It would be bad for you to mind what is convenient and forget what is necessary. Let Mary's one thing be preferred before Martha's many.

(vii) *Love God and his Law much.*

In so doing your thoughts will be much upon him and it. The love of God will find your heart work enough to do. He who delights in God and his Law will find opportunity enough

[235]

to meditate therein, and pleasure enough in meditating therein day and night (Psalm 1. 2; Psalm 119. 97). Your soul will be where it loves, and where your treasure is there your heart and thoughts will be (Matthew 6. 21). Set your affections on things above and when once your love is settled, your thoughts will centre and dwell there. Love will make you watchful and fearful, lest you should offend the Beloved of your soul. It will make you angry with, and cause you to hate all the sinful thoughts that would attempt to withdraw you or to divert you. It will make you like a tree planted by the riverside, exceedingly and beautifully fruitful, for so will you be in your season. It is meditation that is there likened to the watering of the river, and that meditation flows from delight, and that from love, as you may see (Psalm 1. 2, 3). Thus you will grow up and prosper, so much so that your leaf shall neither fade nor wither (verse 3). Thus I have endeavoured to show the sinfulness of sinful thoughts, and endeavoured to prevent them.

### 2. *A warning against sinful words.*

As I have endeavoured before to clear the heart, so that there might not be an evil thought in it; so now my aim is to clear and cleanse the mouth, so that not so much as an evil word might be in it. Too many people are apt to think that words are only wind, things that they shall not be called to account for, and therefore they are so bold and daring as to say, 'With our tongue will we prevail; our lips are our own; who is Lord over us?' (Psalm 12. 4). We may speak what we will, they say, and we will speak what we may. What an unruly tongue has that man who can say that his tongue is his own! Patient Job in a fit of passion said, 'Let me alone that I may speak, and come of me what will' (Job 13. 13). Alas! Is it not thus with many? When you tell them of the sinfulness of sin and of the sins of the tongue, they fly in our faces and say, Hold your peace, we will speak, let there come on us what will. How desperate they are!

But if you will be a little serious I would ask you, when

you are cool and calm, this question, Would you not live and
see good days? Yes! we would. Who is there that does not
desire life, and to see good days while he lives? Many say,
who will show us any good? And everyone says, Life, Life,
Skin for skin, and all for life. 'Come, ye children, hearken unto
me, and I will teach you the fear of the Lord; what man is he
that desireth life, and loveth many days that he may see
good? Keep thy tongue from evil, and thy lips from speaking
guile' (Psalm 34. 11–13). O that all the parents in the world
would call their children together to give them such lectures
as this! Many say, Come my children, I will teach you the
way to grow rich and great, how to be fine and in fashion.
But few call them and say, Come my children, I will teach
you the fear of the Lord, the best wisdom and godliness, the
best and most enriching trade, which is good for this life and
that to come. O that they would ask them, Would you see
life? Yes, you say, but how? Why, if you seek for life and
good days, keep your tongue from evil and guile. This is confirmed in the New Testament (1 Peter 3. 10). The best way to
live and live well is to keep a good tongue in our heads, as
our proverb says, and to have no evil words in our mouths.
For, as the wise man assures us, 'whoso keepeth his mouth and
tongue, keepeth his soul from troubles' (Proverbs 21. 23).
This is not only a political but a divine assertion, and is true
between God and man, as it is between man and man.

Holy David was so afraid of his tongue, lest he should
offend with it, that he put a bridle into his mouth (Psalm
39. 1). Surely the tongue is an unruly thing that it must be
bridled like a horse or an ass! Indeed it is so unruly that one
may better rule horses and manage them, and more easily
turn such unwieldy things as great ships are than keep the
tongue in order; therefore St. James pronounces him a perfect
man who offends not in word, and one that is able with ease
to bridle the whole body, when he has the mastery of his
tongue (James 3. 2–4). It is a rare thing to use the tongue
well!

Now to help you against this evil, that you may not sin

with your mouths, tongues or lips (which are all one in signification), let me beg you to consider that,

(i) *Sinful words are wholly forbidden us and their opposites are enjoined upon us.* God has told us what we shall not, and what we shall say, what words we ought not, and what we ought to use. As to the negative, 'let no corrupt (filthy, rotten, unsavoury) communication proceed out of your mouth; but (affirmatively) that which is good to the use of edifying, that it may minister grace unto the hearers' (Ephesians 4. 29). Again, in the same epistle, 'But fornication, and all uncleanness, or covetousness, let it not be once named among you, as becometh saints; neither filthiness, nor foolish talking, nor jesting, which are not convenient : but rather giving of thanks' (Ephesians 5. 3–4). These things should not be the subject and matter of your conversation and talk, but rather the giving of thanks, that is, that which is graceful and thankworthy, fit to season and edify others by ministering grace to them, as was said before. 'Let your speech be alway with grace, seasoned with salt' (Colossians 4. 6). It should be such as becomes saints, graceful and comely, seasoned and savoury, that which may not defile any but edify all. Though a Christian is not always to talk of grace, yet he is always to talk so as to show himself a gracious person. Our very table talk, as well as our meat, should be seasoned with salt; it should be with the first and second course. For salt is the first to be put on, and the last taken off, that all may be seasoned and savoury. And so should all our speech be, not like salt that has lost its savour, which has no value even for the dunghill (Luke 14. 35).

(ii) *Unless a man take heed to his words and bridle his tongue his religion is vain, and consequently in vain.* It is unprofitable, idle and impertinent (James 1. 26). He only seems to be religious, and thereby both flatters and deceives himself. It is too much to seem to be evil, and too little only to seem to be good. Appearance in evil is too much, but appearance in good is not enough. If a man seems to be religious, and does not bridle his tongue, notwithstanding his seeming to be, he is not religious. A seeming religion is worse than none, as vanity is less than nothing (Isaiah 40. 17). He who has a form and only a form of godliness, denying the power thereof, is worse than the man who has not so much as a form, or makes no profession of godliness. How this should oblige us to take heed of tongue-sins!

(iii) *Sinful words are evidences of sinful hearts.* Words are the image of the mind and the declaration of it; as a man is known by his picture, so is a heart by its words. 'Thou art a Galilean, thy speech beways or discovers thee.' We may know of what nationality men are by their language, whether French or Dutch, etc., and likewise whether they are of the heavenly or the hellish world. It is out of the abundance, that is, the fulness and overflowing, of the heart that the mouth speaks (Matthew 12. 34). Broach a full cask, and what is in will come out; words are like a broaching of the heart and giving it vent, and then out comes that which was within. It is indeed both possible and common for people to speak well when they mean ill; peace is in their mouth when war is in their heart. But that heart is hypocritical, and out of such a double heart which is full of hypocrisy, they speak with their tongues (Psalm 12. 2; Jeremiah 42. 20). If wicked men speak well, yet it is still from an evil heart of hypocrisy, and out of that abundance of the heart the mouth speaks.

(iv) *Evil words corrupt men and their manners.* Our great care should be not to be corrupt, and next to that, not to corrupt others; but evil words corrupt both. They corrupt and defile ourselves: what goes into the mouth, that is, meat, does not defile the man, but what comes out of the mouth, that is, evil words, proceeds from the heart, and they defile the man. The tongue is but a little member, yet it boasts great matters; it is only as a spark of fire, but it kindles a great deal of wood, a world of iniquity, the whole course of nature, and defiles the whole body (James 3. 5, 6). Not only does it defile a man's own body and course of life, but the body and the community of them with whom we have to do; a little leaven leavens the whole lump. 'Be not deceived: evil communications corrupt good manners' (1 Corinthians 15. 33). What kind of bad language or evil communication does the Apostle mean here? It is that which he had mentioned in verse 32: 'Let us eat and drink; for tomorrow we die.' Such statements as this, of a loose, epicurean and atheistic kind, debauch men and their manners. Many an innocent and promising person has been corrupted by such bad statements. They who use evil communication show no good conduct; people of evil words are seldom people of good manners. If they are so for a while, for no one is suddenly wicked or as bad as possible at first, yet they degenerate and grow more immoral and increasingly guilty of bad behaviour. Frequent lying eventually makes men so unfamiliar with truth that they scarcely think that there is any difference between them. They jest for so long that they forget what it is to be in earnest, until awakened by the quarrels that these things beget in and among themselves.

(v) *The tongue is either man's glory or his shame.* It is either worth much or nothing, according to whether it is good or evil. God made man's tongue his glory but sin makes it his shame. Holy David says to his tongue, 'Awake up, my glory' (Psalm 57. 8), and 'My glory rejoiceth' (Psalm 16. 9); the Apostle, following the Septuagint, renders this, 'My tongue was glad' (Acts 2. 26). And when is our tongue our glory but when it speaks to the glory of God? Then, its words are savoury and gracious. If, on the other hand, our tongue is a lying tongue, a slandering tongue, or in any other way evil, then it is our shame. What a vast difference there is between a good and a bad tongue! 'The tongue of the just is as choice silver (a precious commodity): the heart of the wicked (and therefore his tongue) is little worth' (Proverbs 10. 20). He who pays even a farthing for that which is worth nothing pays a farthing too much. A bad tongue is worth so little that he cannot tell how little; it is worth nothing, or if you will, it is worse than nothing in being nothing. Again, 'There is that speaketh like the piercings of a sword: but the tongue of the wise is health' (Proverbs 12. 18). We talk of speaking daggers, or dangerous and killing words; the tongue of the wise, on the contrary, is not only a medicine and wholesome, but, in the abstract, health. There is as much difference between a good and bad tongue as between soundness and wounds, health and sickness. Yet again, 'A wholesome tongue is a tree of life (which is for healing): but perverseness therein is a breach in the spirit' (Proverbs 15. 4). A wounded spirit who can bear? Who can bear up under a broken spirit?

(vi) *God will judge us for and by our words*, as well as by our works and actions. There is a place in Scripture which should make us tremble and engage us to take heed to our words so long as we have even a day to live: — 'But I say unto you, that every idle word that men shall speak, they shall give account thereof in the day of judgment. For by thy words thou shalt be justified, and by thy words thou shalt be condemned' (Matthew 12. 36, 37). If we must give an account of idle words, what account shall we give of filthy and harmful words! Of words that are corrupt and corrupt others! For this reason Solomon tells us that death and life are in the power of the tongue (Proverbs 18.21); a man shall be judged and sentenced according to it. There is such a connection between heart, tongue and deed that he who is judged by one is judged by all of them, for they agree in one. It is noticeable in Psalm 50 that all or most of the charge against men is for words, the sin of the tongue. They have abused God's good word, used their own bad words, giving their mouth to evil. Yet though this is so, the heart was consenting and the hand executing, and therefore there was a concurrence and co-working of all three. Thus, after speaking of their words, God says, 'These things hast thou done' and then 'thou thoughtest' (Psalm 50. 21). 'But I will reprove thee', he goes on, that is, for all this, and especially for your words. This is according to what is said elsewhere, 'Behold, the Lord cometh with ten thousands of his saints, to execute judgment upon all, and to convince all that are ungodly among them of all their ungodly deeds which they have ungodly committed, and of all their (note this!) hard speeches which ungodly sinners have spoken against him' (Jude 14, 15); that is, they have spoken against him in his members. It is also said that their mouths speak great swelling words, as murmurers and complainers do (verse 16). They will jeer at the people of God and taunt them with the name of holy and spiritual, and utter hard speeches against them. But when Christ comes to judgment, he will call them to account for all the hard speeches and all the great swelling words which by way of complaint they have spoken against his members; or by way of flattery and admiration for lucre's sake, they have spoken in commendation and praise of wicked and cruel men. Take heed, therefore, of the sins of the tongue!

When Dives was in Hell, it seems that the part that was most tormented was his tongue; for he begs water to cool his tongue. This gives us some reason to think that, even in relation to Lazarus, he had sinned much with his tongue, and used hard speeches against poor Lazarus; for it was by him that he would have had the water brought. In what we sin we smart and are pained and plagued, as Dives was with and in his tongue. If the tongue is set on fire of Hell while on earth, how will it be set on fire when it is in Hell! The sins of the mouth cry for vengeance with an open mouth, and make others cry for it too. In Psalm 59, the holy writer – not yet a king but still a prophet – prays, 'Scatter them, bring them down, O Lord!' (verses 11–13). Why, David? Why are you so severe? What have they done? O, it is 'for the sin of their mouth and the words of their lips', for their cursing and lying. Then he is at it again, 'Consume them in wrath, consume them'. The sin of their mouth drew forth against them this dreadful imprecation from this merciful and good person, and made him beg God to execute it upon them. Men will have a sad account to give for speaking iniquity, as well as for working it.

Let me therefore entreat you to take heed to your words:

(i) *Let your words be few.* This should be so, not only in

your dealings and conversation with men, but in your addresses to God: 'God is in heaven, and thou upon earth, therefore let thy words be few' (Ecclesiastes 5. 2). This is largely the force of the prayer which our Saviour taught his disciples (Matthew 6. 6–9). There is a vanity which attends men in religion; they think they will be heard for their loud and much speaking; silence would be better than speaking amiss, indeed, many times better than much-speaking. It is true, there is a time to speak, as there is to be silent, and happy are they who improve it well; yet it is seldom that a multitude of words are without sin, and therefore he that refrains his lips is wise (Proverbs 10. 19).

Silence reveals wisdom, and conceals ignorance, and it is so much a characteristic of wise men that the oracle tells us that a fool, when he holds his peace, is accounted wise, and he that shuts his lips is esteemed a man of understanding (Proverbs 17. 28). As a very worthy and noble author expresses it, 'If silence were as much in fashion as it is charitable to mankind to wish it, the regions of Hell would be far more thinly populated than now they are likely to be.' Many have repented for using their tongues too much. Now it is true, a man who holds his peace may offend with his tongue, but it is a more scarce and rare crime than that of much, which is usually too much, speaking. It is Gospel-doctrine which teaches us to be swift to hear and slow to speak (James 1. 19). Moses' imperfection or defect would be an excellence in some people, that is, to be slow of speech. And it would be well with some if they had got such a cold as would keep them from speaking! O, the prittle-prattle that abounds among the busybodies of this world! There are many who are not only vain but unruly talkers, so that a man has more patience to hear them than to hear the beating of a rattling drum (Titus 1. 10).

Alas, it is not only the chatter and tittle-tattle of idle gossips (as in 1 Timothy 5. 13) who speak unbecomingly and of things which they ought not. But much of the talk that wastes the time of men, who would be loth to drink and swear it away, consists of talk that flatters the present or detracts from the absent, censuring superiors or despising inferiors. What empty, ridiculous and frothy conversations (that excite to carnality) are the common pastime, even among those who pretend to better things! And what is such company and conversation good for, except to quench zeal and fervour! Indeed it is the easy way to lose credit and good name, and if not innocence, yet always time, which is too precious to be squandered away and lost, much more to be sinned away! 'Should a man full of talk be justified?' (Job 11. 2). No! Much talk is full of folly; 'for a dream cometh through the multitude of business; and the fool's voice is known by multitude of words' (Ecclesiastes 5. 3). 'In the multitude of dreams and many words there are also divers vanities: but fear thou God' (Ecclesiastes 5. 7); it is as if the multitude of words were inconsistent with the fear of God. We cannot very well speak too little, unless we speak by command from God, and in obedience to him.

(ii) *If we must speak, let us speak as we ought.* Let our words be wholesome words, such as carry medicine and health in them. Let them be safe and sound speech that may neither be gainsaid nor reproved, that may do no hurt but may do good. We should speak that which is good to edify men, that which is good for ourselves and others, either naturally, civilly, morally or spiritually good, as opportunity offers and requires. I do not intend any particular enumeration of the sins of the tongue which are to be avoided, nor a detailed discourse about speaking and ordering our tongues; but only to hint at these things in general, leaving the particular application and improvement to be made by every man, as his own case calls for. Therefore to conclude this, I shall commend but two things in relation to this:

(a) *Look well to your hearts.* If they are not well kept, your tongues will be badly kept. Therefore it is said, 'Keep thy heart with all diligence' (Proverbs 4. 23); or, as it is in the Hebrew, 'above all keeping'. It needs more keeping than anything else, for all the rest of the faculties and members are at the heart's disposal. Therefore keep a strict watch and strong guard over your heart. The speaking of the tongue is from the musing of the heart, which is as fire in the bosom that cannot be hid, but will break out into a flame of words (see Psalm 39. 3). When you are heart-full, your mouth will run over; and if the fountain of your heart is bitter, the streams of your words cannot be sweet. When David prays that the words of his mouth might be acceptable, he prays for this in relation to it, Let the meditations of my heart be acceptable (Psalm 19. 14). If the latter, that is, our meditations, are not acceptable, then the former, that is, our words, are not likely to be acceptable. When our heart speaks our words, our words speak our heart, and it is only one thing. No sooner does our heart indite a good matter, but our tongue will be as the pen of a ready writer (Psalm 45. 1). 'The heart of the wise teacheth his mouth' (Proverbs 16. 23); the Hebrew is, 'maketh his mouth wise'. The fool speaks with an open mouth anything that comes into his head, but a wise man opens his mouth and speaks gravely, wisely, and with deliberation. The mouth needs to go to school, and if we would have it wise, let us get it a wise heart to be its tutor, to teach it the art and grace of speaking wisely and well. 'The heart of the wise teacheth his mouth.'

(b) *Pray to God*. For prayer is the general means for preservation and sanctification of heart, tongue and life. Lift up your heart and soul to him and pray, 'Let the words of my mouth, and the meditation of my heart be acceptable in thy sight, O Lord' (Psalm 19. 14), of which I have just spoken. Say, 'O Lord, open thou my lips, and my mouth shall show forth thy praise' (Psalm 51. 15). 'Let my mouth be filled with thy praise and with thy honour all the day' (Psalm 71. 8). 'Set a watch, O Lord, before my mouth; keep the door of my lips. Incline not my heart to any evil thing' (Psalm 141. 3, 4). That which God keeps is well kept, and if he does not keep the city, the watchmen watch in vain. Commit yourself to the Keeper of Israel, and all will be well (Proverbs 16. 1–3).

### 3. Beware of sinning in deed.

Before I speak directly about living in the practice of any sin, I crave leave to say some things about and against sins of omission. This is a thing too seldom treated or taken notice of, though there is scarcely any guilt more common than this.

(i) *Take heed of sins of omission.* It is a sin to omit any good which is commanded, as well (or ill) as to commit any evil which is forbidden; not to do what we ought, as well as to do what we ought not. We are not only to eschew evil, but to do good also (1 Peter 3. 11). I insist on this the rather because many are more apt and prone to omit duties, to be negligent at doing good, than to commit gross and palpable evils. Withal, they look upon it as a less evil, if any at all, for there are so many trifling excuses ready for it, as you may see (Luke 14. 18–20). I would urge you therefore to consider these things:

(a) Some of the best men have been guilty of this, and have suffered by it. I will give but two examples. First is Jacob, who was most tender of telling a lie, although it was to get a blessing (Genesis 27. 11, 12). Yet this same Jacob was so forgetful of, and for so long neglected and omitted to pay his vow, which he had made at Bethel, that God reminds him of it (Genesis 35. 1), and for the omission of which it is supposed that the afflictions mentioned in the former chapter befell him. The other instance is Hezekiah, a good man and a good king, who did not render to the Lord according to the benefit he had received, nor answered the end of it, but was guilty of not being humble or thankful enough, though he sang a song of praise, it would seem annually, to God. Therefore wrath was upon him (2 Chronicles 32. 25 with Isaiah 38. 20). Alas, how prone good men are to neglect duties, and especially that of returning thanks! For the sake of these things the wrath of God comes on his own children, as it comes on the children of disobedience for gross sins (Ephesians 5. 5, 6). How dearly it cost the spouse when she did not open to her beloved (Canticles 5. 6, 7)!

(b) Yet generally it is a great affliction to good and godly men to be forced to omit duties, though the omission of them in this instance is no sin of theirs, as in time of sickness or in case of flight. How David mourns while he is in the wilderness, having been persecuted and driven there! How he laments his absence from the assemblies of them that kept holy day (Psalm 42. 1–4). Though God in such cases of necessity dispenses with his Sabbath, and consequently his instituted worship on that day, holy men will still lament this necessity and mourn that they are restrained from sharing with others, and that they are forced to do that which otherwise would not be lawful to do on a Sabbath day. It is for that reason (not to exclude others) that, I conceive, our Saviour bade the disciples pray that their flight might not be on the Sabbath day (Matthew 24. 20); for then the usual ordinances of the day could not be enjoyed, nor the ordinary duties of the day practised and performed.

(c) Just as it should be an affliction to be in a necessity, so it is a sin to be willing to omit a duty. It is an affliction not to have a head or hand, but a sin not to have a heart for duty. It is a sin to will evil, and a sin not to will good. But to be willing not to do good is more than sin. Too many people are glad of diversions, as schoolboys are when they have no mind to their books; anything will serve to put off a duty. When the flesh was weak and the spirit willing, Christ himself excused his disciples (Matthew 26. 41), but if the spirit is unwilling, it is no excuse, no matter how weak the flesh is. It was some comfort to St. Paul that though to do he had no power, yet to will was present with him (Romans 7. 18). But not to will, though we have no power, and much more not to will when we have power, is a sin. The reason why the wicked bade God depart from them was because they had no mind or desire to be acquainted with his ways (Job 21. 14). They did not like to retain God in their knowledge (Romans 1. 28), or to pay acknowledgments to him. They had no mind nor will nor desire to do it. This is sin, as well as the other sins with which they are charged.

(d) One omission makes way for another. He who, under pretence of unfitness for duty, puts it off, makes himself fit for nothing more than to omit again. He prepares and fits himself to be unfit for duty, and so to omit duty. To fast too much and for too long takes away and deadens the appetite. So he who omits one duty is likely to omit another and then another, until he omits all and gives up his very profession, and when that is gone, the man's religion dies and he becomes twice dead. Omissions make way for commissions, as in the case of our first parents.

It will be worth our while to observe a few texts which speak of sluggards, for from such an attitude sins of omission generally arise. 'By much slothfulness the building decayeth; and through idleness of the hands the house droppeth through' (Ecclesiastes 10. 18). The house not only lies open to wind and weather, but at last falls down, when the repairs are neglected and omitted. Our bodies are called the temples of God, of which our souls are, as I may say, the holy of holies, or as we call it, the chancel; and it is through sloth that this glorious fabric decays so much. 'He also that is slothful in his work is brother to him that is a great waster' (Proverbs 18. 9). He who is a prodigal, a spendthrift, who spends more than he gets and more than was given him, is a man who will come to nothing and be worse than nothing very soon. This is true, and it is as true that his brother, the slothful man, will not hold out much longer than he. 'The sluggard will not plow by reason of the cold; therefore shall he beg in harvest, and have nothing' (Proverbs 20. 4). A prodigal comes to nothing, and so does the sluggard.

Love is a laborious thing; we read of the labour of love (1 Thessalonians 1. 3), and love never grieves to be obedient (1 John 5. 2–3). Now idleness argues a lack of love, for when the angel of Ephesus left his first love, he left also his first works (Revelation 2. 4, 5). When love grows cold, practice becomes dead. 'The slothful man saith, There is a lion in the way' (Proverbs 26. 13). If you ask him, Why do you not rise up and walk with God? Why do you not go forth and serve

God? O, he says, there is a lion in the way; there is danger in it. But this is only his imagination (see verse 16). 'As the door turneth upon his hinges, so doth the slothful upon his bed' (verse 14). How is that? Why, first one way, then another; he cannot rest on his bed of idleness, and yet he is loth to rise, and therefore he turns this way and that. And if after much ado and many a yawn he does get up, he 'hideth his hand in his bosom (it is cold weather); it grieveth him to bring it again to his mouth' (verse 15). He is grieved to bring it twice to his mouth, though it is to feed himself. This is the guise of idle and slothful people, indeed of professors. We are to do what we do with our might, and how can that be while our hand is in our bosom? Take it out for shame! For as is the case with the man who, having put his hand to the plough, looks back, so also with the man who does not put his hand to the plough at all. Both will be found unfit for the work and kingdom of God; they shall beg in harvest but have nothing. In the great day of recompense, these slothful ones will learn to pray and beg, saying, Lord, Lord, open to us, but they shall have nothing, that is, of that which they beg; no door will open to let them into the House of God, where there is bread enough.

I remember I said that sins of omission make way for sins of commission, and it is only too true. When Job's friends heard such unbecoming language from him as cursing, they concluded that he omitted praying: 'Thou restrainest prayer before God' (Job 15. 4). When men neglect duty, they usually fall into sin. Let us continue with the story of the slothful: 'I went by the field of the slothful, and by the vineyard of the man void of understanding' (Proverbs 24. 30). And what did he observe? 'And, lo, it was all grown over with thorns, and nettles had covered the face thereof, and the stone wall thereof was broken down' (verse 31). Alas, Eden becomes a wilderness, and Paradise a desert; the poor soil is under the curse; it brings forth grieving thorns and pricking briars and stinging nettles, and is again nigh unto more cursing for bringing this forth (Hebrews 6. 8). Sin advances by degrees; it

[249]

seems modest at first: just omit, then it grows bold and bids you commit, and so from omission to commission, until at last the man becomes a man of sin and a son of perdition, a hopeless, desperate, lost and undone man. Moreover, such people are frequently given up (Romans 1. 21). Their first sin was a not glorifying God as God; and then, not being thankful, they became vain; being vain they were darkened; from that they became fools, and so on to abominable idolatries, and at last it came to this, that God gave them up (verse 24). Such is the danger of sins of omission! One makes way for another, and from that they proceed to commission, until they are given up and cursed.

(e) The more knowledge of any duty we have, the more clear it is and the more we are convinced of it, the more aggravated is the omission of that duty. The clearer the light is, the greater the sin of not receiving it; this is *the* condemnation (John 3. 19). If Christ had not come, their sin had not been so great; but now not to believe is to be without excuse (John 15. 22, 24). If God had not told us what we ought to do, we might have made excuse and said that had we known better we would have done better. But God hath shown thee, O man, what is good (Micah 6. 8), and that not only by his works, but by his Word. And if the knowledge of him by them only aggravated men's sin, as it did (Romans 1. 21), how greatly will their sin be aggravated who neglect so great salvation, which at first was preached by the Lord Jesus Christ, and afterward confirmed by them that heard him, God bearing them witness with signs and wonders, divers miracles and gifts of the Holy Ghost (Hebrews 2. 3, 4).

To him who knows to do good and does not do it, to him it is a sin, a great sin, a heinous sin, sin with a witness. It may be sin to another who does not know to do good, but not so great a sin as it is to him who knows. Therefore he who did not know his master's will was beaten with only a few stripes, but he who knew it and did not do it was beaten with many (Luke 12. 47, 48). The Jews were accustomed to abate one of the forty stripes which the law allowed; this they did even to St. Paul, much as they hated him, for of them twice he received forty stripes save one (2 Corinthians 11. 24). But the man who knows his master's will and does not do it, nor prepares himself, shall be beaten with many stripes, with the full number without abatement or mitigation; the total sum required by the law shall be inflicted on him.

(f) Sins of omission, if done in the sight of others, are bad examples, just as sins of commission are. A man may do a great deal of harm by not doing good. We are commanded to let our good works shine before others (Matthew 5. 16), and to be examples of faith and charity to others, to be presidents of good works (Titus 3. 8), for that is what the word signifies in that text. The world is led by the eye as much, if not more than by the ear. Men are as much prevailed with by examples as they are by precepts. They are, on the other hand, most inclined to think that they may do what others, especially their betters, do. If rich men give but little, others who are not so rich and yet able to give, think they may be excused if they give nothing to the poor. If parents neglect prayer, the children scarcely think it their duty to pray.

It is indeed an excellent thing to be an exemplary Christian; it shows that religion is practicable, for it draws men on. It is a listless hack which will not follow and strive to keep pace when another mettled horse leads the way. Similarly, it is sad to be an exemplary sinner; for such an one has more sins to answer for than his own, even those of other men which were committed through his example. It is a common plea, Such and such learned and educated men do so and so, and why may not I? O, do not follow a multitude, however wise and mighty it is, to do evil! Let us therefore provoke one another to love and good works by our example. Let us not only show, but lead the way.

(g) Consider that sins of omission are sins which God has severely judged men for in this world, and for which He will judge men in the great day. It is observable how severe God has been to men who have omitted what he commanded them to do, though they have claimed to do it for God's sake. We have an instance of this in Saul (1 Samuel 15). God sent Saul to destroy Amalek, root and branch, king and people, from head to foot, from throne to threshold, and not to leave one person alive; man, woman, infant and suckling, all must die; oxen and sheep and so on, none must escape. But Saul spared Agag and the best of the sheep and oxen, and would not utterly destroy them. The result was that the Lord repented of having set up Saul to be king (verse 11). Though Saul pretended that it was done for a sacrifice to God (verses 15, 22) yet it is charged against him as rebellion and witchcraft (verse 23); and his not obeying the voice of the Lord is called doing evil in God's sight (verse 19). So he who omits a good, commits an evil; the omission of good is the commission of evil, and is judged accordingly. How dearly this sin of omission cost Saul!

Another remarkable instance is that of Eli. He is charged with honouring his sons above God (1 Samuel 2. 29). How so? Eli was a good old man, and can it be thought that he preferred his sons above God? What should the meaning of this be? It is cleared up, however, in the next chapter, where God says, 'I will judge his house forever for the iniquity which he knoweth; because his sons made themselves vile, and he restrained them not' (1 Samuel 3. 13). He did not give them so much as a sour look, or, as the Hebrew reads, he did not frown upon them. And yet let me tell you that Eli went so far that, had his children had any honesty or any respect to the rebukes of a priest and father, one would have thought that he had said enough. For the old man very gravely expostulated with them, 'Why do ye such things? For I hear of your evil dealings by all this people. Nay, my sons; for it is no good report that I hear: ye make the Lord's people to transgress. If one man sin against another, the judge shall judge him: but if a man sin against the Lord, who shall intreat for him?' (1 Samuel 2. 23–25). Thus he lays their sin and danger before them pretty roundly, and yet God says, that he restrained them not; there was an omission and neglect of more severe discipline. And this omission cost him dear, as dear almost as the sins of commission cost his sons, which were not to be purged with sacrifice (1 Samuel 3. 14).

Another instance is that concerning the Ammonites and Moabites, who were a bastard brood, and like bastards were not to enter into the congregation of the Lord till the tenth generation (Deuteronomy 23. 2–4). The reason given is the sin of omission, because they did not meet Israel with bread and water, when they came out of Egypt. It is a dreadful thing to be excommunicated from, and a dreadful thing not to be admitted into, the congregation of the Lord; and you see that a sin of omission may keep men out for a long time.

But God will also judge men for sins of omission in the great and terrible day of his righteous judgment. Not only the wicked, but the slothful servant will be judged, and the slothful will be judged wicked. We have it from the mouth of Truth itself, 'thou wicked and slothful servant' (Matthew 25. 26), wicked because slothful. He was no waster, but a brother to one (as we previously noted) because he was slothful. For omitting to improve his talent, he was called and judged a wicked and slothful servant, and his punishment was, beside the loss of his talent, to be cast into outer darkness, where there is weeping and gnashing of teeth. He had not turned the grace of God into wantonness, yet for being unprofitable he is sent to Hell. And again, 'He shall say also to them on the left hand, Depart from me, ye cursed, into everlasting fire' (Matthew 25. 41); it is, says Christ, for your sins of omission, because when I was hungry and thirsty, you, like the Ammonites and Moabites we have just mentioned, you brought me no bread or water, you gave me no meat and drink. Some are ready to justify themselves thus, We never did any man harm; we have wronged and oppressed no man. Yes, but God will condemn them who have not done such evils, because they have not done good. Think of these things, then, and beware of sins of omission.

(ii) *Take heed of sins of commission.* We should be careful not to omit our duties, for besides all that has been said, I might add this, that to omit the weightier things of the law, though we observe the lesser, is a sign of hypocrisy (Matthew 23. 23). But we should be no less careful to keep ourselves from the evil that is forbidden, from all kinds and sorts of sins, the enumeration of which would be endless.

(a) Watch against that which may be most properly called your own sin, that to which you are most inclined, and which most easily besets and conquers you. It was David's crown of rejoicing, that he had kept himself from his iniquity, 'I was also upright before him, and I kept myself from mine iniquity' (Psalm 18. 23). He kept himself not only from that which was charged upon him by others to be his iniquity in relation to Saul, but as most interpreters take it, that which was the sin of his inclination; as one might say, from the sin of my particular complexion and constitution, my nature's darling sin. Are you young? Then avoid the sins common to this age; 'flee youthful lusts' (2 Timothy 2. 22) or the lusts of youth. There are some lusts almost peculiar to youth: (i) ambition, vainglory and pride (1 Peter 5. 5), which is most evident in their odd, fantastic dress and eccentric manners, as that text implies, and especially in not submitting to the elders. (ii) the gratifying of the sensual appetite and carnal inclination. They are much for the lust of the eye and of the flesh too, as well as for the pride of life. Ecclesiastes tells us that they are much set upon pleasure, the young man's favourite (11. 9 and 12. 1). The prodigal, who was the younger brother, in this way wasted his estate, his time and himself; he spent all on back and belly, on riotous living. It was a young man whom Solomon saw going away to her house (Proverbs 7. 7) which leads to hell. (iii) Another lust of youth is self-conceit, too much proneness to be wise in their own eyes. They think old men fools, but old men know that they are fools. Their conceit puffs them up and makes them incapable of instruction and very unteachable – Rehoboam and his young counsellors will save us the labour of giving other examples (1

Kings 12). It is for this reason that the Apostle would have Titus exhort young men to be discreet or sober minded. Flee then all these and any other youthful lusts. Make the most haste you can from them; do not only creep or go or run or ride, but flee.

Are you old? Hear then, you old men (Joel 1. 2). What shall we hear?, you will say. Take heed of the sins and lusts of old age (Titus 2. 2). When men are dying and have one foot in the grave, when they are about to give up the ghost, yet, like the thief on the cross, they will be sinning. Take heed of Solomon's old-age sin, a kind of dotage which suffered him to apostatize (1 Kings 11. 3). Be sound in the faith (Titus 2. 2). Take heed of the peevishness of old age; be patient, says the text. Take heed of the covetousness of old age; be charitable, says the text. Be fruitful in your old age, that your latter end may be better than your beginning, and the better because, it may be, your beginning was bad. Seek that your last days may be your best days, and so you may die in a good old age, which may be best done when you die good in old age, and are such as St. Paul the aged who had finished his course. It is a crown and glory to be an old good disciple, as Mnason was (Acts 21. 16).

(b) Take heed of the sins which men and women are guilty of, as relatives, and as they stand in relation to one another. Are you a husband or a wife? Beware of being false, or only feigning love. Are you a parent or a child? Are you a master or a servant? Beware of the sins which attend any of the relationships in which you stand. I had, indeed, intended to have detailed the sins, but they are so commonly written of and known that I shall forbear, and only suggest this direction and counsel, which I have often thought may be of great and good use, namely, that every relative person, such as husband or wife, etc., should read and, if they can, write out and pray that God would write in their hearts the several directions which the Scripture so frequently and abundantly gives to all relations; that they may keep them before their eyes, that they may walk in the truth. Relative duties are too little minded, and if we only considered that we are really that which we are relatively, it would immensely oblige and quicken us to be good in our relationships. It is not likely that they are good Christians who are bad husbands or wives, bad parents or children, bad superiors or inferiors in their places.

(c) Take heed of the sins of the age, country, and places where you live. There are sins as it were particular to some ages and countries, as to them of the latter and last days (1 Timothy 4. 1–4 and 2 Timothy 3. 1–5). When sin becomes an epidemic, it is the less abstained from, for few people care to be different. When sins are as it were the custom and fashion of the country, most will be sinners, especially if sin is countenanced by the example of great ones. But as we should not be conformed to this world at large, neither should we to any part of it. Is there any sin by which the land is defiled, for which the land mourns, and is ready to spew out the inhabitants thereof for it? (Leviticus 18. 27, 28); take heed, then, that you are not found guilty. But be one of the mourners, whom God will set a mark upon (Ezekiel 9. 4). When formality, hypocrisy and apostasy are in fashion, be cautious not to sin in any of these ways, any more than by swearing, drunkenness and uncleanness, though they are common and uncontrolled.

Beware lest you regard the favour and praise of men more than, or without, the favour and praise of God, which hypocrites and only hypocrites do (John 12. 42–43). Daniel and the three children would not sin for the sake of fashion, not even though they were commanded to sin. And the Apostles made their appeal to them that would have had them sin, saying, 'Whether it be right in the sight of God to hearken unto you more than unto God, judge ye' (Acts 4. 18–20). It is God who judges, and not man, and he only has absolute authority over us, to command what he pleases, and therefore our chief care should be to please him. We shall find that the best way to please all, or to displease any with least danger, is to please him who is all in all. Therefore, if any think it strange that ye run not with them to the same excess of riot, and speak evil of you (1 Peter 4. 4), answer them as Joseph did his mistress, 'How can I do this great wickedness, and sin against God?' (Genesis 39. 9). Tell them as the Apostle does that you and they must give an account to him who is ready to judge the quick and the dead; seeing therefore that the end of all things is at hand, let us be sober and watch unto prayer (1 Peter 4. 5, 7). This David did, when they spoke evil of him, fought against him without a cause, and for his love became his adversaries (Psalm 109. 2–4).

(d) Take heed of the sins that attend your callings, occupations and trades. I would premise certain things here:

(i) *Every man should have a calling to follow, and should follow his calling,* as was mentioned above. God has given no man a dispensation to be idle. The rule is, and that by commandment, that if any will not work, that is able to work, neither should he eat (2 Thessalonians 3. 10). If this rule were observed, I am afraid that more rich than poor would go with hungry stomachs and empty bellies. Of idleness comes no good, but certainly a great deal of evil. They who are at work are not at leisure to sin, but they who are idle are at leisure to do nothing but to sin. Adam in innocence, that better than golden age, had his calling and employment: he was a gardener, a cultivator of the ground or a husbandman (Genesis 2. 15). The angels of heaven are not without their calling; when they are abroad (here on earth), they are ministering spirits (Hebrews 1. 14), and when at home in heaven, they cease not day or night from praising God. As one of the Greek Fathers expresses it, their service and calling is to sing songs and psalms of praise. I may therefore say, take heed of the sin of being without a calling, or of having no calling, especially you who are young and strong to labour.

(ii) *No man's calling necessitates him to sin.* There is many a trade of which I would not scruple to say that it is no calling; many make a livelihood out of trades which are no calling. Harlotry and thieving are no callings; for we are called not to uncleanness but to holiness. As to lawful callings, to sin is but accidental, and springs more from our inclination than from the callings themselves. Necessities are things that few men are competent judges of; many things are called so which are far from being so; and nothing should be called so that is a sin. He who cannot follow a calling without sinning had better lay aside his trade than live by sinning. That there is sin in callings is not from our vocation but from our corruption; it is not our calling, but our evil heart that makes us sin. There is no need to tell a lie or to steal or to cheat. There are many other better ways to live, and if we were not distrustful of God, and indulgent to the baseness of our own hearts, we might find them out.

(iii) *Yet there are snares in our callings.* The Devil lays his nets and baits everywhere; he lays his snares to entangle us, not only in our general, but particular callings, to turn all our duties into sins. Many men sin, and most men are liable, being tempted, to sin in their callings. There are many temptations that attend and wait on every calling. Were I to speak to men of any calling, I would follow the example of John the Baptist, who spoke to everyone according to the sin he was guilty of, or to which he was tempted in his place (Luke 3. 10). The publicans were very great oppressors, and therefore he calls upon them to exact no more than their due, their stated and appointed allowance. The soldiers were boisterous and unruly, and therefore he speaks to them to do violence to no man or, as it is in the margin, to put no man in fear; do not decoy men and falsely accuse them; do not plunder and steal, but be content with your pay. But since I cannot speak to every condition, I will lay before you some things in general, which may be applied to each and every one.

(a) Take heed of lying and equivocating. This is a thing grown so common in buying and selling, that it passes as a matter of course: – It cost me more, and yet I will sell it for less; I cannot afford it, yet take the money; I will get nothing by you – as if men could buy and sell, and live by the loss! Do you think that men believe this, or do you yourselves believe it without one or another equivocal distinction? I will not undertake to tell you the words which you should use, but I tell you from the Lord that you should use but few, and speak in truth. In a multitude of words there wants not sin. For the seller to extol a commodity with a variety of words, and tell men that it is the best in town, and that there cannot be a better bought for gold is many times only a courtesy of trade. So for the buyer to say it is nought, it is nought, and when he is gone, to boast, is not short of a sin (Proverbs 20. 14), or to say that he will give no more, though he intends to do so.

Words are precious commodities, and should not be exposed at such risks. What is beyond yea and nay, and reaches to excess, comes of evil, and evil comes of it (Matthew 5. 37; James 5. 12). If you tell untruths and lies, it is as bad as stealing; 'ye shall not steal, neither deal falsely, neither lie one to another' (Leviticus 19. 11). He who lies virtually steals; and the Apostle joins liars and stealers and perjured persons together, and tells us that the law is against them all, and that they are contrary to sound doctrine (1 Timothy 1. 10). If man's law were as God's, there would be a recovery and restitution for what is gained by lying, as well as for what is stolen (Leviticus 6. 1–5). Before you can come to God with your offering, you ought to restore that which is gained by fraud as well as that which is gained by force.

Indeed, to lie is a thing inconsistent with being a child of God. Without, among the dogs, are liars, and they shall, unless they repent, have their part in the lake which burneth with fire and brimstone, which is the second death (Revelation 21. 8; 22. 15). 'The getting of treasures by a lying tongue is a vanity tossed to and fro of them that seek death' (Proverbs 21. 6). He who is not delivered from the way of lying on earth will never be delivered from lying in Hell. Surely, God says of his people, they are children that will not lie (Isaiah 63. 8); that is, to be sure, they will not make a trade of it nor live in or by lying. And it is added, 'so he was their Saviour', as if God would not save a cheating hypocrite and a lying professor. Nor will he without repentance, for 'lying lips are abomination to the Lord: but they that deal truly are his delight' (Proverbs 12. 22). Which would you rather be, abhorred or delighted in by God? Think of this in your warehouses and shops, or when you go out to buy and sell, that you may do everything in truth. Methinks I hear your wives and children begging you, Oh! do not lie to be rich; do not risk going to Hell to leave me riches! Thus I deal plainly and truly with you, that you may do so with all men, and I hope that you will not take it amiss that I endeavour to do you good. If you do, I say with the Apostle, Forgive me this wrong.

(b) Take heed of putting men off and paying them with false and unlawful money. Just as you should not buy stolen and unlawful goods, so you should not pay unlawful money, that which you would not take, and know that others will not receive, if it is discerned. The children of Abraham should be like him, who, when he had bought, weighed or told out his silver, current money with the merchant (Genesis 23. 16). And this sin of paying brass and false money is so much the worse because it usually falls into the hands of the poor, who can least discern, and who suffer most by receiving it. Do as you would be done to, and do not pay that which is not payment, but an abuse and a wrong.

(c) Do not use false weights or measures, or keep your books falsely. Take heed of writing down more than was delivered or bargained for, or writing greater prices than were agreed upon. As to false weights and measures, they are utterly forbidden (Leviticus 19. 35, 36; Deuteronomy 25. 13–16). You are to have a standard measure, and not to think it enough to have one only when the King's officer calls, but throughout the year; otherwise you, as well as your weights and measures, are an abomination to the Lord (Proverbs 20. 10). There is a good saying, and I wish it were made good, You shall have your weight or measure or number, even though you buy it for a penny or a farthing. God says, 'Shall I count them pure with the wicked balances, and with the bag of deceitful weights?' (Micah 6. 11). No! No! However great professors they are, I will not count them pure, but an abomination.

(d) Beware of counterfeit and false lighting. Alas, one can hardly see day by day in many men's shops: they either shut out the light, or one can scarcely see how they let it in, so that men may seek for light at noonday. Men have learnt to draw up or let down so much by the ell or by the yard, that people can scarcely see what they look at with their eyes. That which seemed very fine and fair by a false light is found to be far otherwise by a true one. Now by the same reason that weights are, lights are an abomination to the Lord, that is, because they are false and deceitful. If you tell me that it is the custom of the city and all the world, I ask you, will that answer God and make it no sin?

(e) Take heed of breaking bargains and agreements, when you see that you can buy cheaper from or sell dearer to someone else. I am almost afraid that this practical kind of religion is with many like an old almanack out of date; it is as if religion were confined to the first table – some duties to God – and the second table – duties to man – were of little concern or consequence. Yet most frequently in Holy Writ the characters of godly men are drawn from their obedience to the commands of the second table. And this that I am dealing with is one of these commandments: 'He that sweareth to his own hurt, and changeth not' (Psalm 15. 4). This ought to hold good in promises as well as oaths, in bargaining as well as swearing; for a man ought to be just, though he has not sworn to be so. But woe to them that promise and swear to, yet are not just but both false and perjured!

(f) Take heed of carnal and sinful compliance with customers and tradesmen in their swearing and drinking to excess. 'Have no fellowship with the unfruitful works of darkness, but rather reprove them' (Ephesians 5. 11); do this even though you profit by those who work them. You shall not suffer sin upon your brother, nor upon yourselves (Leviticus 19. 17). Otherwise it is to hate him in your heart, which is a great sin; for he who hurts his brother is a murderer

(1 John 3. 15). Perhaps you will say, this is the best way to lose our customers, and we may as well shut up shop and go away. If that happens, it is better to part with any one than God, and to lose anything rather than his favour and loving kindness, which is better than life, and therefore much better than a livelihood. But it may not so transpire; it is better to trust God than to be beholden to the Devil and sin. Do as you ought to do, and if bad men do not become your customers, then good men may. When your ways please the Lord, he can and will make your enemies to be friends, and at peace with you (Proverbs 16. 7).

Whatever you do, keep a good conscience towards God and man, and though the children of this world shall call you fools, yet they will call themselves fools another day for calling you so now. It is undoubtedly better and more profitable to please God than men. And what will it profit you to gain the world and lose your soul? We are too prone to comply with, and to be drawn away by those from whom we make a living, and we therefore have a kindness for them. But consider what God said, 'Take heed to thyself, lest thou make a covenant with the inhabitants of the land whither thou goest, lest it be for a snare in the midst of thee', that when they 'sacrifice unto their gods, and one call thee, thou eat of his sacrifice' (Exodus 34. 12–15). Intimacy and familiarity and trading together may be a snare (Genesis 34. 21). And when a good customer calls you, covetousness is likely to make you behave like him. Rather than men will lose their gain, they will cry up Diana, though they cry down godliness and God himself (Acts 19. 23–28).

(g) Take heed of abusing and grinding the faces of the poor (Isaiah 3. 15).

(i) By taking advantage of their necessity. You know they must have it because they need it, and their necessity is urgent. O, do not be cruel to them! You know that they must sell at the end of the week to buy bread, or at the end of the quarter to pay their rent. Do not oppress them and add affliction to their affliction by making them under-sell the sweat of their brow and the labour of their hands. Woe to you, if the spoil of the poor is in your house (Isaiah 3. 14–15). Nor must you take advantage of their ignorance, to over-charge and defraud them. Ignorance should be pitied and the unskilful should be well treated; perhaps he refers himself to you. O, do not put a bad for a good commodity into his hands!

(ii) By keeping back the wages of poor workmen. Do not think of growing rich by the poor man's money. Do not put him off till tomorrow, when you have it by you. If you should not do it in the case of charity, much less in a case of justice. This is a crying sin, as you may read (James 5. 4). Poor souls! They have worked hard, and when they have done, they go home and cry for lack of money to buy bread. Truly this cry of theirs enters into the ears of the Lord of Hosts, for so 'Sabaoth' signifies. Though you are too mighty for the poor, yet you are no match for the Lord of Hosts who takes their part and will not always bear with your covetousness and oppression. O, pay off the poor as soon as they have done their work!

(iii) By forcing on them swindling and trashy wares, because they are in your debt. You often complain that your tradesmen go bankrupt, and it is to be feared that they may complain that you break them, either by forcing too much or by putting very bad goods into their hands, which they cannot sell except to their own great loss. They are in your debt, and for fear of your displeasure, lest you should arrest them, they are willing to submit to you. But oh, for the sake of the poor, for God's sake, and for your own and for your family's sake, do not grow rich by the poor man's poverty! And if you know any more wrongs besides these, for I have but little knowledge of your mysteries, I beg you to take heed of them. If you say in your heart that he is a silly fellow who cannot tell the danger of all this, I do not care to answer your objections.

I would say this, however, that you can never evade your consciences, where it is indelibly written that you ought to do as you would be done by in justice. If you would not that others should wrong you, do not wrong them. If your conscience can be bribed, yet God cannot, and what will you do when he rises up to judgment? How will you answer God to whom you must give an account? Be not deceived, God will not be mocked. It is as cheap as it is easy to laugh at and put off such a poor thing as man is; but believe it, conscience and God will not be put off in this way. Thus I have in this matter also endeavoured to discharge my own soul and to save yours, as well as to be free from your blood. Therefore, consider! If you are not guilty, I have not condemned you, but I speak thus that you may not be guilty, and that you may pray to God to be kept from, and praise him if you have been kept from, such crying sins.

(e) Beware of such sins as the world calls little sins, peccadilloes. Some men reckon great sins to be only little ones, and little ones to be none at all or very venial. They say, what harm is there in an innocent lie or a pious fraud? Alas, what a contradiction this is! Can a lie be innocent, and fraud pious? Woe to them who call evil good, and join good and evil as if they were one, or agreed in one! Another says, oh, it is only a trick of youth. Yes, but it is such a trick as may cost you a going to Hell. Another deceives his neighbour and, laughing while he strikes, says, 'Am not I in sport?' (Proverbs 26. 19). Yes, but he who sins in jest or makes a jest of sin may be damned in earnest.

Consider that no sin against a great God can be strictly a little sin, though compared with a greater one it may be. But however little it is, to account it so makes it greater. And the nature of the greater sin is in the least; a spark of fire, a drop of poison have the nature of much more, indeed, of all (James 2. 10). God has severely punished sins that have been looked upon as little sins, indeed, some of them well-meant sins, as when Uzzah took hold of the Ark when the cart shook (2 Samuel 6. 6, 7). When men only looked into the Ark, it cost them dear (1 Samuel 6. 19). Gathering a few sticks on the Sabbath was severely punished (Numbers 15. 32–36). These seem to be small matters, but in sin we must not consider so much what is forbidden as why it is forbidden, and who forbids it.

Besides, a little sin makes way for a greater, as a little boy-thief entering a house, makes way for a man-thief to enter. It is hard to sin once and only once, to commit one little sin and only one. Give the devil and sin an inch, and they will take an ell. Vain babbling increases to more ungodliness. A little leak in a ship may by degrees fill it with water and sink it. The Devil does not much care by what sins we go to Hell, whether small or great, formality or profaneness.

To conclude—he who makes no conscience of little sins makes conscience of no sins. He who breaks the least of God's commandments has none or very little love for God; for herein is love that we keep his commandments, and they are not grievous, no, not the greatest of them, much less the least (1 John 5. 3). To have respect to all the commandments of God is a proof of a sound heart, and excludes shame (Psalm 119. 6, 80). A good conscience is a universal conscience. If a man makes no conscience of little sins, to which the temptations can be only little, how little conscience is he likely to make of great sins, to which there are greater temptations? If Judas betrays his Lord for thirty pieces, what would he not do for more? Consider what our blessed Saviour said, 'He that is faithful in that which is least is faithful also in much: and he that is unjust in the least is unjust also in much' (Luke 16. 10). Beware then of little sins.

(f) Take heed of what men call secret sins. There are only too many who bless themselves in their wickedness because, as they think, no one knows how wicked they are. They are drunkards, but it is in the night; they are unclean, but it is in the dark. Their mystery of iniquity trades in the works of darkness and in the dark. Indeed, if men could sin and no eye see them, they might seem to sin securely; but this is a falsehood as well as a mistake. I have met with two stories, which may perhaps help you in some way. One is of a maid who was tempted to be unchaste and unclean. The person who solicited her promised to do great things for her if she would yield. I will, he said, do anything for you. Will you? she said, then burn your hand in the fire. Oh, that is unreasonable, he answered. But, she replied, it is much more unreasonable that I should burn in Hell for your sake. Who would venture his soul to torment, to gratify his own or another's pleasure and lust? The other story, which suits the case in hand, is of a maid solicited to this same folly, who would not give her consent unless he would bring her to a place where no eye could see them. Whereupon he brought her to a very dark place and repeated his request, saying, Here nobody can see us. Oh, she said, but here God can see us.

Oh, that we would tell all the tempting courtships of men and devils, that we can never sin but there will be two witnesses present to observe and register it, our own selves and God himself. We owe a great deal of reverence to ourselves, and though no one were present. we should revere our consciences and ourselves. What, shall we be witnesses against ourselves, and be condemned by our own testimony? Yet if our hearts condemn us, God, who is greater than our hearts and knoweth all things, will much more condemn us. When St. Paul knew nothing of which to condemn himself, yet it made him very modest that the Lord was to judge him (1 Corinthians 4. 4). We cannot escape the sight, any more than we can escape the judgment of God. He sees us, and what we do when under the figtree, though like Adam and Eve we cover ourselves with figleaves. And he will one day call to us, as he did to them, Adam, sinner, where art thou? If you go up to Heaven, he is there: it is his throne. If down to Hell, he is there: it is his prison. You cannot go from his presence. You may more easily hide from man and yourselves than from God. Therefore that you may not be so foolish and wicked as to sin in secret, or to think any thing or place secret from God, I urge you often and seriously to read the 139th Psalm. Then I hope you will say, for I am sure you will see cause to do so, How shall I do this wickedness and sin against God!

(g) Take heed of the occasions and even the appearances of

this evil, sin. Abstain not only from apparent evil but from all appearances of evil (1 Thessalonians 5. 22). Do not be so irreligious as to go into temptation, when you have been so religious as to pray God not to lead you into temptation; this is mock-prayer. Keep out of harm's way. 'Enter not (put not a foot) into the way of the wicked' (Proverbs 4. 14, 15). And if you have been so foolishly froward, yet do not go on in the way of evil men; but avoid it, pass not by it, turn from it and pass away. You cannot stand at too great a distance from sin. If you will not sit in the seat of the scornful, do not stand in the way of sinners nor walk in the counsel of the ungodly (Psalm 1. 1). Touch not pitch lest you be defiled. Do not gaze, like one enamoured, on the wine, when it looks well and dances in the glass. Make a covenant with your eyes, lest by looking too much on beauty, your eyes become sore and sinful. Abhor not only the flesh or the spot, but the very garment that is but spotted with the flesh (Jude 23). Indeed, abstain from what is inexpedient as well as from what is unlawful; for in being inexpedient, it tends to become unlawful. If it is not a sin, yet if it looks like a sin, beware of it. It is next to being a sinner to be like one; to being proud and wanton to seem so or look so. An appearance of good is too little, but an appearance of evil is too much. It is the hypocrite's sin that he appears better than he is, and it may be a good man's evil to appear worse than he is. A rod is for the back of fools, and it will be laid on a wise man's back if he is found in a fool's coat.

(h) Take heed of being in any way or in any degree guilty of other men's sins. Alas, have we not many sins of our own? But will we have other men's sins to answer for? They are our-other-men's sins, as I may call them. Take heed of being an occasion of, a partaker of, or only accessory to other men's sins. God forbids it, that it may not be (Ephesians 5. 7-11; 1 Timothy 5. 22), and sharply reproves and punishes it where he finds it to be (Psalm 50. 18; 2 Samuel 12. 9; 1 Kings 21. 19). In the last two places, King David and King Ahab are found guilty of murder which was done by other hands, but, alas, by their commission. It is sad to sin against God ourselves but sadder to make others sin against God too. In this way the world is made worse than it would otherwise be. Men are too prone to be vile enough of themselves, were there no Devil to tempt them, but when they have companions and brethren in iniquity, they are apt to sin more lustily.

St. Augustine confesses that he used to boast of sins he was not guilty of, that he might seem to be as bad as his companions, who thought them the best that were worst. O what sins, many and great, are committed in, with, and for company, that would otherwise probably never have been committed! There would be no stealers were there no receivers; and therefore the receiver is as bad as the thief. There would be no adulteresses, were there no adulterers. Many in Hell would probably have been less wicked than they were, and so have had less torment than they have, had they not been furthered by others their companions. Though all sins come from the heart, and may be indulged there when men are alone, yet as to the act, some sins cannot be committed by people alone, but every such sin has a double sinner, if not a greater number.

Besides, in this way men are confirmed and hardened in their wickedness. Where all go naked, none are ashamed. Examples and company steel men in their sins who were iron enough of themselves, and sometimes embolden those who were modest and tender before. 'If any man see thee which hast knowledge sit at meat in the idol's temple, shall not the conscience of him which is weak be emboldened?' (1 Corinthians 8. 10); the Greek is, edified or built. He takes it for a good example, and makes a kind of conscience to do so too, as if you had instructed him to edification, when alas, it edifies him only to wound and put him in danger of perishing; for it follows, 'Ye sin against Christ', as he also does, for you make him offend (verses 11–13).

So hereby we become guilty of other men's sins, and we are likely sooner or later to regret this very grievously. Indeed, though we ourselves may be saved at last, it will certainly pain us to think that any went to Hell in whose sins we had a head or hand, and maybe a heart. Besides, it is very usual that we partake of their plagues whose sins we partake of; we are given warning of this by no less than a voice from heaven (Revelation 18. 4). 'For because of these things cometh the wrath of God on the children of disobedience. Be not ye therefore partakers with them' (Ephesians 5. 6–7). It is sad to be found on the Devil's ground; as the Devil said, he found the woman (whom he possessed) when at a play. Yet to be more specific, we may be guilty of other men's sins in several ways:

(1) In giving occasion for it beforehand. It may more than probably be said that such sins would not have been committed but for such occasions being given.

(a) By neglecting what might and ought to be done for its prevention. He who, when he can and ought, does not hinder a sin, contributes to its production, as when men neglect to instruct or teach those who are under their charge, whether they are ministers, parents or heads of families (Ezekiel 3. 17–20). It was the apostle's rejoicing that in this case he was pure from the blood of all men (Acts 20. 26, 27). Many a child and servant, when they have come to prison and execution, have made this sad complaint, My parents or my master never gave me warning; they never showed me the danger of sin or instructed me in the way of the Lord, the way of righteousness and holiness! Beware of this! And when sin begins to bud and blossom, nip it by reproofs and discipline, or else you may be charged with sin as old Eli was (1 Samuel 3. 13). Crush the cockatrice while in the egg; dash the brats against the wall while young! If you are silent or indulgent, children and servants take it for consent and approbation, as men misinterpreted God's holding his peace (Psalm 50. 21). Inclinations will come into acts, and acts into customs and habits, if not checked and restrained. But if you thus deal with them early, you may prevent a great deal of sin; indeed, it is the best proof of your love (Proverbs 13. 24). And it may be that they will say, as David did to Abigail, 'Blessed be the Lord God of Israel, which sent thee this day to meet me: and blessed be thy advice, and blessed be thou, which hast kept me this day from coming to shed blood, and from avenging myself with mine own hand' (1 Samuel 25. 32–33). In the same way someone may say, I would have been an adulterer today, and another may say, I would have been a drunkard today, if you had not given me counsel and correction; if you had not given me a helping hand, I would have sinned today; oh, blessed be thou of the Lord! Think of it, is it not better to hear them blessing you than cursing you? Therefore prevent sin all you can.

Solon, a heathen, gives good advice, 'Do not spoil your children, lest you weep in future.' Too many people laugh at their children's cunning shifts, their fibbing and lying; but this laughing may cost you weeping, when you (and before they) are old. It was a law among the Lacedaemonians, that if any of the ancients saw a young one sinning, and did not reprove him, they should undergo the same punishment with the offender.

(b) We may occasion other men's sins and be guilty of their crimes, by doing something which we ought not to do; thus acting we further other men's sinning. If we are superiors we may do this by way of command. Some men are so wicked that they command others to be wicked, who are so wicked as to obey their commands. Absalom commanded his servants to kill his brother Amnon and they obeyed (2 Samuel 13. 28). Jezebel wrote letters in Ahab's name to certain elders to hire sons of Belial – for so false witnesses are called – that they might accuse Naboth of blasphemy and then stone him to death (1 Kings 21). Indeed, David himself was guilty of this sin, and therefore it is spoken of as his only sin (1 Kings 15. 5). Some have made laws to command men to sin, as if they should sin *cum privilegio* and with authority (Daniel 3. 10; 6. 7–9). And how many masters command their servants to say they are not at home when they are, and to commend their commodity for one of the best no matter how bad it is, and to do that which it is not lawful to do on the Sabbath day. Now, since poor servants are under awe and stand in fear, they tend to obey. Therefore, take heed what you command your servants; for every sin they commit by your command will be charged on you, as on them, if not more so.

(c) We may also be the occasion of other men's sins by counselling them to sin. They who cannot command may counsel, which is the next thing to it. In one chapter of the Bible it is recorded three times, in three successive verses, that Ahaziah walked in the ways of Ahab, and did evil in the sight of the Lord by the counsel of Athaliah and the House of Ahab to his destruction (2 Chronicles 22. 3, 4, 5). Amnon sinned according to the counsel of Jonadab (2 Samuel 13. 5, 6). Jonadab is called his friend, and friends take sweet counsel together; but what bitter counsel is wicked counsel! Never counsel anyone to sin under the pretence of friendship, for it is a killing kindness. As Rebecca told Jacob, when she counselled him to lie and deceive, that upon her should the curse be (Genesis 27. 6–13), so say I to you, that the curse will be on you if you advise others to sin.

(d) We may occasion other men's sins by example, and the more eminent the example, the more infectious it is. Great men cannot sin at a low rate because they are examples: the sins of commanders are commanding sins; the sins of rulers ruling sins; the sins of teachers teaching sins. There is a kind of sorcery and bewitching power in such examples (Galatians 2. 12, 13). When Peter and the rest of the Jews dissembled with him, Barnabas, though a good man and full of the Holy Ghost, was also carried away with their dissimulation, that is by their example and in compliance with it. Similarly, that example of which I spoke earlier, concerning a man sitting at meat in an idol's temple, has given us an example of something very catching and infectious (1 Corinthians 8. 10). The world is more easily exampled into sin than into goodness, for sin finds a party within. Abraham's faith, Moses' meekness, Job's patience and Peter's courage are not so easily followed as their contraries. Therefore give no bad examples.

(e) By tempting and provoking to sin. The trumpeter does not fight, but when captured he fares as badly as the soldiers who do, because he stirs them up. When Ahab's wickedness is reckoned up, it is with this remark, that his wife Jezebel incited or stirred him up (1 Kings 21. 25). There was none like Ahab—he had no peer or fellow, and was second to none in wickedness, and he was irritated and provoked to this by his wife. Take heed of tempting or stirring up anyone to sin. Some men's corruptions would sleep more than they do if others did not awake and stir them up. Some are so wicked as not to sleep or to let others sleep until they have done mischief. Then they tempt others to sin in several ways.

*By enticement and solicitation.* It is a sad employment to be sin's solicitor, yet there are all too many of them. They are pimps, and bawds; they pander for lust and sin. And though the solicited person does not sin, as Joseph did not, yet the one who solicits is a sinner, as Joseph's mistress was. There are sinners who, like the Devil, go up and down to entice others to sin (Proverbs 1. 10–16). Even flattery has force in it, and offers a kind of violence (Proverbs 7. 21).

*By importunity.* Delilah made poor Samson almost weary of his life; she never left him until she had undone him. He stood it out a great while, but her importunity prevailed at last (Judges 16. 16, 17). Moreover, it was by much fair speech or importunity that the harlot prevailed with the young man, who perhaps was going about his business and thought no harm until she importuned him (Proverbs 7. 13–21).

*By lying to men in the name of the Lord,* as the old prophet did to the young (1 Kings 13. 18). The Name of the Lord is a great argument, and very taking with those who fear him. Therefore some false prophets make pretension to it and turn themselves into Angels of Light, though they are of the Devil. They quote God's authority as the Devil had the impudence to do, though falsely, to our Saviour himself (Matthew 4. 3, 4). This is a shrewd way of temptation.

*By using improper language, and offering insults to men.* Some men have lavish tongues and can hardly answer without a 'you lie'. Such is their pride and passion that they answer rudely and give such ill language as would anger a saint, as the saying is. People of quality and honour who are used to, and deserve civility will not bear such provoking words; they will not take them except on the point of their rapiers and return them to the giver's throat. Great sins are committed from such beginnings. Therefore Solomon tells us that a soft answer turns away wrath (Proverbs 15. 1), as it did in Judges 8. 2, 3, but grievous and fierce words stir up anger, as they did in 2 Samuel 19. 43, compared with 20. 1. God will not allow parents to provoke their children to wrath (Ephesians 6. 4). As well as ungenerous words, bad and unbecoming behaviour, abuses and affronts tempt men to sin. When Jacob's sons had deceived and thereby slain the Shechemites —as the Law did Paul, for so he says (Romans 7. 11)—they made this surly answer as an excuse to their father, 'Should he deal with our sister as with a harlot?' (Genesis 34. 31). It was as if Shechem's sin justified theirs, and they did well to be angry! They could not put up with such an abuse and dishonour! Therefore, do not use provoking language, to make men sin.

(f) By sending others to ensnare and trap them. Those who employ such decoys are in part guilty of their sin; and Christ Jesus called it tempting, when men of this kind were employed to entangle and ensnare him. The Pharisees sent the Herodians who should feign themselves just men and praise him into a snare and tempt him into a crime against Caesar. They pretend a case of conscience, but our Saviour says to this sort of men, 'Why tempt ye me, ye hypocrites?' They who were thus employed sinned, and so did those who employed them —see the story (Matthew 22; Luke 20). There are only too many more things of this kind, by which we may occasion other men's sins. But I will add only one more thing.

(g) By declaring a thing otherwise than the truth is, by mincing and equivocating. There are more than enough examples wherein good men have been guilty of this. I mention them, that saints as well as sinners may hear and fear and not do wickedly. Abraham prevailed with Sarah to say she was his sister, by which Pharaoh concluded that she was

[273]

not his wife, and took her. But when God plagued Pharaoh for so doing, he reasoned the case with Abraham, 'What is this that thou hast done to me? Why didst thou not tell me she was thy wife? So I might have taken her to be my wife . . .' (Genesis 12). He severely expostulated with and upbraided him, and yet Abraham is at it again in Chapter 20, and meets with a more plain and homely rebuke, and is charged with no less than sin by Abimelech, 'Thou hast brought on me and on my kingdom a great sin. Thou hast done deeds unto me that ought not to be done' (Genesis 20. 9). He lays the sin at Abraham's door, and Sarah also for her suppleness had a reproof from him (verse 16). Yet after all this, Abraham's son Isaac is found remiss in the same thing, and meets with the same rebuke, and that from one who did not pretend to so much religion as Isaac did (Genesis 26). Alas, how many, by taking false oaths and bearing false witness, give occasion to judges to justify the wicked and condemn the righteous! Much more might be spoken of these things, but a word to the wise is sufficient.

(2) Take heed of being partners in other men's sins when they are committed, as co-helpers of them:

(a) *As instruments to execute others' sinful designs or commands*. Thus Doeg was, in executing the priests (1 Samuel 22). So are any others who serve the lusts of men. All persons who are to be obeyed, such as father and mother, are to be obeyed in the Lord (Ephesians 6. 1). Whosoever's will is left undone, God's will should be done, and never left undone to fulfil that of another or our own. They who put unrighteous decrees into execution are under the same woe with them who decree them; for without the execution the decree would do no harm to them against whom it was made (Isaiah 10. 1, 3). Those who put wicked commands into practice and execution are wicked, and are partners in the wickedness of those who command wickedness (1 Kings 12. 30).

(b) *As confederates with others*. Though the sin is not committed by you who are confederates, yet your being such makes you partakers of their sin. The counsellors and com-

[274]

biners are judged equally with the practisers (Psalm 83. 3–9). 'Blessed are they who walk not in the counsel of the ungodly' (Psalm 1. 1). And the prophet says, 'The Lord spoke thus to me with a strong hand' – not simply the word of the Lord came to me, or the Lord spake to me, but he spake with a strong hand! Why? 'Say ye not, a confederacy, to all them to whom this people shall say, a confederacy' (Isaiah 8. 11, 12). The men of the league and association fare, because they sin, alike (Psalm 2, with Acts 4. 26–28).

(c) *As consenters, giving your consent to other's sin;* whereas if you had denied it, perhaps they would not have sinned. 'When thou sawest a thief, then thou consentedst with him, and hast been partaker with adulterers' (Psalm 50. 18). An adulterer is a thief, for he steals water from another's cistern, and to consent with him is to be a partaker. Therefore, 'If sinners entice thee, consent thou not' (Proverbs 1. 10); enter your dissent and do not let your soul have anything to do with their secrets.

Consent may be signified by complying actions. Paul speaks of this as being once his own case: he consented to the death of the martyr Stephen, and witnesses both that he stood by and that he kept the raiment of those who slew him (Acts 22. 20). In the same way, many consent to the sin of others by standing guard and watching the door; in this way they do not only wink at, but encourage and embolden others to sin.

Consent may be given by silent connivance, when we see people about to sin and do not witness against it. Silence, we say, gives consent. So it does often, though not always; for it may be the case that it would only be to throw pearls before swine to speak to some scorners. Some speak too gently, as if it were a matter of no great consequence, but will not put forth the power they have to prevent sin. Pilate seemed to witness against the Jews when they cried out for the crucifying of Christ Jesus, and washed his hands to testify his innocence (Matthew 27. 24). Yet because he did not put forth his power, he is reckoned among the number of them who killed him (Acts 4. 27).

Consent may be given openly and notoriously by word of mouth. Saul, afterwards Paul, gave his voice (Acts 26. 10); his vote went with the rest, and he gave it with a voice, a loud voice. If anyone brings false doctrine, and a man bids him Godspeed, this man is partaker of his evil deeds (2 John 10, 11). When men say, as Jehoshaphat did to Ahab, 'I am as thou art, and my people as thy people; and we will be with thee in the war' (2 Chronicles 18. 3); when we thus give consent, it is notorious.

(3) Do not be accessory to other men's sins after they are committed. You may be guilty of this in many ways, but I shall name only four.

(a) *In not grieving for other men's sins.* All sin is against God, and for that reason he who truly grieves for his own sin will grieve for other men's too. It was the great commendation of Lot that his righteous soul was vexed with the filthy conversation of the Sodomites; it was a torment, a kind of hell to him (2 Peter 2. 7). David could not prevent men sinning and therefore he grieved for it, so much so that his eyes ran down with rivers of tears (Psalm 119. 136). And this made the prophet Jeremiah wish his eyes fountains, that he might weep day and night. All these people were remembered by the Lord in mercy, when others were rewarded with misery. There is scarcely another way like this, to be kept from partaking in the ruin of sinners. God will set a mark on his weeping and mourning people, and as for the rest, they will be found as accessories if not principals in wickedness, and judged accordingly (Ezekiel 9. 4–6). Oh, that there were more crying persons, when there are so many crying sins! They who grieve not and mourn not are guilty, as the apostle tells us (1 Corinthians 5. 1, 2); but by mourning they were cleared of this matter (2 Corinthians 7. 11).

(b) *By concealing that which we ought to reveal and make known.* This may be easily proved from Scripture: 'If a soul sin, and hear a voice of swearing, and is a witness, whether he has seen or known of it; if he do not utter it, then he shall bear his iniquity' (Leviticus 5. 1). 'Whoso is partner with a thief hateth his own soul: he heareth cursing, and bewrayeth it not', which he ought to do (Proverbs 29. 24). Yet again, 'If thy brother, the son of thy mother, or thy son, or thy daughter, or the wife of thy bosom, or thy friend, which is as thine own soul, entice thee secretly, saying, Let us go and serve other gods, which thou hast not known, thou, nor thy fathers . . . thou shalt not consent unto him' (Deuteronomy 13. 6, 8). Is that enough? No! 'nor hearken unto him'. Is that enough? No! 'neither shall thine eye pity him'. Is that enough? No! 'neither shalt thou spare'. Is that enough? No! 'neither shalt thou conceal him'. Is that enough? No! 'thou shalt surely kill him (by revealing him to the judges); thine hand shall be first upon him to put him to death.' But you will say, is this not un-natural? What! betray a brother, one from the same womb, the son of my mother? Indeed more, my own son! Indeed more, my wife, and most of all, my friend! No matter! for all that, thou shalt not conceal him. To conceal such a sinner would be to partake of his sin (2 John 10. 11). These spirits, these soul-stealers, must not be concealed, lest the receiver and concealer be reckoned as bad as the thief.

(c) *In not separating from other men when God calls you to it.* Remember Lot's wife, who was loth to withdraw, and was turned into a pillar of salt – to season us, as one of the fathers said. There are people with whom we should not eat (1 Corinthians 5. 11). To join in communion with known sinners is the greatest testimony you can give, either that they are saints or that you are sinners; you bear a false witness for them and a true witness against yourselves. When the apostle had reckoned up a whole troop of sinners, of whom self-love led the van, and a form of godliness brought up the rear, he adds, 'from such turn away' (2 Timothy 3. 5). You may hear a voice from heaven, saying, 'Come out of her, my people, that ye be not partakers of her sins' (Revelation 18. 4). Be not therefore unequally yoked with unbelievers (2 Corinthians 6. 14).

(d) *If instead of reproving other men's sins, we approve of them.* 'Have no fellowship with the unfruitful works of darkness, but rather reprove them' (Ephesians 5. 11). Not to reprove them, but instead to have fellowship with them, is to approve. Besides this, we declare our approbation when we take pleasure in the actions or the actors. 'The prophets prophesy falsely, and the priests bear rule by their means; and my people love to have it so' (Jeremiah 5. 31); they love to have it so, that is to say, they set their seal to it, to approve and confirm what the prophets and priests do. Of the same import is the statement, 'who knowing the judgment of God, that they which commit such things are worthy of death, not only do the same, but have pleasure in them that do them' (Romans 1. 32). Men are said to help on the afflictions of God's people and to approve them by saying, Ha! Ha! we would have it so (Ezekiel 25. 3; 26. 2). To take pleasure in such things as others do is to be accessories, as if we had done them ourselves. When the apostle Paul tells of other men's sins he does it with weeping (Philippians 3. 18), and so frees himself from the least degree of approbation. But when men laugh at, take pleasure in, and make sport of other men's sins, it is, by construction, an approbation of them. Approbation of other men's sins is also to be inferred when men flatter others and speak peace to them in their evil ways. That is, when men say 'Peace' where God says there is none, that is, to the wicked. God and man will curse him who says to the wicked, Thou art righteous (Proverbs 24. 24). 'Because they have seduced (flattered) my people, saying, Peace, and there was no peace; and one built up a wall, and, lo, others daubed it with untempered mortar, and they sewed pillows under their elbows; therefore, God says, will I pull down the wall, and will tear your pillows and kerchiefs' (Ezekiel 13. 10, 14, 18, 20, 21). And the reason given is, because they made the heart of the righteous sad, and strengthened the hands of the wicked, that he should not return from his wicked way verse 22). There is a woe against such people.

Approbation is also declared when men defend and excuse the sins of others, as if they were retained like lawyers and

[278]

had their fee. They who justify the wicked are equally an abomination with them who condemn the righteous (Proverbs 24. 17). Some are so wicked that they defend other men's wickedness – not only like lawyers but like soldiers – by sword and force of arms; as was done for the man who had abused the Levite's concubine (Judges 17. 15). But to plead for other men's sins is to be as guilty as are they who commit them.

I might add many more things, but I will forbear, because I have been somewhat lengthy on this subject. But I was more willing to do this, because it is a thing too seldom treated and too little taken notice of and laid to heart, that is, the share that we too often have in the sins of other men.

# CONCLUSION

As I come to the close of the whole matter I would wish with my soul that there might never be an occasion for me or any other to preach on this subject again. Shall I now entreat you to consider what has been said, and to think what an abominable and ugly thing sin is? It is the worst of evils, worse than the worst of words can express. I have shown you how it is contrary to God and man. For proof of this I have brought witness from Heaven, Earth and Hell. I have shown you how dearly it cost Christ Jesus who died for it, and how dearly it will cost you, if you live and die in it. Therefore stand in awe and sin not. Lay up the Word of God's command, promise and threatening, that you may not sin against him. Take heed of sinning, for at once you sin against God and your own selves.

I have entered into your closets and your hearts, to tell you of your secret sins. I have told you of, and warned you against, the sins of your lips and of your life. I have told you of your shop – and calling – sins, that you might beware. And what shall I say or do more for you? I have preached to you, prayed and wept for you. I have shown you the way of repentance, faith and holiness. And were I to die for you, I hope I should not account my life dear to me, that I might save your souls by losing it. Let me again, then, entreat, beseech and beg you for God's sake and for your souls' sake not to sin. These things are written, that ye sin not. But 'hear ye, and give ear; be not proud: for the Lord hath spoken. Give glory to the

Lord your God . . . but if ye will not hear it, my soul shall weep in secret places for your pride; and mine eyes shall weep sore, and run down with tears' (Jeremiah 13. 15–17). If you do not hear, you make this to be sad work for me and others who teach you, but, alas, much sadder for yourselves! You make us weep on earth, but you, if you do not repent, will weep in Hell. I beseech you therefore, learn what the grace of God teaches you, to deny all ungodliness and worldly lusts, to live soberly, righteously and godly in this present world (Titus 2. 11, 12), or as it is in Luke 1. 75, 'Serve the Lord in righteousness and holiness all the days of your life.' 'Having therefore these promises (which according to Peter are the greatest and most precious) let us cleanse ourselves from all filthiness of the flesh and spirit, perfecting holiness in the fear of God' (2 Corinthians 7. 1).

Shall we commend holiness in those who are dead, and yet not like holiness in ourselves while we are alive? Holiness is the beauty of earth and Heaven, without which we cannot live well on earth, nor shall ever live in Heaven. Certainly they who jeer and scoff at holiness and rejoice that they are none of the holy ones, might as well make bonfires, ring the bells and give thanks that they shall never be saved. For if they are not holy, saved they cannot be. As one puts it, they who shall be in Heaven will be in no danger of being derided for the sake of piety, for those who deride will not be admitted there. As for the wicked, God will turn them into Hell, and all the nations (all them of any nation) that forget God (Psalm 9. 17).

Poor soul, think a little, indeed, think much of the great day of your account and God's judgment. Though you put it far from you, yet it will surely come, and woe unto you, if it ever takes you unawares and as a thief in the night (1 Thessalonians 5. 3, 4). Seeing this may be, and that will be, what manner of persons ought we to be in all holy conversations and godlinesses! For it is plural in the Greek (2 Peter 3. 10, 11). What more shall I say? I will close the whole matter with what was long since excellently spoken by a great Doctor in our Israel, which is worthy to be written in the hearts of all men and often to be before their eyes and in their thoughts.

At the last, he says, there will come a day when all mankind shall be summoned naked (without differences or degrees) before the same tribunal; when the crowns of Kings and shackles of prisoners; when the robes of princes and the rags of beggars; when the gallants' finery, the peasants' home-spun, the statesmen's policy, the courtiers' luxury and the scholars' learning shall all be laid aside; when all men shall be reduced to an equal plea, and without respect of persons shall be judged according to their works. Then those punctilios and formalities, cuts and fashions, distances and compliments which are now the darling sins of the upper end of the world, shall be proved to have been nothing else but well-acted vanities. Then the pride, luxury, riot, swaggerings, interlarded and complemental oaths, sophisticated and quaint lasciviousness, newly-invented courtings and adorations of beauty, the so much studied and admired sins of the gallantry of the world, shall be pronounced out of the mouth of God himself to have been nothing else but glittering abominations. Then the adulterating of wares, the counterfeiting of lights, the double weight and false measures, the courteous equivocations of men greedy of gain, which are now almost woven into the very art of trading, shall be pronounced nothing else but mysteries of iniquity and self-deceivings. Then the curious subtleties of more choice wits, the knotty questions and vain strife of words, the disputes of reason, the variety of reading, the very circle of general and secular learning, pursued with so much eagerness by the more ingenious spirits of the world, shall be all pronounced but the thin cobwebs and vanishing delicacies of a better-tempered profaneness.

Lastly, then, the poor despised profession of the power of godliness, a trembling at the Word of God, a scrupulous and conscientious forbearance not only of oaths but of idle words, a tenderness and aptness to bleed at the touch of any sin, a boldness to withstand the corruptions of the times, a conscience of but the appearance of evil, a walking humbly and mournfully before God, an heroic resolution to be strict and circumspect, to walk in an exact and geometrical holiness in the midst of a crooked and perverse generation, which the world esteems and scorns as the peevishness of a few silly impolitic men, shall in good earnest from the mouth of God himself be declared to have been the true and narrow way which leads to salvation; and the enemies thereof shall then, when it is too late, be driven to that desperate and shameful confession: 'We fools counted their life madness, and their end to have been without honour. And now they are reckoned among the saints and have their portion with the Almighty!'

'Consider what hath been said, and the Lord give thee understanding in all things' (2 Timothy 2. 7).

# SOME OTHER
## PURITAN
## PAPERBACKS

# THE TREASURES OF JOHN OWEN
## FOR TODAY'S READERS

# COMMUNION WITH GOD

John Owen (1616–83) believed that communion with God lies at the heart of the Christian life. With Paul he recognised that through the Son we have access by the Spirit to the Father. He never lost the sense of amazement expressed by John: 'Our fellowship is with the Father and with his Son, Jesus Christ.' In this outstanding book he explains the nature of this communion and describes the many privileges it brings.

*Communion With God* was written in a day, like our own, when the doctrine of the Trinity was under attack and the Christian faith was being reduced either to rationalism on the one hand or mysticism on the other. His exposition shows that nothing is more vital to spiritual well-being than a practical knowledge of what this doctrine means.

Until now, *Communion With God* has been read by only small numbers of Christians with access to the 275 closely printed pages in *The Works of John Owen*. Now Dr R. J. K. Law has produced a splendidly readable abridgement which brings Owen's rich teaching to a much wider readership.

Here is one of the greatest Christian classics of all time in a new format and more easily readable style.

ISBN 0 85151 607 6
224pp., paperback

# ALL THINGS FOR GOOD

*Thomas Watson*

Thomas Watson of St Stephen's, Walbrook believed he faced two great difficulties in his pastoral ministry. The first was making the unbeliever sad, in the recognition of his need of God's grace. The second was making the believer joyful, in response to God's grace. He believed the answer to the second difficulty could be found in Paul's teaching in Romans 8.28: God works all things together for good for his people.

First published in 1663 (under the title, *A Divine Cordial*), the year after Watson and some two thousand other ministers were ejected from the Church of England and exposed to hardship and suffering, *All Things For Good* contains the rich exposition of a man who lived in days when only faith in God's Word could lead him to such confidence.

Thomas Watson's exposition is always simple, illuminating and rich in practical application. He explains that both the best and the worst experiences work for the good of God's people. He carefully analyses what it means to be someone who 'loves God' and is 'called according to his purpose'. *All Things For Good* provides the biblical answer to the contemporary question: 'Why do bad things happen to good people?'

ISBN 0 85151 478 2
128pp., paperback

# A LIFTING UP FOR THE DOWNCAST

*William Bridge*

These thirteen sermons on Psalm 42:11, preached at Stepney, London, in the year 1648 are the work of a true physician of souls. In dealing with believers suffering from spiritual depression, Bridge manifests great insight into the causes of the saints' discouragements such as great sins, weak grace, failure in duties, want of assurance, temptation, desertion and affliction. A correct diagnosis is more than half the cure but Bridge does not leave his readers there. He gives directions for applying the remedy. For example in dealing with 'great sins' he says, 'If you would be truly humbled and not be discouraged; not be discouraged and yet be humbled; then beat and drive up all your sin to your unbelief, and lay the stress and weight of all your sorrow upon that sin.' The general causes of spiritual depression are the same in every age. Downcast Christians of the twentieth century can find help here as surely as did past generations.

ISBN 0 85151 298 4
288pp., paperback

*For free illustrated catalogue please write to:*
## THE BANNER OF TRUTH TRUST

*3 Murrayfield Road,*      *P.O. Box 621, Carlisle,*
*Edinburgh EH12 6EL*      *Pennsylvania 17013,*
*U.K.*      *USA*